Teachir Video Games

A Strategy Guide

Teacher Guide

by Zachary Hartzman

First Published in 2022 by Leyline Publishing
1650 West Rosedale Street, Suite 305, Fort Worth, TX 76104

 Leyline Publishing, Inc.
1650 West Rosedale Street, Suite 305
Fort Worth, Texas 76104

www.leylinepublishing.com | https://www.geektherapeutics.com/

Printed in the United States of America

10 9 8 7 6 5 4 3 2 1

Library of Congress Cataloging-in-Publication Data is available upon request.

ISBN 978-1-955406-02-4 (E-book)

Editing and Proofreading by Anthony M. Bean
Copyediting by Madeline Jones
Text Design and composition by Asya Blue Design
Printed by Versa Press
Cover Design by Kelsey Hargrove

Table of Contents

The Games **34**

Foreword

When we think of the word or concept *play*, we conjure images in our mind of beautiful young children pretending to be astronauts, pilots, teachers, mothers, fathers, or princes and princesses. The images of children playing make-believe are endless, and in our society they are wholeheartedly acceptable – they are just so cute! However, this encouragement of play never stretches into teenage and adulthood. In the later years, the word *play* turns into something juvenile – or even dark or perverse. Parents say to their pre-pubescent child "stop acting like a baby, you're ten years old now," or, "stop crying and act like a grownup." In both instances, the common word used is *act* or *stop pretending*, or *stop imagining*, and the messages become clearer that in order to walk into adulthood you have to leave your sense of wonder behind. It becomes hard, in our society at least, to separate the idea of play in adulthood with negative or sexual undertones. Teenagers are in desperate need of age-appropriate play.

Play should be viewed as a valuable classroom activity that enables children and youth to develop a wide variety of social and academic skills. Through play, children and youth learn how to get along with others, solve problems, inhibit their impulses, and regulate their emotions. Play helps to develop well-rounded healthy citizens. While there is plenty of research to support the importance of play in the developmental life of a child, there just isn't enough opportunity to play beyond age 12, particularly for teenagers who are in the most crucial part in their lives and where experimentation and imagination is so very much a part of their everyday life experiences. Wouldn't it be in the best interest of educators to incorporate more opportunities for adolescents to continue to expand their minds, experiment and imagine safely, and extend their childhood onward into their adult lives.

"A light heart maketh merry," Shakespeare once wrote. With the many challenges our young people face economically, socially, and politically, they are the thermometers of society. As violence, drug use, depression, and suicide continues to increase in this age group, why not incorporate some intentional play in the part of their lives they spend the most time in: the classroom?

Play and classroom are two words that inherently do not go together as the age of the child increases, and are antithetical by high school. To play in a high school classroom is supposedly akin to childishness. To someone who loves the outdoors, books, paper, antiquities, and art, the idea of learning through video games was blasphemy. However, my career as a high school principal schooled me rather quickly on the importance of being up to date with what my teenagers are being exposed to daily. As I observed the young people at my school quickly becoming subsumed by social media and video games, I realized there was an opportunity to use the very vehicle that so enthralled them as a means to educate them. A teacher at my school, Zachary Hartzman, helped me to see that. He had already realized how so many of our students benefit from gaming in their own time, and that it is the job of educators to access this medium in a meaningful way. It might be a different way of learning, but that makes it all the more exciting. As an educator, prolonging, encouraging, and maintaining child-like wonder for education is tantamount to keeping my young people engaged within the traditional four walls of a classroom, and games are an invitation to explore. I am a proponent of fun and am an individual who is always looking for innovation that will reach our young people. So I became a gambler and placed my bets on Zachary's intelligence, creativity, and genuine ability to connect with his students.

As I reflect on my journey to becoming a believer in the usefulness of gaming and its place in classroom play, I think of my own children. My staunch opposition to exposing them to any video games was actually limiting them, by cutting off yet another way to play and socialize with other children their age. My son, who is an avid lover of building and who finds every opportunity to build a ship, a car, an airplane out of whatever materials he finds, can technologically build cities with unlimited resources in different environments when he plays *Minecraft*. His imagination has been expanded and his interest for building has increased, not decreased. My daughter, a born social butterfly who thrives on interactions with others, has found a way to maintain social connectedness and be whoever she wants with multiple peers from her school on *Roblox*, an online game creation platform. There are moments where it is hard to believe there are no physical children in our home, with their peals of laughter or shouting at each other to move out of the way or to correct each other when one isn't playing fair. The same behaviors that you would come to expect in a playground manifest themselves on the virtual servers. Furthermore, in the midst of pandemic social life, having virtual opportunities for my children, as well as my students, has made a difference in maintaining a sense of community and togetherness. There is a sense of comfort in hearing a familiar voice on the other end of the phone, or being able to see each other on Facetime while playing, that has helped to temper the feeling of loss when you physically can't be together. Gaming has a place in the lives of our youth, whether at home or at school, and not recognizing their influence is to miss an opportunity to understand our students better.

- Norma A. Vega
Principal, ELLIS Preparatory Academy

Introduction

The Legend of Zelda: Ocarina of Time - Learning in Unexpected Places

"Hey! Listen!"

Navi - *The Legend of Zelda: Ocarina of Time*

It was February 1997. A young boy named Groose had just turned seven and could not wait to get his hands on a new fighting game for his Nintendo 64. Although he did not remember the name of the game at the time, he figured an employee at the local Toys R' Us would know exactly what he wanted. The game on his mind was *Mortal Kombat Trilogy*, but it turned out that Groose was not the best at describing what he wanted. The employee, a teenager, thought he must have been talking about this new game that had come out a couple of months earlier, *The Legend of Zelda: Ocarina of Time*. He reluctantly agreed that it might be the game that he wanted, so his father grabbed it and proceeded to check out. The employee's praise of the game has been etched into his mind to this day: "This game took me three months to beat. It's just awesome." And even though this was not the game he originally wanted, it would forever become a core part of this Groose's identity.

For a long time, *The Legend of Zelda: Ocarina of Time* was not a game that most people would think of when they heard about video games and education. This game, however, had a tremendous impact and shaped an entire generation of gamers. There is clear evidence that video games are not a waste of time, as many kids have grown accustomed to hearing. So many people have learned a tremendous amount from just this one game and continue to via future and continual installments of the franchise. The Legend of Zelda: Ocarina of Time contains an amazing, hidden curriculum. When you take a closer look, there is obvious educational value found throughout the game.

The first thing this game teaches kids is how to listen. In many of the Zelda games, you, the player, are accompanied by some sort of companion who is meant to help the protagonist, Link (you), on your journey. In *Ocarina of Time*, this companion comes in the form of a little fairy named Navi. Whenever Navi wants your attention, she shouts "Hey! Listen!" This has become a meme over time because of how frequently this happens in the game. Playing it today, it can seem annoying to have this high-pitched voice calling out for you constantly. Remember, though, that this game was massively popular in its time, especially for a child or adolescent like the one in the story above. He would play with his older brother, who was nine at the time, but neither was exceptionally good at navigating through a large fantasy world. Kids can be smart, but they are not always the best critical thinkers. Groose loved when Navi called out because there was a very good chance he and his brother were lost and needed help finding their next destination. The Internet was still in its infancy (unlike today, when hints and instructions for games can be found instantly online) and they did not have a guidebook to aid them on their quest. They really had nowhere to look for help. Navi, while annoying by today's standards, was an exceptional guide. A teacher, essentially. Groose often wondered how many times his teachers had said something similar to "Hey! Listen!" while at school. Teaching children to actively listen can be challenging. It is not always a skill that comes naturally, nor is it easy to keep their attention in the classroom, like video games can. This game ingrained in Groose that he had to listen carefully because he did not want to miss something important and get lost (and that happened a lot). However, Navi was always there as a helpful guide and teacher to remind what he had already learned and how to use it in the current problem.

An added benefit is that the game does not have full voice acting. The story and dialogue are told through text, which encourages its players to read. Groose's parents used to force him to read every day even, though he absolutely dreaded his time spent with most books. He would fight it and try to avoid it as much as possible, except in video games and game guides - he devoured those. Obviously, kids still need to read books, but remember that there are various ways to go about getting kids interested in reading. There are plenty of students who hate reading anything given to them in class, but will happily read video game guides and reviews online. *The Legend of Zelda* franchise, and Nintendo games in general, are interesting in that all in-game dialogue is told through text. They only just recently added voice acting in their *Breath of the Wild* cutscenes. For *Ocarina of Time*, Groose had to read everything: dialogue, signs, maps, notes, letters, etc. to make his way through the perilous dungeons and fantasy world. The magic was that the amount of text in the game never annoyed him. Besides the books that his parents and teachers forced him to read, some big contributors to fostering his literacy were video games and comics which have gone on to inspire and foster his choice in career paths.

There is a lot more value to be found in video games than what is traditionally considered educational. Video games can do more than just build one's literacy; it can teach mechanics, problem-solving, rules, narrative speaking, and even foster relationships with others. The Open-World genre is one of the more popular video game genres these days; see *Assassin's Creed, Ghost of Tsushima, Cyberpunk 2077, The Legend of Zelda: Breath of the Wild, Fallout, Horizon Zero Dawn*, and thousands of other examples. The player is basically plopped into a world and given a lot of freedom to go wherever they want. There is usually a story that guides the player in a main direction, but the player can just explore most of the map and complete side quests as they please. The player is never obligated to follow the main story at all times. *Ocarina of Time* toyed with this concept before Open World was even a genre. After the introductory segments of this game you enter Hyrule Field, and the game just opens up into a massive field that you have the ability to explore till your heart's content. It gives players a sense of freedom that no other game really ever offered before this. The grandness of this game was almost too much for kids like Groose above to handle alone. It actually forced him to do something that is incredibly difficult for many kids: he needed to collaborate with others.

Groose and his older brother fought a lot when they were younger. Hanging out together did not always come naturally, as brothers tend to have difficulty relating to one another. It was a lot easier, however, when they were playing video games. Being the younger brother, the Groose was often relegated to Player 2 or just watching in the background. But he was always able to provide input in order to help his brother progress in the story. They basically shared the same save file for the *Ocarina of Time* gameplay. They needed to work together if they had any hope of beating the game. They even had to sneak and print guides (hundreds of pages - think of all of the extra reading they had to do!) from GameFAQs behind their parents' back. After playing for hours together, they would talk about the game with their friends at school. At one time, they even brought their copy of the game to a friend's house because their friend told him his older brother was able to beat the Forest Temple, which he and his brother were really struggling with.

There were whole communities of kids built around this focus, just trying to figure out how to get through games like *Ocarina of Time*. It was a type of collaboration, in-person and online, that many kids had never experienced before. Video game communities still thrive online, and every new game comes with a full guide on a number of websites. One never actually needs to seek help from others in-person anymore. If someone is lost in a game, they are just a couple of clicks away on Google from reading about where they need to go next. The technological limitations of 1998, while magical for the time, forced kids to collaborate with others. Even though the game was not multiplayer, there was still this multiplayer aspect to it that does not really exist with single player games anymore. Even though kids today have it easier, you can still find hordes of them talking video games in the cafeteria at any school around the world. And let's be honest, they are talking about them during your classes, as well. They may not need each other's help figuring out where to go in a game, but they are definitely debating various strategies they use in whichever game they are playing, constantly comparing and contrasting ideas and strategies.

The *Legend of Zelda: Ocarina of Time* is always brought up whenever there is a conversation around the greatest or most influential games ever made. *Ocarina of Time* changed video games as a medium. It fostered a generation of gamers who still buy every new iteration of the franchise because of the impact this game had on them. It was the first time a video game really made kids want to embark on a grand adventure to save the world. This game made Groose a gamer - a part of his identity that has impacted every facet of his life, including his eventual decision to incorporate video games into his teaching practice. There is learning to be found in unexpected places - if we are willing to look. For a long time, video games were these unexpected places. As the medium continues to grow, more people and educators are becoming aware of the fact that video games can become an integral part of a student's education. There is more educational value in allowing a student to play an entertainment game like *The Legend of Zelda: Ocarina of Time* than forcing them to read a book written a hundred years ago. The video game interacts with the player and vice versa to create an interactive journey and dialogue.

Ocarina of Time is a classic tale of a hero's journey. A young boy is thrust into the unknown to save the Kingdom of Hyrule. In order to complete his journey, he must first learn what it means to wield power, become courageous, and gain wisdom. These three aspects of the Zelda franchise resonate in our own society as kids journey through life. We all have the power to overcome the challenges that lie ahead of us. Courage pushes us to try something new and different. Wisdom is our reward as we learn from these experiences. What is wonderful is how *The Legend of Zelda: Ocarina of Time* does not alone lay claim to the ability to inspire their players to grow. Just as the boy Groose above has grown alongside Link, he has grown alongside a number of other video game characters from various franchises. He may fight the Dark Lord Ganondorf one day, but traverse through the trenches of World War I the next, and save his home in yet another epic tale.

So, if you have not guessed yet, that young boy was me, and I still consider buying *The Legend of Zelda: Ocarina of Time* instead of *Mortal Kombat* as the best mistake I ever made. I can still visualize myself in my parents' basement the first time my brother and I booted the game up. The music still rings in my ears as I think about the opening title screen. This was clearly a far cry from the brutal bloody fighting game I had wanted, but it seemed really cool. I certainly did not realize that I was about to start one of the greatest games ever made or that it was going to shape my future as it has. The trials and tribulations laid the foundation for a passion of resolving issues and problems in my own life. And more importantly, it taught me how to ask for help and listen to others when I am unable to resolve a problem by myself.

When I first decided to pursue a career in education, my close friends joked that I would be the teacher who watched movies and played video games with his students. I always knew in the back of my mind that both of those activities, especially video games, could be a real asset. My hope in writing this book is that you and other educators will be both inspired and prepared to teach with video games in your own classroom. To be clear, this book is not about educational video games. There are many video games out there that were created with the sole purpose of education in mind. This is not a guide to video games like *Reader Rabbit, The Oregon Trail, or Math Blaster*. This is not a book about gamification or how to gamify a student's learning environment. This book is a strategy guide that will show you how the video games we all know and love can be utilized as an effective teaching resource. They are not meant to replace your current curriculum, but rather to supplement and reinforce what you are already teaching and help get your students excited to learn alongside you. When you decide to try teaching with video games, do not let anyone tell you they are a waste of time. As *Shigeru Miyamoto*, the creator of *The Legend of Zelda* franchise once said, "Video games are bad for you? That's what they said about rock and roll."

References

Bean, A. M., Johnson, D., & Johnson, S. (2019). Foreword. In *The psychology of Zelda: linking our world to the Legend of Zelda* series (pp. IX-IX). foreword, Smart Pop.

Pedagogy

"Be proud of your Death Count!
The more you die,
the more you're learning.
Keep going!"

Postcard, *Celeste*

Games and Learning

Game Based Learning

Game-based learning (GBL) is a type of play tied to specific learning outcomes. Generally, GBL is constructed to balance content with gameplay and the ability of the player/student to retain and apply the subject matter to the real world. Games have always been used in the classroom as a form of play or sport. They are often competitive, but can also be collaborative experiences that the students are drawn to and heavily engage in. Most people can remember at least one time where a teacher of theirs had them play Jeopardy in class. These games and play mediums have always been important for learning.

Video games, like Jeopardy, can be a good addition to many classrooms because they offer a unique way to engage with the curriculum in your class. Like film, television, and comics before them, video games are the perfect supplement to reinforce what is already being taught in the classroom. They are a unique experience that can transform how people learn, and it is the job of educators to access their potential in a meaningful way for our students. There are not many mediums out there that combine aspects of play and learning at the same time. It is a different way of learning, but that is what makes it so fun. Greg Miller, a man who has made his living talking about video games, describes them like this:

> To me, video games mean imagination. Growing up, I played with action figures a lot, and it was my way of creating stories with narratives, branching paths, and histories. Games are that on a far grander scale. Games are a chance to get lost in a world someone else has created and discover all the backstories that make a scene tick. They allow us to go to places we've never been, talk to people we could never talk to, and literally walk a mile in someone else's shoes. Games have taught me compassion and empathy by showing me experiences I could never have for myself. Games give us all an intimate glimpse into someone else's life.

Every student dreads the teacher that forces them to read primary source documents all day. Every teacher dreads creating a boring curriculum that adheres to some standardized test. So change things up a bit and make learning just a little bit more fun. Every classroom has a Greg Miller in it, and video games can be the perfect tool to get them engaged with the lesson. It may not be easy for everyone. There is an acquired literacy that gamers have cultivated over their many years of gaming. Just like how it takes time to learn how to read or walk, it might take some time to learn how to play a video game. But hey, you have already taken the first step by reading this book.

PRINCIPLES OF LEARNING

Utilizing students' hobbies as a way of making learning fun is a great way for teachers to foster positive relationships between themselves and their students. Bring in a comic book if a kid is into comics, show a movie for those who are into film, and play a video game with the kids who stay up too late at night playing online with their friends. To understand how video games can transform education, we first need to change the perspective that games are just entertainment. Most products that were created for entertainment also hold educational value. James Paul Gee, a Professor of Literacy Studies and a Regents' Professor at Arizona State University, once wrote that learning can be broken down into sixteen parts. From there he breaks down how good video games incorporate each of those learning principles. They are as follows . . .

1) Identity	Identifying with content is an important facet of learning. Real learning is more difficult to attain if the student does not see the value in the content.
2) Interaction	Interacting with what is being studied is essential for learning to take place. This is why so many students struggle with only reading books. Books can be amazing, but they do not literally respond to the readers.
3) Production	The process of creating something helps students apply and hone their newly developed skills.
4) Risk Taking	Students need to feel comfortable taking risks. They need to be even more comfortable with the prospect of failure. Failing and learning from one's mistakes is essential to overcoming obstacles.
5) Customization	Teachers need to differentiate and scaffold all of their lessons in order for the material to be accessible to every student in their classroom.
6) Agency	Students often need to feel in control of their own actions and learning. It is important to provide students with choices so that they can have their own voice.
7) Well-Order Problems	This is a reference to how skills build on one another. A teacher cannot expect a student to write a well-structured essay without first teaching them how to create an outline or how to write a thesis statement.
8) Challenge and Consolidation	Through trial and error, alongside meaningful teacher feedback, students can consolidate the skills they have learned into a final product. They can take these newly acquired abilities and even apply them to other contexts.
9) "Just in Time" and "On Demand"	Information needs to be provided to students in the proper context. Students need to be ready for the information, to want to use it, and to actually be able to put it to use.
10) Situated meanings	Learning new information is easier to remember when it is attached to another medium. It is easier to learn the definition of a word if it comes alongside an image, for example.
11) Pleasantly Frustrating	Challenge is a good thing. It can be fun to overcome challenges. An issue arises when something is too difficult and becomes overly frustrating. A problem should feel doable even if a student fails on a first or second attempt.
12) System Thinking	Instead of memorizing individual facts, it is important to understand the relationships between ideas and concepts within a system. This allows for different forms of analysis like "Cause and Effect" and "Compare and Contrast."
13) Explore, Think Laterally, Rethink Goals	As the saying goes, "it's about the journey not the destination." Allow students to take their time with new information. Let them explore and play around with it rather than trying to get to the destination as quickly as possible.

14) Smart Tools and Distributed Knowledge	Smart tools are commonplace in schools and workspaces. It is important that students have the ability to navigate the smart tools they have at their disposal. They do not need to know how Google works, but they do need to learn how to navigate it in order to find reliable resources.
15) Cross-Functional Teams	Most schools advocate for group work to be a central aspect of learning. This way students can serve as various functions that come together in a final product.
16) Performance Before Competence	Practice makes perfect. Students need to be able to perform before they are competent at something and they need to be able to do so without being evaluated.

So how do video games relate to the above sixteen points? If you read through them all again from a gamer's perspective, it should be clear that good video games are adept at implementing each and every one of these metrics - even better than mediums like books, comics, movies, or TV. This is not meant to advocate teaching with video games over books, but it does show that video games should be taught alongside other traditional means of learning. So let's run through the sixteen parts of learning again while looking at specific gaming examples.

1) Identity	Players can hop into the shoes of an already well established identity like Link from *The Legend of Zelda*, or create a new identity from the ground up in an RPG like *Fallout*.
2) Interaction	Video games directly interact with their players. They verbally respond and even fight back during certain situations. There is a feedback loop that helps the player grow over time.
3) Production	Players can often produce just as much content in a game as they consume. One can choose their own path in a plethora of open world games or games that dabble in dialogue choices and narrative trees. Players can even create entire worlds in games like *Minecraft*, *Super Mario Maker*, *Dreams*, and *Fortnite*.
4) Risk Taking	Students need to feel comfortable taking risks. The entire point of most video games is to take risks, die, and try again. Some games like *Celeste* even make that an essential part of the gameplay that is interwoven into its narrative.
5) Customization	So many video games, especially more modern ones, have a number of accessibility options available to the player. One can modify and tweak their experience as they see fit. That way each student or class can customize their ideal experience.
6) Agency	Many games thrust agency upon its players. Telltale games are a great example of this. Games like *The Walking Dead*, *The Wolf Among Us*, and even *Batman* the *Telltale Series* demand that the player makes their own choices. Students can be in complete control of the decisions made by the protagonists. They can shape the narrative whichever way they think makes the most sense.

7) Well-Order Problems	Many video games are built based on levels. Tasks start off easy to teach basic concepts. Then things will become more difficult as the player becomes capable of consolidating all their newly acquired abilities.
8) Challenge and Consolidation	Games will often require its players to take a skill learned early on in a game and apply it in a different context later. Something that seems like a mundane task may become an important aspect of defeating a boss down the line. Check out the different rune abilities in *The Legend of Zelda: Breath of the Wild*.
9) "Just in Time" and "On Demand"	Ever play a game where you find potions right before a boss fight? Or run out of arrows and bullets the second you finish up clearing a room of zombies? Video games do a good job of providing its players with the necessary tools at just the right time. "Tools" can be information and lore as well.
10) Situated meanings	Video games always provide words, themes, and morals in context. What one hears also takes some kind of visual or audio form on screen.
11) Pleasantly Frustrating	Players can easily stay in their comfort zone. Between different difficulty settings and accessibility features, games can be tailored so that they are never so challenging that students will just give up and walk away. (Unless it is *Dark Souls*.)
12) System Thinking	Players need to always think of "cause and effect." Their decisions directly impact the system they are working within. From simple actions like shooting an enemy, which alerts them to your location, to sparing someone's life, which may actually change the plot and ending of a game.
13) Explore, Think Laterally, Rethink Goals	Video game developers do not want the players to rush to the ending. They have spent years crafting a piece of art that they want everyone to spend time with. People can explore, play, and rethink what it is they are actually learning from the experience. And then they can start all over again when they finish and try things differently. Many games implement a New Game + feature to do exactly this.
14) Smart Tools and Distributed Knowledge	Video games almost never require players to know every aspect of the content they are playing. *Assassin's Creed* will never require the player to memorize the map of its ancient locations. The game will help guide the player where they need to go, but they must learn the basics in order to navigate those systems.
15) Cross-Functional Teams	This is more apparent in multiplayer games that require collaboration. One teammate often can't carry the rest to victory in games like *Overcooked*, *Overwatch*, or *League of Legends*. Each person has a role play and they need to work together to win.
16) Performance Before Competence	Video games almost always give people the chance to perform before judging their abilities. Whether it comes in the form of tutorials, or repeated gameplay mechanics, the player should always be ready for that final section or boss fight.

Teaching with Video Games

Is every video game worth bringing into school? Absolutely not. It should be clear though that many can easily find their place within a school's curriculum, assuming careful thought and consideration has been put into a game's selection. The wonderful part is that a substantial portion of many schools' student bodies is already video game literate. They know how to navigate the various systems found in video games across different genres. Even a student who only plays *Call of Duty* can quickly adapt to the playstyle of a walking simulator like *Gone Home*, or a third person action adventure game like *Tomb Raider*. Accessing students' prior knowledge is teaching 101. It is a default that needs to be a part of every educator's practice. Obviously not every teacher needs to find ways to teach with video games, but every school should at least have a space for gaming. Many schools have comics and graphic novels embedded into English language arts curriculum. There are many elective classes where students have the opportunity to study film and TV. Why is it then, that video games are still a rarity in schools?

While video games have flourished across the word, they still have ways to go before becoming commonplace in educational systems. By 2022, experts forecast that the gaming industry will produce $196 billion in revenue. That is more than the movie and music industries combined. Tons of teachers already find ways to incorporate movies and music into their practices, so it is really only a matter of time before video games become more integrated. They still have many obstacles to overcome, however, before they can play a central role in classroom learning, such as skepticism about video games as a medium, and the lack of gaming literacy among current teachers. Luckily, our students are experts and we can rely on them to help with games' incorporation into school curriculum.

TAPPING INTO CULTURE

Many students do not personally connect with their teachers specifically because they are struggling with one of those sixteen above aspects of learning. This can happen because the students' interest and hobbies are not being addressed, leaving them feeling distant. A culturally responsive teacher who wants to reach all of their students may certainly need to find a way to teach with video games at some point. By 2019, 73% of kids 2-17 in the United States play video games. A medium played by so many people can no longer be ignored as a serious educational resource. A whopping 97% of teenagers play video games, whether through computers, consoles, or portable handheld systems. Despite what many people may think, there is not that big of a difference between the playtime of different genders. 99% of boys and 94% of girls play video games. Most gamers also engage in multiple genres. One week they may be playing a fast-paced, first-person shooter and then engage with a more story-driven walking simulator the next. Gaming is a vast culture that is inherent in many of our students' lives and it is the job of the teacher to tap into that.

Teachers are meant to be culturally responsive educators, and while most teachers mean well, they can be doing their students a disservice by not tapping into all of their prior knowledge. Students are experts of all different facets of culture, especially pop culture. They often teach even the most educated of teachers about the latest trends, music, movies, and video games. Pop culture is a vital aspect of most students' lives. Their hobbies and the way they spend their time usually center around an aspect of popular culture. Unfortunately assumptions about the value of pop culture has for a long time kept that part of students' lives outside of their classrooms.

The value of these video games cannot be understated. Video games have the enormous potential to immerse players in complex systems, and by playing in those systems, students can learn from the points of view of the characters, and perhaps even develop their own identities within the systems. A teacher can have their students placed in the shoes of soldiers from during World War I in *Valiant Hearts: The Great War*. They can take a museum tour through Ancient Egypt and Greece in *Assassin's Creed Origins* and *Odyssey*, respectively. A soon-to-be graduate can preview the difficulties of maintaining contact with their friends after attending different colleges in *Emily is Away*. In each of these scenarios the student is an active participant in the learning process. Best of all, students can play the games together so that students can process and grow together.

Dr. Kurt Squire believes that studying games can contribute to engaging students of the digital age. Games are unique because they enable intellectual and social growth that persists over the long term. The skills one learns from games also transfer to one's other academic skills. Teachers and educators need to be able to tap into these resources since so many students are already well versed in video games. He noted that "any time that we turn a child off to learning rather than awakening their intellectual curiosity, we've failed." And even for those students who do not have a history playing games, many are more than willing to engage with them as a new means of learning. Dr. Squire notes that video games are now, more than ever, being taken seriously as a form of art and culture, as more academics recognize video games' ability to create interactive narratives. Ignoring video games and their role in society would be just as detrimental as ignoring the impact of comics and film. Lately you can find entire sections dedicated to comics and graphic novels in many school libraries. Bringing pop culture into schools is to participate in the lives of one's students. Video games are cultural worlds that provide a space for people to learn by combining aspects of critical thinking, social interaction, and new technologies.

Dr. Squire's note that the skills learned from video games can transfer to one's academic life is important. A growth mindset is the idea that one's identity, intelligence, or abilities are not stagnant- people are flexible, malleable, and capable of growing. Many students come into school with a fixed mindset. They believe that their intelligence is pre-determined and their grades are somehow affirmations of their own, or lack thereof, intellectual ability. How many times has a student uttered the words, "I just don't get math"? How many times has an English language learner expressed that they will never be able to learn English?

Video games offer the perfect resource for teaching and instilling a growth mindset in students. Take a game like *Celeste*, developed by Matt Makes Games. On the surface, the game is about climbing a mountain. The real message of the game, however, comes after playing for a little while and dying several hundred times. As the player progresses through the story, the main character Madeline receives a number of postcards. One such card that shows up early in the game and reads:

> "Be proud of your Death Count! The more you die, the more you're learning. Keep going!"

Yes, the game is about trying to scale a mountain, but it is also about reconciling with one's anxiety, depression, and self-image. It is okay to try something and fail. It is okay to try something and fail more than once. What is important is that one is resilient and able to push through and learn from the experience. It does a remarkable job of using its gameplay mechanics to reinforce the central idea of the game. A game like *Celeste* will never teach a student math, but it can help show them that there is value to be found in their effort and failures. Plus, playing this game is a lot fun and will make for a super engaging lesson in any teacher's classroom.

Teaching with Video Games

The growth mindset is not unique to *Celeste*. Thousands of video games are built with this concept as a gameplay focus. From the infamous "You Died" message after every death in *Dark Souls* to every missed jump from any *Super Mario* game, video games want the players to learn and get better with time. There is no fixed mindset to be found. Any player has an inherent ability to keep practicing and get better. This is even more true as video games these days offer accessibility options that can enable more people to access their content. What is really wonderful is that the educational value of video games expands way beyond just teaching people how to have a growth mindset.

A STUDENT'S PERSPECTIVE

Danny is a recent high school graduate from the Bronx, in New York City. He is originally from the Dominican Republic and emigrated to New York back in 2016. He was already a senior in high school when he made his move to the United States. Instead of transferring into a school at the same grade level, Danny started over again as a freshman with four additional years of high school ahead of him. He, like many immigrants to the country, could not speak English. In order to graduate in New York, a student must first pass the Regents Examination in English Language Arts. Learning a language is not easy, so he, along with many other immigrant students, started high school over to learn the language and eventually a high school diploma. He also had the privilege of enrolling in a video game elective course at his school. He had the following to say when asked about his experience.

> When I had to start high school over, I believed that it would be a waste of time. I really thought that I was too old to be in grade school again. Once I was there, however, I started to like the people I met and believed that I could have a lot of fun for a short period of time, probably just one year or so. I did need to learn English after all. But then someone changed my point of view and I decided I needed to attend all four years and get my high school diploma. It was a wonderful experience and I now know what I want in my life.

> I never considered myself the strongest student. I struggled a lot with procrastination. I would like to do all my work on time but for some reason there was always something holding me back. There was a period of time where I was having a hard time in my life because my parents were on vacation for a long period of time. Since I was alone, I was pretty much doing anything I wanted since there was not someone at home to keep me on track. Yea I'm technically an adult, but it's always good to have the presence of a role model. Luckily a lot of my teachers kept me in check.

> During my senior year, I had the opportunity to enroll in a video game literature course. At the beginning of the class I felt very excited to start learning with something that I love. Video games are one of my hobbies, and may be a part of why I end up procrastinating from time to time. But I really liked the idea of video games becoming a part of my learning at school. It seemed like a great idea to get me motivated to learn. It was good even for those who do not usually play video games. By the end of the class everyone expressed that they enjoyed learning from the video games very much.

> This class inspired me to start looking into game development programs at various colleges. I would often tell my teachers that I was only 75% sure that I wanted to

go to college, even though that was kind of a lie. Senioritis hit me hard and I really wasn't sure if I wanted to continue school, especially since I had started school over and would only just be starting college at twenty-two years old. But then my teacher for the video game literature course told me that he was taking me and several of my classmates to Boston. Every year there is a big video game convention there called Pax East. My teacher had applied to bring himself and five of us students there to speak on a panel about our experiences learning with video games. We spoke in front of a few hundred people just talking about video games and why we thought they were useful in schools.

It was eye-opening to see how many people cared about what I was saying. They all paid attention to me and after the panel so many of them came up to say "Congratulations," to myself and my classmates. I asked my teacher, "Did you expect it to go that way?" And he said, "You all did better than I expected and I'm so proud of you." After the panel I said to myself, "That's what I want to be, that's what I want to do in my life." So now I want to work on creating games, not only to make him proud, but because it was so clear that video games can help so many people.

Then I got accepted into a very good program of games development with a full ride and my teacher told me, "With this opportunity you should 100% be going to college now." So now I eagerly await the start of college and the creation of my own games. Maybe my teacher will teach with my games in the future. I believe that using video games in school is very beneficial because it definitely gets students like me to work with more passion. Plus it will introduce people who don't play video games to them and they may find a new fun activity for themselves. Using things like pop music, movies, and games is important because they can change the perspective of the people or society. People need to realize that these things are not a waste of time and can be really beneficial for many students and people.

Danny is just one student, but his passion for video games extends beyond just himself. There are so many students who stand to benefit from the inclusion of video games in their learning experience. Not all of them will go on to pursue a career in video games like Danny, but they may end up more passionate about what transpires in their classroom. That reason alone should be enough to find a place for a video game or two in your curriculum.

BEYOND K–12

Video games are not just played by kids either. 43% of adults play video games often; and that number is only increasing. They are becoming a more integral part of people's lives and pop culture as a whole. Rachel Kowert, the Research Director at Take This described video games like this:

To me, video games mean fun and entertainment. They mean getting to collaborate and compete, to witness and experience joy and sorrow, to be part of an interactive story. They give us the unique chance to live many lives from the safety and comfort of our living room couch. To grieve the loss of Aerith with Cloud in *Final Fantasy VII*. To feel the twinge of success after a large raid battle in *World of Warcraft*. And to know what it would feel like to be the lead lemming and accidentally lead your whole village off a cliff to doom!

In my life, video games have been fantastic sources of entertainment and education. I have learned so much from video games. New information (like world history from the *Civilization* series of games), new skills, like effective city planning (From the *SimCity* franchise), and many, many things about social relationships through online play (like, how to effectively communicate with fewer non-verbal cues).

Video games were my childhood. They were my adolescence. And now, they are something that I get to share with my children.

Take This is an organization that helps those struggling with mental health in the gaming community. According to Take This, One-in-two people will be diagnosed with a mental health condition in their lifetime. Take This was founded to let people know that there's help for people with mental health challenges who are also passionate about making games. Rachel Kowert not only played games throughout her childhood and adolescence, but she merged her passion for video games and a her skills as a phycologist into a career dedicated to helping others. In an industry with hundreds of thousands of employees, there are a number of different ways that one's love for video games can impact their professional career.

Rachel Kowert is not the only person whose passion for video games led to a successful career. Reggie Fils-Aime's career was also impacted by his love for video games. For those of you who do not know, Reggie is the former President and COO of Nintendo of America. Some of your students might know him since he has long been an internet meme. He studied finance and business while attending Cornell University from 1979 to 1983. Upon graduating he ended up pursuing marketing and sales. He worked with a number of companies before ultimately ending up at Nintendo in 2003. Not every kid who loves video games will immediately find a job in that industry, but that passion can come back to help them down the road. Reggie said the following when asked, "What do video games mean to you and what have you learned from them?"

Before I was a game company executive, I was a video game fan just like you. I played games on Coleco and Atari Systems. I played coin operated games. The very first system I personally owned was the Super Nintendo Entertainment system and I still have that original system and a library of over eighty games. I played games on just about every console and handheld system since the early 90s. So I've always had a passion for this form of entertainment and I believe that came through in my role at Nintendo. It certainly helped me be successful there. I learned from people in the industry like my friends Mr. Iwata and Mr. Miyamoto and I believe you can learn real skills from video games. I believe you can learn skills like strategic and critical thinking, communication, creativity, quick decision making, and relentlessness all from video games."

He has been a fan of video games his entire life. That hobby eventually led him to become the president of one of the most well known and loved video game companies in the world. He has always understood the value in video games and recognizes that they can continue to teach those who play them.

Just as Reggie's passion led him to become the president of a gaming company, many other people entered the industry as video game developers. Two such people are Kyle Seeley the developer of *Emily is Away* and Steve Gaynor, the developer of *Gone Home*. When asked what video games meant to him Kyle Seeley had the following to say:

Video games mean a lot. I'm a game developer, so video games are how I express myself. Some people have art or music, but for me it's games. With them I can tell a deeply personal story, convey a complicated idea, or even just make something cathartically fun. I'd be lost without them.

What I've learned, both by making games and playing them, is the power of perspective. That, I think, is video games biggest strength over other mediums. Books let you understand a character, movies immerse you in a narrative, but only games ask the player, "Okay, now what?" And it's that agency, that power to choose, that lets players truly inhabit someone else. Someone with different motivations, different constraints, a different point of view entirely. And that's immensely powerful. Players don't simply experience a story, they're part of it. They don't simply see a new perspective, they form their own new perspective. And I think, especially given all that's going on in the world today, that's an incredibly necessary thing.

Kyle points out the key difference between video games and other mediums. It is not often that people can immerse themself in a narrative that asks the audience to learn and create new perspectives. Teachers often create simulations for their students in to role play. Assuming the role of another person or character is a great way for students to connect and empathize with others. Video games have done the leg work for teachers. Teachers only need to facilitate the conversations that come out of the playtime.

Steve Gaynor of The Fullbright Company and developer of *Gone Home* remarked when asked about what he has learned from video games:

Video games occupy a lot of roles in my life. They're a medium and an activity I've been constantly engaged with as an audience member since I was a child, as well as a creative space that's been my professional vocation since soon after I finished college. So they mean a lot to me. They are an incredible array of unforgettable moments and places that have taken a near-limitless range of forms, stretching back as early as I can remember, that are as vivid as places I've actually been, things I've actually done; they're a professional space where I've gotten to work with inspiring people who taught me everything I know about what I do and challenged me on how to be better at contributing to the body of work that's given me so much.

The human mind is something that can be uniquely elsewhere than where it is, through imagination and engagement with words, imagery and sound. Video games, for me, are places to be other than where we are, to expand the possibilities of what we can experience outside the world we inhabit, as a participant directly inhabiting these places, unique from any other kind of art or entertainment. I've learned a great deal from video games. Some are small, trivial things (how to siphon gas through a hose— Full Throttle, 1995; the definition of the world "simultaneous"— Nintendo Power Magazine, 1980s). But in the bigger picture, both as a developer and player, I've learned to think within, and around, problem spaces defined by consistent rules - and what it means to consider those rules from unique angles, explore the entirety of a possibility space, not just what's on the surface — to test boundaries and discover how the world reacts. To imagine what might be possible and see if it is. Games are an invitation to explore.

Problem solving is one of the most important skills learned by playing video games. Most games

Teaching with Video Games

present a problem that needs to be solved. More importantly, they do so in a safe environment where failure is expected and even encouraged. Even beyond that, there is a vast array of vocabulary that many kids learn in video games. Gaynor learned "simultaneous" from a Nintendo Power Magazine. How many other kids have learned words like "evolution" from *Pokémon*, "potion" from *The Legend of Zelda*, "polytheism" from the *Civilization* series, or even "accessibility" from more modern games like *The Last of Us Part II* that allow the player to tailor the gameplay to match their preferred experience? Visual cues are especially beneficial for English language learners, as they allow those students to put new vocabulary words in context. The way games situate meaning is essential for language learning. Words and language are associated with images, actions, and dialogue. Allowing learners to attach words to an appropriate context is a much more meaningful experience than studying definitions. As James Paul Gee puts it, memorizing definitions "may be good for test taking, but it is not good for deep understanding." Engaging with new vocabulary in a game environment allows for a deeper understanding of language.

A number of passionate educators are currently utilizing video games for all of the reasons above. Some of them include Steve Issacs, the International Society for Technology In Education Outstanding Teacher of the Year in 2016; Peggy Sheely, who has her sixth grade humanities class learn by playing the massive multiplayer online (MMO) video game *World of Warcraft*; and Paul Darvasi, a veteran teacher who has authored a number of articles around game-based learning and even wrote *Empathy, Perspective and complicity: How digital Games Can Support Peace Education and Conflict Resolution* for UNESCO's Mahatma Gandhi Institute for Education for Peace and Sustainable Development (MGIEP). When asked about what he has learned from video games, Dr. Paul Darvasi said:

> From my early memories, video games felt like magic, and that feeling has never faded. I am still amazed that I can enter and play in these interactive paintings, and each of the countless virtual worlds I have inhabited left their mark: I learned about the importance of crop cycles in my early forays into Intellivision's *Utopia*, I paid the consequences for poor zoning decisions in *SimCity*, and I struggled to maintain a fresh water supply in my offworld colony in *Oxygen Not Included*. As an educator, however, I have become more interested in how video games teach as opposed to what they teach. In a video game, a player begins by carrying out simple tasks and, within a few hours, they are proficiently managing a matrix of complex activities. This is achieved through a potent elixir of engagement, autonomy, choice, scaffolding, safe trial and error, and accelerated learning through doing. I am convinced that once schools learn to effectively apply these hallmarks of popular video games, the kingdom of education will be a better, happier and, perhaps, more magical place.

That sounds nice, right? Engagement, autonomy, choice, and scaffolding are aspects of education we hold dear.

Education is malleable. It is an ever-changing system that has never held any perfect form. It is always being molded and modified by those that wish to see it be a welcoming and nurturing environment for people of every background. Since COVID-19 brought education systems around the world to their knees, it is imperative to find new and engaging ways to get our students excited to learn. Video games are not the only answer, but they are an additional tool that educators can harness. And you never know: some of your students may embrace and utilize these experiences when they become a game developer, a psychologist, a teacher, or the next President of Nintendo. Hopefully this book will help get you started on your game-based learning journey.

References

Davis, V. (2014, October 13). *A Guide to Game-Based Learning.* https://www.edutopia.org/blog/guide-to-game-based-learning-vicki-davis.

Fandom. *Endings.* Undertale Wiki. https://undertale.fandom.com/wiki/Category:Endings.

Farber, M. (2018). Introduction. In *Game-Based Learning in Action: How an Expert Affinity Group Teaches With Games* (pp. 1–1). introduction, Peter Lang Inc., International Academic Publishers.

Fils-aime, R. (2007, November 18). *Life as the Regginator.* The New York Times. https://www.nytimes.com/2007/11/18/jobs/18boss.html.

Gee, J. P. (2013). Games for Learning. *Educational Horizons, 91,* 16–20.

Gee, J. P. (2007). Good Video Games and Good Learning. *University of Wisconsin-Madison and Academic Advanced Distributed Learning Co-Laboratory.* https://doi.org/10.3726/978-1-4539-1162-4

Heller, E. (2018, December 17). *GOTY 2018: #5 Celeste.* Polygon. https://www.polygon.com/best-games-2018/2018/12/17/18126327/best-games-2018-celeste-games-of-the-year.

Hilliker, E. (2017, May 18). *Top Five Vocabulary Strategies for English Language Learners.* Tch-svg. https://www.teachingchannel.com/blog/top-five-vocabulary-strategies-for-english-language-learners.

Keller, D. S., Squire, K., Giroux, H., Bekerman, Z., & Burbules, N. (2008). Critical Education in an Interactive Age. In *Mirror images: popular culture and education* (pp. 105–110). essay, Lang.

Perrin, A. (2020, May 30). *5 facts about Americans and video games.* Pew Research Center. https://www.pewresearch.org/fact-tank/2018/09/17/5-facts-about-americans-and-video-games/.

Pew Research Center. (2020, May 30). *Teens, Video Games and Civics.* Pew Research Center: Internet, Science & Tech. https://www.pewresearch.org/internet/2008/09/16/teens-video-games-and-civics/.

Pino-James, N. (2015, December 11). *Golden Rules for Engaging Students in Learning Activities.* Edutopia. https://www.edutopia.org/blog/golden-rules-for-engaging-students-nicolas-pino-james.

Plunkett, L. (2017, April 4). *The Weird Words I Learned From Video Games.* Kotaku. https://kotaku.com/the-weird-words-i-learned-from-video-games-1676172328.

Popova, M. (2020, February 16). *Fixed vs. Growth: The Two Basic Mindsets That Shape Our Lives.* Brain Pickings. https://www.brainpickings.org/2014/01/29/carol-dweck-mindset/.

Rucker, N. W. (2019, December 10). *Getting Started With Culturally Responsive Teaching.* Edutopia. https://www.edutopia.org/article/getting-started-culturally-responsive-teaching.

Riley, D. (2019). *What Percentage of Kids Play Video Games.* The NPD Group. https://www.npd.com/wps/portal/npd/us/news/press-releases/2019/according-to-the-npd-group—73-percent-of-u-s—consumers-play-video-games/.

Ritzhaupt, A., & Pleasant, R. (2011). Video Games and Learning: Teaching and Participatory Culture in the Digital Age. *International Journal of Gaming and Computer-Mediated Simulations.*

Shaffer, D. W., Squire, K. R., Halverson, R., & Gee, J. P. (2004). Video games and the Future of Learning. *University of Wisconsin-Madison and Academic Advanced Distributed Learning Co-Laboratory.*

Squire, K. (2006). From Content to Context: Videogames as Designed Experience. *Educational Researcher, 35*(8), 19–29.

Take This. (2020, July 1). *About Take This.* Take This. https://www.takethis.org/about/.

Steinkuehler, C. (2014). Games and Learning. Handbook of the Learning Sciences (2nd Ed.).

Team, W. by E. (2013, April 23). *What is GBL (Game-Based Learning)?* EdTechReview. https://edtechreview.in/dictionary/298-what-is-game-based-learning.

Webb, K. (2019, October 1). *The $120 billion gaming industry is going through more change than it ever has before, and everyone is trying to cash in.* Business Insider. https://www.businessinsider.com/video-game-industry-120-billion-future-innovation-2019-9.

Woodard, C. (2019, November 17). Using Undertale to teach evidence gathering for argumentative essays/thesis writing [web log]. https://www.heylistengames.org/teacherslounge/the-teachers-lounge/using-undertale-to-teach-evidence-gathering-for-argumentative-essays-thesis-writing.

Teaching Toolkit

"It's Dangerous to Go Alone! Take This."

-Old Man, *The Legend of Zelda*

What You Need to Get Started

You are in luck! Bringing video games into your classroom is much easier than you think. There are myriad ways to play video games with your students. What is fun about game-based learning is there is no right method of teaching in this way. Interviewing ten teachers who teach with games will provide ten different methodologies. Some teachers utilize a flipped classroom method where students play the games at home and then use class time to discuss and analyze their experiences. A handful of schools will provide students with individual copies of a game so they can play at their own pace. Some teachers even have students stream games online, now that many schools are engaged in remote learning. Other teachers prefer to play together as a class, with one student playing at a time while the game is projected in the front of the classroom. Depending on the game, this is probably the easiest method of implementing game-based learning, since many schools can't ensure every student has the necessary technology to be able to play their own copies at home.

The method you choose to use will ultimately depend on the type of game you plan on bringing into your classroom. If it is narrative-heavy, takes several hours to complete, and requires a console to play, then consider playing together as a class. If the game is free to play, only lasts fifteen to twenty minutes, and runs in a web browser, then it makes a lot more sense to have students play individually, assuming that enough computers are available.

If you are just starting out, I recommend that you play a game together as a class. That way, only one console/computer is needed and only one copy of a game needs to be bought. There is definitely merit to having each student play their own save file, but it can be a lot harder to manage. Playing together as a class allows for students to have ongoing conversations and debates about what is happening on screen. Think of it like the many times you have read a book together in an English language arts class, or the times you watched a movie in a history class. Not every student needs to actually play the game. The teacher can rotate player turns, and not every student identifies as a gamer; some would much rather watch others play than play themselves. Watching video games is an extraordinary popular activity; millions of people watch others play on Youtube and Twitch.

This chapter will detail all of the materials, resources, and tools you need to start teaching with video games.

PERSONAL COMPUTER

This is the easiest place to start for teachers who do not have a gaming console. Most people at least have their own personal computers (PC) or are provided one by their school. This book is not going to delve into the specificity of different types of computers and which is the best, but if you have a computer with a hard drive then you should be fine. The only drawback to a personal computer is that some video game consoles have games exclusive to their platform, although even those are slowly becoming more available on PCs.

Steam

If you know what game you want to play and have a computer, then Steam is the easiest place to start. Steam is a video game digital distribution service created by Valve that can be downloaded to any computer. You may recognize Valve as the developer of classics like *Half Life, Portal, Left 4 Dead,* and *Team Fortress.* The

Steam platform is the largest digital distribution platform for PC gaming. Most games worth teaching with can be found on Steam. All you really need is your computer, a HDMI cable, and some type of screen that you can connect to your computer. Most schools these days have SMART Boards or Promethean Screens, so it should be easy to have any game projected in the front of the room. There are also a number of projectors that can attach to a computer via HDMI if you need to go about purchasing one. Most games on Steam are played with a mouse and keyboard, but the platform does have Bluetooth support if you prefer to have your students play with a controller. Steam has their own branded controller, but any modern Nintendo, Playstation, or Xbox controller can easily be linked to the platform.

Steam is by no means the only platform out there through which to buy games, but it is the most recognizable. Chances are a couple of your students already have their own accounts.

itch.io

itch.io is a website for its users to host, sell, and download video games. The wonderful aspect of itch.io is its focus on indie games. There are no AAA games to be found here. Instead, there is a catalogue of thousands of smaller-scale, independently made games. Many beginner developers start off on itch.io. Indie games are unique in that they often focus more on narrative and storytelling mechanics instead of gameplay because the development teams often consist of just one or a couple of people. This site is especially useful for those of you in search of smaller experiences. Most of the games available here are pretty short: less than a half hour of playtime. Even better, many of the games available on itch.io are free to play. This makes it a low-stakes entry point for those of you who are not ready to financially invest in this method of teaching – though there is always a donation option for the developers of these games that you should consider if you do continue to utilize their products.

The games that are free to play can usually be played in two different ways. Some of them need to be downloaded directly to a computer, just like with Steam. Others, however, can be played in any web browser. This is where it is easy to have each student play their own copy of the game. A large number of schools these days fill their classrooms with iPads, Chromebooks, and other learning devices. If each student has access to a device, then all the teacher needs to do is share the link with them and make sure the internet is working. We all know how unreliable that can be at times. A lot of the games can be played on mobile phones, but most games are optimized for computer use, so they may not run perfectly on an iPhone or android device.

No Platform is perfect, and you should choose one that you are most comfortable with. Steam is easy enough and definitely popular enough that some students may be able to help you when needed. Itch.io is a great entry point with low financial risk. Plus many of the games there are really special and deserve more attention. Other digital distribution platforms one can utilize are . . .

Gamersgate	Green Man Gaming	GOG	Humble Store
Origin by EA	Ubisoft UPlay	Epic Games Launcher	Bethesda Launcher
Microsoft Store	Apple App Store	Blizzard Battle.Net	Discord Store

Teaching with Video Games

They each have their own benefits with their own exclusives and occasional deals. You will need to do your homework to find out what is truly the best service for you and your students. Steam and itch.io are good entry points for those of you who may find all of this information daunting.

NINTENDO

Everyone knows Nintendo. Everyone has that one family member who just refers to all video game consoles as Nintendos. Nintendo has an extensive library of consoles, but the Nintendo Switch is perfect for those teachers interested in game-based learning. It's Nintendo's most recent video game console – a hybrid console that acts as both a handheld system and one that can be connected and played on any TV. The system itself is a tablet with two Joy Con controllers attached to either side. When someone wants to play on a TV, all they need to do is slip it into a dock that it comes with. Even better, you can buy multiple docks so that noone has to carry a dock around. That means a teacher can have a dock at school and a second one at home. This is a lot easier than lugging an entire Playstation or Xbox back and forth. The Joy Con controllers also function as either one controller, or two separate controllers. As a home console, the Nintendo switch is probably the easiest and most accessible to work with.

Just like itch.io, the Switch is a wonderful place to find and play indie games. The independent scene has been going through a renaissance of sorts, partly due to the success of the Switch. Nintendo has embraced and marketed the many independent games, partly to make up for the lack of big budget AAA games available on the console (see their Nindies Showcases). As a tablet, it's naturally less powerful than other home consoles and computers, but the amount of indie games available is wonderful for teachers, and a great place to start looking for games to play with their students. Indie games are great because they are usually under five hours long. Instead of creating a massive cinematic experience, they often focus on telling a strong short story that does not overstay its welcome. This is ideal for a classroom setting since it can be challenging for teachers to set aside class time for larger games. This focus on pure storytelling makes them a particularly good fit for English language arts (and other countries' equivalent) or social studies classes. The indie scene is also particularly amazing about producing games that deal with social emotional health. Many schools have advisory classes that focus on checking in with students and their personal and emotional lives. Playing these games can foster healthy, open conversations between the students. These games also tend to be less mechanically demanding. An indie game like *What Remains of Edith Finch* is much easier to control than a AAA game like *Assassin's Creed*. Using a controller, or mouse and keyboard, is definitely challenging if one did not grow up playing games. If the controls are easier, then the game becomes more accessible for all of the students who want to play.

If you are not an experienced gamer, then the Switch is a great way to dip your toes in the water. Depending on the context of your class there is an entire library beyond just the Switch that can be accessed. There are thousands of games across Nintendo's entire console history. If you can find a way to make a lesson out of a Nintendo 64 game, go for it! There is no reason to pigeonhole the curriculum to just the modern consoles, but it is easier on the tech side of things. And remember, only with a Nintendo console can you bring the *Mario* and *Zelda* franchises into your classroom.

PLAYSTATION

Playstation is a juggernaut. As of May 2020, lifetime sales for the Playstation 4 have passed 110 million consoles. Odds are you have several students with a Playstation 4. And if not a Playstation 4, then definitely a Playstation 2, 3, or the newly released 5. A Playstation is realistically just as good as having a personal computer or a Nintendo Switch in your classroom. The only real downside is that you may end up lugging a full-sized console back and forth to your school. If you are willing to put up with that minor inconvenience, then there is a lot to be gained from using a Playstation console. It also has an extensive library of games including a vast library of indie games. On top of that, Playstation has invested heavily in its exclusive content. Only on a Playstation console can you find franchises like *God of War, Uncharted, The Last of Us, Horizon Zero Dawn, and Spider-Man. The Last of Us* franchise in particular is one destined to have entire college courses dedicated to its discussion and analysis. *The Last of Us Part II* is already the fastest selling Playstation exclusive game of all time with over four million copies sold in just three days.

Playstation also has the added benefit of the Playstation Virtual Reality (PSVR) headset, if you really want to get crazy and experimental. It is another several hundred-dollar investment and can be a little challenging to set up, but virtual reality offers an entirely new form of storytelling and experiences that can easily aid a teacher's curriculum. In a typical video game the player gets to control the protagonist in a story. Well, in virtual reality the player can actually be the protagonist.

You cannot go wrong with Playstation. Playstation is constantly at the forefront of the gaming industry, pushing the boundaries of what video games can accomplish. Even better, nearly every classroom will have at least one student well versed in the Playstation ecosystem. It is always a good idea to tap into the skills and background knowledge students already have. Bringing a Playstation into a classroom will instantly turn some students into experts.

XBOX

Xbox is very similar to Playstation. The Xbox One has the same access to AAA games, with the added benefit of being a slightly more powerful console than the Playstation 4. So if graphics, framerate, and fidelity are super important for you, then Xbox is the way to go. The new Xbox Series X only improves upon all of these details. The only real issue with Xbox is that, of the three home consoles, it offers the fewest exclusive games. There are a couple of great franchises like *Halo* and *Gears of War*, but they are both shooters, which are less likely to be used in schools. Incorporating a shooter into a curriculum can happen in the same way teachers show war movies like Saving Private Ryan in class, but playing a game that incorporates gun violence can be controversial. Doing so would most likely require the explicit permission of each student's parents. Microsoft has acquired Bethesda Softworks so Xbox will end up with many more exclusives in the long run. Popular franchises like Fallout, The Elder Scrolls, and Doom are all a part of Xbox's future. These are some of the most well known intellectual properties in gaming. Buying an Xbox now is solid investment for the future.

The cool thing about Xbox though is that it is by far the most accessible in terms of backwards compatibility. Both the Nintendo Switch and Playstation 4 are unable to play games from their previous generations. The Xbox One and Xbox Series X, however, are able to play a large number of games from both of its predecessors: the original Xbox and the Xbox 360. That immediately makes the library available on the console larger than its competition. The Playstation 5 can play Playstation 4 games, but cannot play games from any earlier generations.

Another reason to keep Xbox in mind is their Game Pass service. Xbox Game Pass is a service unlike any other currently in the video game industry. Think of it as a Netflix for Games. It is a monthly subscriptions service that gives the user instant access to a large library of video games. It is full of indie games, but also contains a decent number of AAA games. The average AAA game costs around $60, which was equal to about six months of this service. It more than pays for itself as long as the user plays a couple of games a year. Uniquely, if someone does not have an Xbox, they can also use this service on a PC. For those of you worried about the cost of teaching with video games, this provides a low entry cost, and you are sure to find something worth bringing into your classroom.

MOBILE

Playing on a mobile phone is actually a lot easier than one might think. It may also be an easy place for a teacher to start. There are thousands of games available to play on smartphones. Many of them are absolute garbage, but there is a handful of story-based games worthy enough to teach with. They can also be played together as a class, as with the other home consoles. Any smartphone can actually be projected on a screen in the front of a classroom, assuming there is a SMART Board, Promethean Screen, or any other kind of television set. One option would be to buy an HDMI adapter that connects a smartphone directly to a screen. This would mirror whatever is on the phone screen to the screen in the front of the classroom. One student can play on the phone while the rest of the class watches the projected version of the game. There are also ways of using Google Chromecast or Apple TV to stream whatever is on a smartphone to a larger screen. That is, however, a larger monetary investment.

As noted, not every student needs their own copy of a game, but many students these days do have smartphones. As these devices have advanced so have the games available to play on them. Playing mobile games is a good idea if a teacher is absolutely set on each student having their own copy of a game. A lot of mobile games are also free to play. Just make sure that your students do not spend money on in game purchases and microtransactions. That is where they get you.

TWITCH - YOUTUBE

An interesting thing about video games today is that many people who identify as gamers may not actually play video games themselves. Video platforms like Twitch and Youtube have revolutionized how video games are consumed. Many people these days opt to watch other people (streamers) play games. Globally, people watched over fifty billion hours of video game content on Youtube in 2018 alone. Most of those people probably also play games themselves, but watching gaming content has become a staple of the industry. Twitch, the largest live streaming service available has over fifteen million daily active users. Nearly half of these users are between the ages of 18 to 34, and 21% are ages 13 to 17. Nearly a quarter of all people watching video games on Twitch are of middle and high school age. These numbers are important. Video game culture was for a long time something that had a price tag. You needed to be able to afford a console, computer, and games in order to participate in that culture. Twitch and Youtube changed this. They are both free to use and have allowed anyone to consume video game content even if they are not paying for and playing the games themselves.

So how does this all relate to teaching? First and foremost, gaming is a method to catch up students who may have been absent or missed a class. Teachers always need a backup plan and a way to catch students up if they missed something. Not every student needs to be the player when using a game in class. Any student can easily watch a video clip on Youtube from a portion of a game that they missed. Certain games also have branching dialogues where the actual narrative will change depending on the player's choices. A large number of games even have different endings. A teacher can use Youtube to find clips of the various endings in order to show a student exactly what they missed, if the game was shown in class with one ending.

Twitch will be more helpful when students are not in the classroom. The platform lets a user stream content live on the internet. People can visit a player's page and watch them as they play through a game. There is even a chat box that lets users speak to each other while watching.

COVID-19 has changed education. Schools across the world are now engaged in remote learning. Even as schools return to in person learning, remote teaching will continue to be an option for many of those who need. It has shown the world that there can be different ways to schedule school. If remote learning continues to play a part, during a quarantine or not, then Twitch works perfectly. A student who has a console or personal computer at home can stream a game online. Then the rest of the class can watch and engage in the online chat. This allows everyone to experience the game together even when they are not in the classroom.

There is no one right way to teach with video games. There is no one right way to teach in general. It is ultimately up to the educator to try and refine different methods. It should be a tailored experience that best reaches the students. When you do decide to start your game based learning journey all you need is one means of playing a game and screen to project the game in the front of the room. The rest is a group experience just like any other lesson.

References

25 Useful Twitch Stats for Influencer Marketing Managers [Infographic]. Influencer Marketing Hub. (2020, June 10). https://influencermarketinghub.com/twitch-stats/.

Austin, P. L. (2019, March 4). *How Nintendo's Embrace of Indie Games Is Helping the Switch*. Time. https://time.com/5531065/nintendo-switch-indie-games/.

Hernandez, P. (2019, August 16). *The people who watch video games, but never play them*. Polygon. https://www.polygon.com/2019/8/16/20807731/youtube-twitch-fandom-video-games-cosplay-fan-art.

Join Xbox Game Pass: Xbox. Xbox.com. (2020). https://www.xbox.com/en-US/xbox-game-pass.

Lempel, E. (2020). The Last of Us Part II sells more than 4 million copies [web log]. https://blog.playstation.com/2020/06/26/the-last-of-us-part-ii-sells-more-than-4-million-copies/.

Minotti, M. (2020, May 13). *PlayStation 4 sales reach 110.4 million*. VentureBeat. https://venturebeat.com/2020/05/12/playstation-4-sales-reach-110-4-million/.

Twitch Advertising. (2021). *Over 2,500,000 are watching Twitch right now*. Twitch.tv. https://twitchadvertising.tv/audience/#:~:text=Nearly%20half%20of%20all%20Twitch,are%20ages%2013%20to%2017.

Xbox One Backward Compatibility List: Xbox. Xbox.com. (2020). https://www.xbox.com/en-US/xbox-one/backward-compatibility.

The Games

"If you're ready to be kind
and receive kindness in return,
please sign here!"

Ella – *Kind Words*

Video Games as Texts

Hey Listen Games was created because there is a lack of resources out there for those who are interested in teaching with video games. There is a large community of game-based educators, but there are very few resources that provide actual lesson plans, curriculum, and handouts for teachers. There are organizations out there that provide spaces for educators and developers to collaborate and bounce ideas off each other, but none that puts those lesson plans in your hands. That's where this book comes in - it provides lesson plans, curriculums, and handouts for teachers. Hey Listen Games can act as a starting point to understanding how and why a teacher uses video games in their classroom. From there, any teacher can take those lesson plans and modify or adapt them to best match their own learning environment. Playing video games is a very normal activity for many students and it is important for teachers to bring that sense of normalcy into their classrooms.

This portion of the manual will provide a detailed list and explanation of the games you can teach with. You will find a rationale and instructions for teaching with a collection of different video games found on Hey Listen Games. These are all games that were made for entertainment purposes, many of which your students are already playing on their own time. Not all of them will match your exact needs, but you may come across one that fits perfectly in your classroom. These are all individual lessons that should not be taught on their own. They are lessons and activities that you need to teach in conjunction with what is already a part of your curriculum. Most can be completed within a week and none of them take up a full unit. You probably have mandated texts and standards that you need to teach cover, depending on your district and state. While these games are Common Core aligned, they are not meant to replace your current texts, but to supplement them. You'll need to make sure the context of your curriculum is appropriate for the following lessons. These games are also by no means the only ones you can teach with. There are thousands of games out there just waiting to be used in a classroom. Finding the best games to use can be tough, so consider this your entry point.

Some of these summaries will include student work samples while others will include sample handouts. Note that all student work provided was completed by students of mine who are English language learners (ELLs) and that you may need to modify/adapt for your own students. All age ratings are listed according to Common Sense Media. The full lesson plans and curriculum are all available for free at Hey Listen Games (https://www.heylistengames.org). So head over there if you see something that may be worth playing with your students.

Papers, Please

SEE PAGE 2 IN THE STUDENT PACKET

- Content Area/s: Social Studies
- Developed by Lucas Pope
- Available on Microsoft Windows, OS X, Linux, iOS, PlayStation Vita
- Rated: 15+

WHERE TO PLAY

- Available on Microsoft Windows, OS X, Linux, iOS, PlayStation Vita

CONTEXT

This lesson should take place during a unit on

- Immigration
- Refugee Crises
- The Holocaust

DO AHEAD - PREP

- Decide if you want to buy the full game or download the free beta version
    - > The beta does not include the whole game, but it does have more than enough if you do not plan on teaching with the entire game.
- Choose the texts that you want to teach alongside this game. Some examples are as follows
    - > The Immigration Act of 1924 (The Johnson-Reed Act)
    - > Syria Refugee Crisis Explained
    - > Holocaust and Human Behavior Curriculum

OVERVIEW

Immigration and border security are often at the front of political discussions in the United States and around the world. In Papers, Please you take on the role of a border security agent who controls the flow of migration into your country, Arstotzka.

Papers, Please is a game of making choices and facing the consequences of one's actions. It is a great way to get students to interact with many different types of restrictions placed on immigrants and migration. It is an easy, non-threatening, lesson to get students thinking critically about issues that actually exist in our world. The game tasks the player with observing documentation of incoming migrants and ultimately making the decision if they can enter the country. You can follow the rules, or you can begin letting in people who are not legally allowed to enter. These choices will have lasting effects throughout the game. Do you turn away everyone, including refugees, or do you show compassion for those who need entry? The latter action will put you and your family at risk. *Papers, Please* is, at its core, a puzzle game. The player must sift through the paperwork of each immigrant, investigating whether or not the people are wanted criminals or smugglers, are using stolen or forged documents, even if their vaccinations are up to date. If their papers are in order, then they can enter. Otherwise they are denied.

The game may be fictional, but it is grounded in reality. Think of moments in history like the Immigration Act of 1924 in the United States, a law that dramatically restricted the flow of immigration into the United States through the use of a national origins quota. Specifically the quota provided immigration visas to two percent of the total number of people of each nationality in the United States as of the 1890 national census. This was a policy that lasted until 1965 with the passage of the Immigration Act of 1965. It is very easy for students in a U.S. History class to play Papers, Please and make connections to the treatment of immigrants throughout United States history. That being said, it can be taught in a Global History class as well. It is also a game that does not need to be played in its entirety. Just playing over the course of one class period will be more than enough time for students to make connections with the content of the unit.

DESCRIPTION OF ACTIVITY

- One copy of Papers, Please needed
- Project the game in the front of the room
- The player's job as an immigration inspector is to control the flow of people entering the Arstotzkan side of Grestin from Kolechia. Among the groups of immigrants, visitors and people looking for work are hidden smugglers, spies, and terrorists. Using only the documents provided by travelers and the Ministry of Admissions's primitive inspection system, search, and fingerprint systems you must decide who can enter Arstotzka, who will be turned away and who will be arrested.
- Documents in Papers, Please contain information that identifies and verifies a character›s ability to enter Arstotzka, allowing the inspector to grant them an entry stamp. The checking and handling of documents occurs every day and forms the core gameplay of the game.
- Will you deny or accept the entry of immigrants and travelers?
- Remember, all places and characters in this game are fiction. This game is simply a representation of how many people feel about migration, immigration, and border patrol.
- Make sure to take note of the decision made by the players and the consequences of those decisions as you play through the game together.
- Provide an accompanying handout before starting the game, as students will be answering questions as they play through the story.

OBJECTIVES

- Students will identify different types of immigration restrictions in the game *Papers, Please*.

- Students will make connections between historical issues of immigration and the game *Papers, Please*.

- Students will make connections between modern day immigration issues and the game *Papers, Please*.

CORRELATION TO COMMON CORE STANDARDS

English Language Arts Anchor Standards

GRADES K-12

- College and Career Readiness Anchor Standards for Reading

  Key Ideas and Details

  > CCSS.ELA-LITERACY.CCRA.R.2

  Determine central ideas or themes of a text and analyze their development; summarize the key supporting details and ideas.

- College and Career Readiness Anchor Standards for Speaking and Listening

  Comprehension and Collaboration

  > CCSS.ELA-LITERACY.CCRA.SL.1

  Prepare for and participate effectively in a range of conversations and collaborations with diverse partners, building on others› ideas and expressing their own clearly and persuasively.

  > CCSS.ELA-LITERACY.CCRA.SL.2

  Integrate and evaluate information presented in diverse media and formats, including visually, quantitatively, and orally.

History - Social Studies

GRADES 6-8

Key Ideas and Details

> CCSS.ELA-LITERACY.RH.6-8.2

Determine the central ideas or information of a primary or secondary source; provide an accurate summary of the source distinct from prior knowledge or opinions.

Integration of Knowledge and Ideas

> CCSS.ELA-LITERACY.RH.6-8.7

Integrate visual information (e.g., in charts, graphs, photographs, videos, or maps) with other information in print and digital texts.

> CCSS.ELA-LITERACY.RH.6-8.9

Analyze the relationship between a primary and secondary source on the same topic.

Teaching with Video Games

GRADES 9-10

Key Ideas and Details

> CCSS.ELA-LITERACY.RH.9-10.2

Determine the central ideas or information of a primary or secondary source; provide an accurate summary of how key events or ideas develop over the course of the text.

Integration of Knowledge and Ideas

> CCSS.ELA-LITERACY.RH.9-10.7

Integrate quantitative or technical analysis (e.g., charts, research data) with qualitative analysis in print or digital text.

> CCSS.ELA-LITERACY.RH.9-10.9

Compare and contrast treatments of the same topic in several primary and secondary sources.

GRADES 11-12

Key Ideas and Details

> CCSS.ELA-LITERACY.RH.11-12.2

Determine the central ideas or information of a primary or secondary source; provide an accurate summary that makes clear the relationships among the key details and ideas.

Integration of Knowledge and Ideas

> CCSS.ELA-LITERACY.RH.11-12.7

Integrate and evaluate multiple sources of information presented in diverse formats and media (e.g., visually, quantitatively, as well as in words) in order to address a question or solve a problem.

> CCSS.ELA-LITERACY.RH.11-12.9

Integrate information from diverse sources, both primary and secondary, into a coherent understanding of an idea or event, noting discrepancies among sources.

TIME REQUIREMENTS

While the game takes about five hours to complete, only thirty minutes to one hour of playtime is recommended for this lesson, which makes it ideal for a lesson in the classroom and for students to complete homework based on the lesson.

SAFETY - TRIGGER WARNING

Papers, Please is a mature game. There are depictions of death and even a terrorist attack at one point, early in the game. Prepare your students for these moments beforehand when needed.

- Beyond the Empathy Games 101: Digging Deep into Empathy, Ethics, and Design with Kelli Dunlap
- An Introduction to Content Warnings and Trigger Warnings

The Republia Times

SEE PAGE 4 IN THE STUDENT PACKET

- Content Area/s: Social Studies - Media Literacy
- Developed by Lucas Pope
- Rated: 10+

WHERE TO PLAY

- Available on Web Browser

CONTEXT

This lesson should take place during a unit on

- The News
- Wartime Propaganda
- Media literacy

DO BEFORE - PREP

- Decide if you want to play together as a class, in pairs, groups, or individually
- Choose the texts that you want to teach alongside this game. Some examples are as follows
  - > What is media literacy, and why is it important?
  - > News Article Analysis - Facing History

OVERVIEW

Many people today get caught in «bubbles» when it comes to the news. Most people check one outlet for the news without consulting other sources. While it is great to be informed even from one source, it is important to remember that every newspaper or tv channel has motives. There is always a bias and always a slant. People need to utilize various sources of news before they can make conscious decisions about current events.

The Republia Times puts us in the shoes of a man in charge of the country›s newspaper and propaganda machine. It teaches us that there can be ulterior motives for the stories that are chosen to be published. It is a great, free game by Lucas Pope in which you play as a minister of propaganda in the imaginary country of Republia. You control the headlines and layout of the country›s newspaper and your aim is to increase both loyalty and readership numbers. It is up to the player to decide whether or not to follow the direct guidelines provided by the government, or to foster disloyalty in order to help an ongoing rebellion. Helping the rebellion, however, will put the player's family at risk. The lesson gives students the opportunity to not only critique newspapers and their influence, but actually interact and take part in said influence.

What is also great about *The Republia Times* is that it is very short, with a normal playthrough only taking about ten minutes. This gives students the opportunity to play multiple times while making different decisions in order to experience the different endings. They can also have discussions with each other to see what they all did differently. Here is an example of student work for a student who played through the game:

DESCRIPTION OF ACTIVITY

- Amount of copies needed is at the discretion of the teacher
  - > The game is free to play in web browsers
  - > The class can play together with the game projected in the front of the room
  - > Students can play in pairs/groups on computers
  - > Or students can play individually on computers
- As the game's name puts it, *The Republia Times* is the national newspaper of a fictional country recovering from a war with a neighboring nation. The game puts the player into the shoes of the editor-in-chief of the newspaper. It is the player's job to increase the loyalty of the public by highlighting good things about the Republian government. *The Republia Times*, however, is run by an Orwellian style government and has no qualms about threatening the lives of your significant other and children if you do not do your job well.
- In managing this newspaper and public opinion, the player selects headlines to place on the front page. Be careful, though: the player must make sure to pick flattering stories like, "The Honorable and Great Leader Awarded Lifetime Glory Medal," and to ignore unflattering stories like, "The Honorable and Great Leader Photographed in Women's Clothes." The size of the headline is important, as well. The larger it is, the more attention it receives from the populace. The game will allow the player the option to choose headlines that adhere to their own political agenda.
- Several days into work at *The Republia Times*, the player is contacted by a rebellion force. They plead with the player to sabotage Republia by turning the public against its government. Sabotaging the government does not only risk the player's life, but that of their family, as well. These different options in narrative lead to different endings, all of which are worth pursuing.
- Provide an accompanying handout before starting the game, as students will be answering questions as they play through the story.

OBJECTIVES

- Students will identify different types of news sources.
- Students will identify bias and how it is used to push an agenda in the news.
- Students will play through The Republia Times at least once. Depending on how far the student progresses, they may be able to attempt a second time.

CORRELATION TO COMMON CORE STANDARDS

English Language Arts Anchor Standards

GRADES K-12

- College and Career Readiness Anchor Standards for Reading

Key Ideas and Details

> CCSS.ELA-LITERACY.CCRA.R.1

Read closely to determine what the text says explicitly and to make logical inferences from it; cite specific textual evidence when writing or speaking to support conclusions drawn from the text.

> CCSS.ELA-LITERACY.CCRA.R.2

Determine central ideas or themes of a text and analyze their development; summarize the key supporting details and ideas.

- College and Career Readiness Anchor Standards for Speaking and Listening

Comprehension and Collaboration

> CCSS.ELA-LITERACY.CCRA.SL.1

Prepare for and participate effectively in a range of conversations and collaborations with diverse partners, building on others› ideas and expressing their own clearly and persuasively.

> CCSS.ELA-LITERACY.CCRA.SL.2

Integrate and evaluate information presented in diverse media and formats, including visually, quantitatively, and orally.

History - Social Studies

GRADES 6-8

Key Ideas and Details

> CCSS.ELA-LITERACY.RH.6-8.1

Cite specific textual evidence to support analysis of primary and secondary sources.

> CCSS.ELA-LITERACY.RH.6-8.2

Determine the central ideas or information of a primary or secondary source; provide an accurate summary of the source distinct from prior knowledge or opinions.

Integration of Knowledge and Ideas

> CCSS.ELA-LITERACY.RH.6-8.9

Analyze the relationship between a primary and secondary source on the same topic.

Craft and Structure

> CCSS.ELA-LITERACY.RH.6-8.4

Determine the meaning of words and phrases as they are used in a text, including vocabulary specific to domains related to history/social studies.

GRADES 9-10

Key Ideas and Details

> CCSS.ELA-LITERACY.RH.9-10.2

Determine the central ideas or information of a primary or secondary source; provide an accurate summary of how key events or ideas develop over the course of the text.

Integration of Knowledge and Ideas

> CCSS.ELA-LITERACY.RH.9-10.9

Compare and contrast treatments of the same topic in several primary and secondary sources.

Craft and Structure

> CCSS.ELA-LITERACY.RH.9-10.4

> Determine the meaning of words and phrases as they are used in a text, including vocabulary describing political, social, or economic aspects of history/social science.

GRADES 11-12

Key Ideas and Details

> CCSS.ELA-LITERACY.RH.11-12.2

Determine the central ideas or information of a primary or secondary source; provide an accurate summary that makes clear the relationships among the key details and ideas.

Integration of Knowledge and Ideas

> CCSS.ELA-LITERACY.RH.11-12.9

Integrate information from diverse sources, both primary and secondary, into a coherent understanding of an idea or event, noting discrepancies among sources.

Craft and Structure

> CCSS.ELA-LITERACY.RH.11-12.4

Determine the meaning of words and phrases as they are used in a text, including analyzing how an author uses and refines the meaning of a key term over the course of a text (e.g., how Madison defines faction in Federalist No. 10).

TIME REQUIREMENTS

A single round of *The Republia Times* takes about fifteen minutes. This lesson can be taught with just one playthrough, but it is worth it to have students play a couple of times so that they can roleplay in different ways and pursue different endings. Allowing students to engage with the game in different ways will help them gain a better understanding of how people can be manipulated by the news.

SAFETY - TRIGGER WARNING

While *The Republia Times* is perfectly appropriate for most teenagers, it still lightly deals with themes of war. Keep this in mind if there are any refugees or students affected by war in your classroom.

- Beyond the Empathy Games 101: Digging Deep into Empathy, Ethics, and Design with Kelli Dunlap
- An Introduction to Content Warnings and Trigger Warnings

Bad News

SEE PAGE 6 IN THE STUDENT PACKET

- Content Area/s: Social Studies
- Developed by Drog In collaboration with the University of Cambridge
- Rated: 14+

WHERE TO PLAY

- Available on Web Browser

CONTEXT

This lesson should take place during a unit on

- The News
- Propaganda
- Media literacy With a Focus on Social Media

DO BEFORE - PREP

- Decide if you want to play in pairs, groups, or individually
- Choose the texts that you want to teach alongside this game. Some examples are as follows
  - > Do tweens and teens believe "fake news"?
  - > How to Spot Fake News (and Teach Kids to Be Media-Savvy)

OVERVIEW

People spend, on average, over two hours each day on social media. Our students are no exception. An unintended consequence of social media is that people tend to place themselves in a bubble of information. We see, like, share, or upvote posts that are in agreement with our own biases or perspectives. Over time we tend to see less and less of the ideas that can potentially challenge these biases. This gradually pushes people further to the fringes of (often political) ideologies. Disinformation plays a large role in this. People are less likely to fact check something that lines up with their own beliefs. The *Bad News* game can help get students thinking critically about the "news" and information they come in contact with on social media. It sheds a light on some of the tactics utilized by people who engage in misinformation and disinformation campaigns.

Developed by DROG, in collaboration with the University of Cambridge, Bad News acts as an introduction to the various strategies that disinformation campaigns employ throughout social media platforms. To quote from their Information Sheet:

> The term "fake news" has become ubiquitous in media coverage. While it certainly has its uses, it doesn't do a very good job at describing the full breadth of the concept. What we call "fake news" refers to news that has been entirely fabricated or

made up. However, a news item doesn't have to be entirely made up to be insidious or misleading. To capture the broader scope of the various ways to mislead audiences, we prefer to use the term "disinformation." Unlike "misinformation," which is simply information that is incorrect, disinformation involves the intent to deceive. Propaganda, then, is disinformation with an explicit or implicit political agenda.

Most people were never taught how to filter the plethora of information with which we come in contact. This game breaks down these concepts in a way that is both accessible and funny. The game puts the player in the shoes of a propagandist. You create your own "fake news" website, foster an army of trolls to help spread disinformation, create bots to help increase your credibility, and attack those who dare to question your posts. The game chooses simple topics that most of us are familiar with (i.e. climate change, vaccinations, flat Earth conspiracies, and Donald Trump) to illustrate the patterns followed by many propagandists. From these topics the player will have the opportunity to choose what to post and how to go about spreading disinformation.

There is no ‹winning› in this game. Any time you try to act morally, the game will stop you and make you act like a troll. The game makes you think of ways to lie to people in order to gain more followers and credibility. There is no room for facts here. Instead, you post controversial headlines from a list of options that are aimed at exploiting people's emotions. Posts that inspire happiness lose followers. You need to make people afraid and angry. You need to be careful, however, because lying too blatantly will lose followers, as well. You need to build up your followers' trust before you start posting anything too crazy.

You earn six badges throughout the game, for impersonation, discredit, polarization, emotion, trolling, and conspiracy. These are six trademark strategies consistently used across ALL social media platforms. Many people learn by doing, and getting students to partake in these actions in a safe and non-threatening way will help them recognize these tactics in their day-to-day lives. The more successful they are at implementing these strategies in the game, the higher their score will be. This also provides some opportunity for competition to see who can gain the most followers. While the topics in the game are political, there are opportunities to present propaganda from the Right and Left of the political spectrum. This is important because while it is okay for teachers to provide their own opinions, they must also provide multiple perspectives. Plus, you don't want to be on the receiving end of any backlash from angry parents.

The information sheet for *Bad News* contains a section on Inoculation Theory. They state:

> that people are able to build up a resistance against false or misleading information by being presented with a weakened version of a misleading argument before being exposed to the "real" information. One can see this as giving people a kind of "vaccine" against misleading information. If you can recognize it, you can resist it. The Bad News game draws on inoculation theory for its theoretical justification.

Playing the game helps build this resistance. These conversations do not stop with the end of the lesson. *Bad News* is merely an introduction to media literacy, which needs to be embedded throughout any Social Studies course. It's not really a choice, if we want our students to be successful critical thinkers.

DESCRIPTION OF ACTIVITY

- Amount of copies needed is at the discretion of the teacher

  > The game is free to play in web browsers

  > The class can play together with the game projected in the front of the room

  > Students can play in pairs/groups on computers

  > Or students can play individually on computers

- "WHY IS DISINFORMATION A PROBLEM? - Bad News Info Sheet

  > Disinformation is commonly used by a variety of parties, including some governments, to influence public opinion. Social media is the perfect place to spread disinformation. To give an example, around 47 million Twitter accounts (approximately 15%) are bots.

  > Disinformation works because many people fail to recognize false information when it's presented to them. Much of this information is shared by friends, whom people trust to tell them the truth. A fake news article shared and shown to someone by a friend is therefore more likely to be seen as trustworthy.

  > The *Bad News* Game - Bad News Info Sheet

  The *Bad News* Game helps build resistance against disinformation by putting players in the position of the people who create it. The players will gain insight into the various tactics and methods used by people in real life.

  The game is very straightforward: players are shown a short text or image (such as a meme or article headline) that they then react to in a number of different ways.

  Their score is measured in two ways: 1) followers and 2) credibility. Choosing an option that is in line with real producers of disinformation increases both the player's followers and credibility count.

  Be careful though. If the player lies too blatantly, chooses an option that is a bit too outrageous, or acts too much in line with journalistic best practices, the player will lose followers away or their credibility will diminish. The aim of the game is to gather as many followers as possible without losing too much credibility.

  The player earns six badges over the course of the game: impersonation, emotion, polarization, conspiracy, discredit, and trolling.

  Make sure you "take part in a study on fake news recognition" in the beginning of the game. You need to do this at the beginning and at the end.

- There will be two playthroughs.

  > Playthrough Part 1

  Play the game and answer the accompanying questions.

  > Playthrough Part 2

  Have the students play through the game a second time using all their knowledge from the first try to gain as many followers as possible.

  THIS PART IS VERY IMPORTANT:

  Page 6-11 of the Bad News Info Sheet has "Badge Breakdown" handouts.

  These pages are not attached here because they were created by Drog, but they are free to access in the link provided above.

Pass out one of these Badge Breakdown handouts to each individual, pair, or group of students. Rotate through the handouts so that there is at least one of each badge in the class.

Answer accompanying questions.

- Provide an accompanying handout before starting the game, as students will be answering questions as they play through the story.

OBJECTIVES

- Students will identify misinformation and disinformation.
- Students will discern fake news from real news.

CORRELATION TO COMMON CORE STANDARDS

English Language Arts Anchor Standards

GRADES K-12

- College and Career Readiness Anchor Standards for Reading

  Key Ideas and Details

  > CCSS.ELA-LITERACY.CCRA.R.1

  Read closely to determine what the text says explicitly and to make logical inferences from it; cite specific textual evidence when writing or speaking to support conclusions drawn from the text.

  > CCSS.ELA-LITERACY.CCRA.R.2

  Determine central ideas or themes of a text and analyze their development; summarize the key supporting details and ideas.

- College and Career Readiness Anchor Standards for Speaking and Listening

  Comprehension and Collaboration

  > CCSS.ELA-LITERACY.CCRA.SL.1

  Prepare for and participate effectively in a range of conversations and collaborations with diverse partners, building on others› ideas and expressing their own clearly and persuasively.

  > CCSS.ELA-LITERACY.CCRA.SL.2

  Integrate and evaluate information presented in diverse media and formats, including visually, quantitatively, and orally.

History - Social Studies

GRADES 6-8

  Key Ideas and Details

  > CCSS.ELA-LITERACY.RH.6-8.1

  Cite specific textual evidence to support analysis of primary and secondary sources.

  > CCSS.ELA-LITERACY.RH.6-8.2

Teaching with Video Games

Determine the central ideas or information of a primary or secondary source; provide an accurate summary of the source distinct from prior knowledge or opinions.

Integration of Knowledge and Ideas

> CCSS.ELA-LITERACY.RH.6-8.9

Analyze the relationship between a primary and secondary source on the same topic.

Craft and Structure

> CCSS.ELA-LITERACY.RH.6-8.4

Determine the meaning of words and phrases as they are used in a text, including vocabulary specific to domains related to history/social studies.

GRADES 9-10

Key Ideas and Details

> CCSS.ELA-LITERACY.RH.9-10.2

Determine the central ideas or information of a primary or secondary source; provide an accurate summary of how key events or ideas develop over the course of the text.

Integration of Knowledge and Ideas

> CCSS.ELA-LITERACY.RH.9-10.9

Compare and contrast treatments of the same topic in several primary and secondary sources.

Craft and Structure

> CCSS.ELA-LITERACY.RH.9-10.4

Determine the meaning of words and phrases as they are used in a text, including vocabulary describing political, social, or economic aspects of history/social science.

GRADES 11-12

Key Ideas and Details

> CCSS.ELA-LITERACY.RH.11-12.2

Determine the central ideas or information of a primary or secondary source; provide an accurate summary that makes clear the relationships among the key details and ideas.

Integration of Knowledge and Ideas

> CCSS.ELA-LITERACY.RH.11-12.9

Integrate information from diverse sources, both primary and secondary, into a coherent understanding of an idea or event, noting discrepancies among sources.

Craft and Structure

> CCSS.ELA-LITERACY.RH.11-12.4

Determine the meaning of words and phrases as they are used in a text, including analyzing how an author uses and refines the meaning of a key term over the course of a text (e.g., how Madison defines *faction* in *Federalist* No. 10).

TIME REQUIREMENTS

A single round of *Bad News* takes about fifteen minutes. The students should play through the game two times since the first playthrough will act more as a practice round.

SAFETY - TRIGGER WARNING

There is no violence to be found in *Bad News*. That being said, the game is overtly political and a lot of the game's narrative is reflective of the Trump administration's influence in the United States. Politics can be a tricky subject so make sure you play beforehand and use it at your own discretion.

- Beyond the Empathy Games 101: Digging Deep into Empathy, Ethics, and Design with Kelli Dunlap
- An Introduction to Content Warnings and Trigger Warnings

Gone Home

SEE PAGE 10 IN THE STUDENT PACKET

- Content Area/s: Social Studies - English Language Arts
- Developed by The Fullbright Company
- Rated: Everyone 15+

WHERE TO PLAY

- Available on iOS, Playstation 4, Playstation 5, Nintendo Switch, Xbox One, Xbox Series X/S, Microsoft Windows, Apple, Linux

CONTEXT

This lesson should take place during a unit on

- Civil Rights
- LGBTQ+ Issues
- Literary Elements

DO BEFORE - PREP

- Decide if you want to play together as a class, in pairs, groups, or individually.
- Choose the texts that you want to teach alongside this game. Some examples are:
  > Facing History: The In Group
  > Facing History: Finding Confidence
  > Facing History: Why I No Longer Hide My Rainbow

OVERVIEW

There are more movies (though still not many) than ever before that tackle the struggle of being LGBTQ+ in the United States or other places. This topic has not yet fully transitioned to video games. Gone Home beautifully brings these conversations to the video game community, a community that has made amazing strides towards acceptance of all people. You play Kaitlin Greenbriar who has spent the year studying abroad in Europe. While abroad, her family moved into a new home, one that could have been the perfect setting for a horror game. Upon returning from Europe, Kaitlin finds her new home completely abandoned by her parents and younger sister Sam. The goal of the game is to investigate the house to determine why. That is the game. There is no fighting, no puzzles, nor scary moments. You just want to find out what happened to your family.

Gone Home is a walking simulator. A walking simulator is an adventure game focused on gradual exploration and discovery through observation, with little in the way of action. The gameplay is to simply walk around and interact with the environment. Played in the first person through Kaitlin's eyes, the player walks around and engages with the narrative at their own pace. This type of game is super accessible to most students. Even students who have never played video games before will most likely be able to learn the controls and engage with the content.

As you begin investigating, you slowly start putting together a story of your sister slowly coming to terms that she is a lesbian and all the conflict she begins to face as a result. This personal story is woven into the exploration of the Greenbriar family home. Kaitlin (the player) needs to conquer their fear of moving through the house while also reconciling with and internalizing this newly revealed information about Sam. Kaitlin might be afraid of this unfamiliar, spooky-looking home, but it is nowhere near as frightening as Sam coming to terms with her own sexuality in the 1990s United States. This takes place during the heart of the "Don't Ask, Don't Tell" era. As Sam normalizes her own feelings, so does Kaitlin, and by extension, so can the player. The students who play this game will share the same struggle as Kaitlin as they make their way through the game, and that struggle can make them more empathetic and open-minded in real life.

DESCRIPTION OF ACTIVITY

- Amount of copies needed is at the discretion of the teacher
  - > The class can play together with the game projected in the front of the room
  - > Students can play in pairs/groups on computers - consoles - smartphones
  - > Or students can play individually on computers - consoles - smartphones
- In *Gone Home*, you will learn the story of your younger sister and the struggles she faces with herself and with her parents.
- After a study abroad trip to Europe, Kaitlin Greenbriar returns to an empty home. She is greeted by a note on the front door reading, "Don't go digging around trying to find out where I am," from her younger sister Sam.
- The player (Kaitlin) obviously ignores the note and begins digging around to figure out why her family has disappeared. And there is plenty to dig through.
- Everything in Gone Home works toward building Sam's story. With every photo, note, cassette tape, and journal entry, more is revealed about Sam as a character.
- This story is fiction, but there are countless examples of people facing similar problems that the class can discuss later.
- There are side stories in the game about the parents, but those are less important than the main story.
  - > You will focus on finding all your sister Sam's journal entries.
- Provide an accompanying handout before starting the game, as students will be answering questions as they play through the story.

OBJECTIVES

- Students will examine one girl's coming out story and map its major moments.
- Students will consider challenges facing the LGBTQ+ community in the United States.
- Students will differentiate the ways in which stories can be told in video games as opposed to other mediums.

CORRELATION TO COMMON CORE STANDARDS

English Language Arts Anchor Standards

GRADES K-12

- College and Career Readiness Anchor Standards for Reading

Key Ideas and Details

> CCSS.ELA-LITERACY.CCRA.R.2

Determine central ideas or themes of a text and analyze their development; summarize the key supporting details and ideas.

> CCSS.ELA-LITERACY.CCRA.R.3

Analyze how and why individuals, events, or ideas develop and interact over the course of a text.

- College and Career Readiness Anchor Standards for Writing

Production and Distribution of Writing

> CCSS.ELA-LITERACY.CCRA.W.4

Produce clear and coherent writing in which the development, organization, and style are appropriate to task, purpose, and audience.

- College and Career Readiness Anchor Standards for Speaking and Listening

Comprehension and Collaboration

> CCSS.ELA-LITERACY.CCRA.SL.1

Prepare for and participate effectively in a range of conversations and collaborations with diverse partners, building on others› ideas and expressing their own clearly and persuasively.

> CCSS.ELA-LITERACY.CCRA.SL.2

Integrate and evaluate information presented in diverse media and formats, including visually, quantitatively, and orally.

History - Social Studies

GRADES 6-8

Key Ideas and Details

> CCSS.ELA-LITERACY.RH.6-8.2

Determine the central ideas or information of a primary or secondary source; provide an accurate summary of the source distinct from prior knowledge or opinions.

Craft and Structure

> CCSS.ELA-LITERACY.RH.6-8.4

Determine the meaning of words and phrases as they are used in a text, including vocabulary specific to domains related to history/social studies.

Integration of Knowledge and Ideas

> CCSS.ELA-LITERACY.RH.6-8.9

Analyze the relationship between a primary and secondary source on the same topic.

GRADES 9-10

Key Ideas and Details

> CCSS.ELA-LITERACY.RH.9-10.2

Determine the central ideas or information of a primary or secondary source; provide an accurate summary of how key events or ideas develop over the course of the text.

Craft and Structure

> CCSS.ELA-LITERACY.RH.9-10.4

Determine the meaning of words and phrases as they are used in a text, including vocabulary describing political, social, or economic aspects of history/social science.

Integration of Knowledge and Ideas

> CCSS.ELA-LITERACY.RH.9-10.9

Compare and contrast treatments of the same topic in several primary and secondary sources.

GRADES 11-12

Key Ideas and Details

> CCSS.ELA-LITERACY.RH.11-12.2

Determine the central ideas or information of a primary or secondary source; provide an accurate summary that makes clear the relationships among the key details and ideas.

Craft and Structure

> CCSS.ELA-LITERACY.RH.11-12.4

Determine the meaning of words and phrases as they are used in a text, including analyzing how an author uses and refines the meaning of a key term over the course of a text (e.g., how Madison defines faction in Federalist No. 10).

Integration of Knowledge and Ideas

> CCSS.ELA-LITERACY.RH.11-12.9

Integrate information from diverse sources, both primary and secondary, into a coherent understanding of an idea or event, noting discrepancies among sources.

English Language Arts

Reading Literature

GRADE 6

Key Ideas and Details

> CCSS.ELA-LITERACY.RL.6.2

Determine a theme or central idea of a text and how it is conveyed through particular details; provide a summary of the text distinct from personal opinions or judgments.

Craft and Structure

> CCSS.ELA-LITERACY.RL.6.4

Determine the meaning of words and phrases as they are used in a text, including figurative and connotative meanings; analyze the impact of a specific word choice on meaning and tone

GRADE 7

Key Ideas and Details

> CCSS.ELA-LITERACY.RL.7.2

Determine a theme or central idea of a text and analyze its development over the course of the text; provide an objective summary of the text.

Craft and Structure

> CCSS.ELA-LITERACY.RL.7.4

Determine the meaning of words and phrases as they are used in a text, including figurative and connotative meanings; analyze the impact of rhymes and other repetitions of sounds (e.g., alliteration) on a specific verse or stanza of a poem or section of a story or drama.

GRADE 8

Key Ideas and Details

> CCSS.ELA-LITERACY.RL.8.2

Determine a theme or central idea of a text and analyze its development over the course of the text, including its relationship to the characters, setting, and plot; provide an objective summary of the text.

Craft and Structure

> CCSS.ELA-LITERACY.RL.8.4

Determine the meaning of words and phrases as they are used in a text, including figurative and connotative meanings; analyze the impact of specific word choices on meaning and tone, including analogies or allusions to other texts.

GRADES 9-10

Key Ideas and Details

> CCSS.ELA-LITERACY.RL.9-10.2

Determine a theme or central idea of a text and analyze in detail its development over the course of the text, including how it emerges and is shaped and refined by specific details; provide an objective summary of the text.

Craft and Structure

> CCSS.ELA-LITERACY.RL.9-10.4

Determine the meaning of words and phrases as they are used in the text, including figurative and connotative meanings; analyze the cumulative impact of specific word choices on meaning and tone (e.g., how the language evokes a sense of time and place; how it sets a formal or informal tone).

GRADES 11-12

Key Ideas and Details

> CCSS.ELA-LITERACY.RL.11-12.2

Determine two or more themes or central ideas of a text and analyze their development over the course of the text, including how they interact and build on one another to produce a complex account; provide an objective summary of the text.

Craft and Structure

> CCSS.ELA-LITERACY.RL.11-12.4

Determine the meaning of words and phrases as they are used in the text, including figurative and connotative meanings; analyze the impact of specific word choices on meaning and tone, including words with multiple meanings or language that is particularly fresh, engaging, or beautiful. (Include Shakespeare as well as other authors.)

Reading Informational Texts

GRADE 6

Key Ideas and Details

> CCSS.ELA-LITERACY.RI.6.2

Determine a central idea of a text and how it is conveyed through particular details; provide a summary of the text distinct from personal opinions or judgments.

> CCSS.ELA-LITERACY.RI.6.3

Analyze in detail how a key individual, event, or idea is introduced, illustrated, and elaborated in a text (e.g., through examples or anecdotes).

Craft and Structure

> CCSS.ELA-LITERACY.RI.6.4

Determine the meaning of words and phrases as they are used in a text, including figurative, connotative, and technical meanings.

GRADE 7

Key Ideas and Details

> CCSS.ELA-LITERACY.RI.7.2

Determine two or more central ideas in a text and analyze their development over the course of the text; provide an objective summary of the text.

> CCSS.ELA-LITERACY.RI.7.3

Analyze the interactions between individuals, events, and ideas in a text (e.g., how ideas influence individuals or events, or how individuals influence ideas or events).

Craft and Structure

> CCSS.ELA-LITERACY.RI.7.4

Determine the meaning of words and phrases as they are used in a text, including figurative, connotative, and technical meanings; analyze the impact of a specific word choice on meaning and tone.

GRADE 8

Key Ideas and Details

> CCSS.ELA-LITERACY.RI.8.2

Determine a central idea of a text and analyze its development over the course of the text, including its relationship to supporting ideas; provide an objective summary of the text.

> CCSS.ELA-LITERACY.RI.8.3

Analyze how a text makes connections among and distinctions between individuals, ideas, or events (e.g., through comparisons, analogies, or categories).

Craft and Structure

> CCSS.ELA-LITERACY.RI.8.4

Determine the meaning of words and phrases as they are used in a text, including figurative, connotative, and technical meanings; analyze the impact of specific word choices on meaning and tone, including analogies or allusions to other texts.

GRADES 9-10

Key Ideas and Details

> CCSS.ELA-LITERACY.RI.9-10.2

Determine a central idea of a text and analyze its development over the course of the text, including how it emerges and is shaped and refined by specific details; provide an objective summary of the text.

> CCSS.ELA-LITERACY.RI.9-10.3

Analyze how the author unfolds an analysis or series of ideas or events, including the order in which the points are made, how they are introduced and developed, and the connections that are drawn between them.

Craft and Structure

> CCSS.ELA-LITERACY.RI.9-10.4

Determine the meaning of words and phrases as they are used in a text, including figurative, connotative, and technical meanings; analyze the cumulative impact of specific word choices on meaning and tone (e.g., how the language of a court opinion differs from that of a newspaper).

GRADES 11-12

Key Ideas and Details

> CCSS.ELA-LITERACY.RI.11-12.2

Determine two or more central ideas of a text and analyze their development over the course of the text, including how they interact and build on one another to provide a complex analysis; provide an objective summary of the text.

> CCSS.ELA-LITERACY.RI.11-12.3

Analyze a complex set of ideas or sequence of events and explain how specific individuals, ideas, or events interact and develop over the course of the text.

Craft and Structure

> CCSS.ELA-LITERACY.RI.11-12.4

Determine the meaning of words and phrases as they are used in a text, including figurative, connotative, and technical meanings; analyze how an author uses and refines the meaning of a key term or terms over the course of a text (e.g., how Madison defines faction in Federalist No. 10).

Speaking and Listening

GRADE 6

Comprehension and Collaboration

> CCSS.ELA-LITERACY.SL.6.1

Engage effectively in a range of collaborative discussions (one-on-one, in groups, and teacher-led) with diverse partners on grade 6 topics, texts, and issues, building on others› ideas and expressing their own clearly.

> CCSS.ELA-LITERACY.SL.6.2

Interpret information presented in diverse media and formats (e.g., visually, quantitatively, orally) and explain how it contributes to a topic, text, or issue under study.

GRADE 7

Comprehension and Collaboration

> CCSS.ELA-LITERACY.SL.7.1

Engage effectively in a range of collaborative discussions (one-on-one, in groups, and teacher-led) with diverse partners on grade 7 topics, texts, and issues, building on others› ideas and expressing their own clearly.

> CCSS.ELA-LITERACY.SL.7.2

Analyze the main ideas and supporting details presented in diverse media and formats (e.g., visually, quantitatively, orally) and explain how the ideas clarify a topic, text, or issue under study.

GRADE 8

Comprehension and Collaboration

> CCSS.ELA-LITERACY.SL.8.1

Engage effectively in a range of collaborative discussions (one-on-one, in groups, and teacher-led) with diverse partners on grade 8 topics, texts, and issues, building on others› ideas and expressing their own clearly.

> CCSS.ELA-LITERACY.SL.8.2

Analyze the purpose of information presented in diverse media and formats (e.g., visually, quantitatively, orally) and evaluate the motives (e.g., social, commercial, political) behind its presentation.

GRADES 9-10

Comprehension and Collaboration

> CCSS.ELA-LITERACY.SL.9-10.1

Initiate and participate effectively in a range of collaborative discussions (one-on-one, in groups, and teacher-led) with diverse partners on grades 9-10 topics, texts, and issues, building on others› ideas and expressing their own clearly and persuasively.

> CCSS.ELA-LITERACY.SL.9-10.2

Integrate multiple sources of information presented in diverse media or formats (e.g., visually, quantitatively, orally) evaluating the credibility and accuracy of each source.

GRADES 11-12

Comprehension and Collaboration

> CCSS.ELA-LITERACY.SL.11-12.1

Initiate and participate effectively in a range of collaborative discussions (one-on-one, in groups, and teacher-led) with diverse partners on grades 11-12 topics, texts, and issues, building on others› ideas and expressing their own clearly and persuasively.

> CCSS.ELA-LITERACY.SL.11-12.2

Integrate multiple sources of information presented in diverse formats and media (e.g., visually, quantitatively, orally) in order to make informed decisions and solve problems, evaluating the credibility and accuracy of each source and noting any discrepancies among the data.

TIME REQUIREMENTS

It will take a minimum of about two hours to complete a playthrough of Gone Home, though it could take longer since there is a lot of optional exploration in the game. If students decide to explore more, then the time needed will be slightly longer.

SAFETY - TRIGGER WARNING

The game will deal with themes of discrimination towards the LGBTQ+ community. This could affect students sitting in your room. While bringing up these themes before the game could potentially spoil some of the story, it might be necessary to front load that information.

- Teaching Tolerance is a great resource for finding these strategies.
- Beyond the Empathy Games 101: Digging Deep into Empathy, Ethics, and Design with Kelli Dunlap
- An Introduction to Content Warnings and Trigger Warnings

Valiant Hearts: The Great War

SEE PAGE 13 IN THE STUDENT PACKET

- Content Area/s: Social Studies
- Developed by Ubisoft Montpellier
- Rated: 13+

WHERE TO PLAY

- Available on Android, iOS, Microsoft Windows, PlayStation 3, PlayStation 4, PlayStation 5, Xbox 360, Xbox One, Xbox Series X/S, Nintendo Switch

CONTEXT

This lesson should take place during a unit on World War I

DO BEFORE - PREP

- Decide if you want to play together as a class, in pairs, groups, or individually
- Choose the texts that you want to teach alongside this game. Some examples are as follows
    > National World War I Museum

    Trench Warfare

    Women of World War I
    > Weapons of World War I
- This game is very puzzle heavy. Play the game enough that you are familiar with the puzzles in the game or have a walkthrough handy in case students get stuck.

OVERVIEW

If you want an engaging way to teach World War I from a non-American perspective, *Valiant Hearts: The Great War* is definitely the text to use. It is a comic book brought to life that portrays the horrors of The Great War, all while remaining accessible to kids. You play as four strangers, accompanied by one dog, whose lives intertwine as they make their way through the trenches of war. The story may be fiction, but the locations and events are all based on fact.

Unlike many games set in a war, this is a game about fighting in a battle. Instead of combat, it is about exploration, adventure, and puzzle-solving. As you play, you will come across artifacts, facts, and diary entries that all add up to a greater portrait of World War I. These were included with the help of Mission Centenaire, a commemorative organization dedicated to education about the war, and Apocalypse World War I, a documentary mini-series about the war.

The game acts as a great conversation starter to get students talking about what a soldier's duty should be in times of war. A German man who has lived in France was deported and forced to join the German military. An older Frenchman was conscripted into the French army. An American decided to join the French before the United States officially entered the war. Finally,

Teaching with Video Games

there is a nurse who decides to help people regardless of their nationality. The game offers a number of different perspectives on the conflict. It is a great jumping off point to then examine the lives of real people. It is also ideal to dive into discussions on the author›s purpose. The way the war is depicted is very intentional. This game specifically highlights the use of chlorine gas, which killed over 90,000 soldiers throughout the war. It also touches on something unexpected: one of the main characters of the game ends up killing his own officer because the officer was forcing his soldiers to continue into enemy territory and through the trenches regardless of how many people were being killed.

DESCRIPTION OF ACTIVITY

- Amount of copies needed is at the discretion of the teacher
  - > The class can play together with the game can be projected in the front of the room
  - > Students can play in pairs/groups on computers - consoles - smartphones
  - > Or students can play individually on computers - consoles - smartphones
- *Valiant Hearts: The Great War* tells the story of:
  - > <u>Emile</u> - A French farmer who, after being drafted into the French army, becomes a POW (Prisoner of War). After being saved by Freddie, he begins to search for his son-in-law, Karl.
  - > <u>Freddie</u> - An American volunteer fighting in the war to avenge his fallen wife.
  - > <u>Anna</u> - A Belgian nurse searching for her father kidnapped by Baron Von Dorf.
  - > <u>Karl</u> - A German, married to Emile's daughter, Marie.
  - > <u>Walt</u> - A Doberman pinscher who interacts with each of the characters during their adventures.
- *Valiant Hearts* is a comic book brought to life. The five characters are on a grand adventure of survival and exploration as they try to reunite with their loved ones.
- This story takes you back to famous WWI locations like Reims or Montfaucon, revisiting historical battles on the Western Front, such as the Battle of Marne or the Battle of the Somme.
- This game is very puzzle heavy. Instead of focusing on combat, you will need to think your way out of different dangerous situations.
- As you play, you will come across artifacts and diary entries that give a greater insight to life during the war.
- The game is broken up into 4 episodes.
  - > Episode 1: Dark Clouds
  - > Episode 2: Broken Earth
  - > Episode 3: The Poppy Fields
  - > Episode 4: Wooden Crosses
- Provide an accompanying handout before starting the game, as students will be answering questions as they play through the story.

OBJECTIVES

- Students will discuss what a soldier›s primary duty should be in times of war.

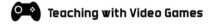
Teaching with Video Games

> Each person in this story breaks off or runs away from their "duty" at some point in the game due to personal interests/vendettas. What should a soldier's primary duty be in times of war? Must a soldier always follow the orders they are given, or were the characters in Valiant Hearts justified in their decisions to defect from their duties?

- Students will examine four characters' stories and map their experiences.
- Students will consider the moral challenges that soldiers face during war.

CORRELATION TO COMMON CORE STANDARDS

English Language Arts Anchor Standards

GRADES K-12

- College and Career Readiness Anchor Standards for Reading

  Key Ideas and Details

  > CCSS.ELA-LITERACY.CCRA.R.2

  Determine central ideas or themes of a text and analyze their development; summarize the key supporting details and ideas.

  > CCSS.ELA-LITERACY.CCRA.R.3

  Analyze how and why individuals, events, or ideas develop and interact over the course of a text.

- College and Career Readiness Anchor Standards for Writing

  Production and Distribution of Writing

  > CCSS.ELA-LITERACY.CCRA.W.4

  Produce clear and coherent writing in which the development, organization, and style are appropriate to task, purpose, and audience.

- College and Career Readiness Anchor Standards for Speaking and Listening

  Comprehension and Collaboration

  > CCSS.ELA-LITERACY.CCRA.SL.1

  Prepare for and participate effectively in a range of conversations and collaborations with diverse partners, building on others' ideas and expressing their own clearly and persuasively.

  > CCSS.ELA-LITERACY.CCRA.SL.2

  Integrate and evaluate information presented in diverse media and formats, including visually, quantitatively, and orally.

HISTORY - SOCIAL STUDIES

GRADES 6-8

  Key Ideas and Details

  > CCSS.ELA-LITERACY.RH.6-8.2

  Determine the central ideas or information of a primary or secondary source; provide an accurate summary of the source distinct from prior knowledge or opinions.

  Craft and Structure

> CCSS.ELA-LITERACY.RH.6-8.4

Determine the meaning of words and phrases as they are used in a text, including vocabulary specific to domains related to history/social studies.

Integration of Knowledge and Ideas

> CCSS.ELA-LITERACY.RH.6-8.9

Analyze the relationship between a primary and secondary source on the same topic.

GRADES 9-10

Key Ideas and Details

> CCSS.ELA-LITERACY.RH.9-10.2

Determine the central ideas or information of a primary or secondary source; provide an accurate summary of how key events or ideas develop over the course of the text.

Craft and Structure

> CCSS.ELA-LITERACY.RH.9-10.4

Determine the meaning of words and phrases as they are used in a text, including vocabulary describing political, social, or economic aspects of history/social science.

Integration of Knowledge and Ideas

> CCSS.ELA-LITERACY.RH.9-10.9

Compare and contrast treatments of the same topic in several primary and secondary sources.

GRADES 11-12

Key Ideas and Details

> CCSS.ELA-LITERACY.RH.11-12.2

Determine the central ideas or information of a primary or secondary source; provide an accurate summary that makes clear the relationships among the key details and ideas.

Craft and Structure

> CCSS.ELA-LITERACY.RH.11-12.4

Determine the meaning of words and phrases as they are used in a text, including analyzing how an author uses and refines the meaning of a key term over the course of a text (e.g., how Madison defines *faction* in *Federalist* No. 10).

Integration of Knowledge and Ideas

> CCSS.ELA-LITERACY.RH.11-12.9

Integrate information from diverse sources, both primary and secondary, into a coherent understanding of an idea or event, noting discrepancies among sources.

TIME REQUIREMENTS

A full playthrough of *Valiant Hearts: The Great War* will take about six to seven hours of playtime. This should ideally be spread over several classes. Depending on the length of your classes, you should prepare to spend about a week or two with this game in class. This will allow for adequate time to both play and discuss each day spent with the game.

SAFETY – TRIGGER WARNING

While *Valiant Hearts* is rated 13+, it is a very mature game. The game is about World War, I which means there are depictions of violence and death. The cartoon animation style makes the game more easily digestible, but it is best to preface this information for your students beforehand in case they want to opt out of this lesson.

- Beyond the Empathy Games 101: Digging Deep into Empathy, Ethics, and Design with Kelli Dunlap
- An Introduction to Content Warnings and Trigger Warnings

Never Alone

SEE PAGE 19 IN THE STUDENT PACKET

- Content Area/s: Social Studies - English Language Arts
- Developed by Upper One Games, E-Line Media
- Rated: 13+

WHERE TO PLAY

- Available on iOS, Mac, PlayStation Vita, PlayStation 3, PlayStation 4, PlayStation 5, Wii U, Windows, Xbox One, Xbox Series X/S, Xbox360

CONTEXT

This lesson should take place during a unit on

- Native American populations in North America
- Ancient Civilizations

DO BEFORE - PREP

- Decide if you want to play together as a class, in pairs, groups, or individually
- Choose the texts that you want to teach alongside this game. Some examples are:
  > *Never Alone* Parents Guide
  > National Geographic: Revealing pictures shine a new light on Inuit culture
  > Minority Rights Group International: Alakan Natives

OVERVIEW

Many teachers struggle to find modern engaging resources about indigenous communities in America. Luckily there is now a game that can help teachers who want to include curriculum about native populations. *Never Alone*, developed by Upper One Games and E-Line Media, is a video game about the Iñupiat Alaskan people. Even better, it was actually developed by a full team of Native Alaskan storytellers.

Never Alone is a puzzle platformer, but the puzzles and jumping mechanics are not the highlight of this game. They are fairly simple and do not really add that much to the experience. Where *Never Alone* shines is in the storytelling. *Never Alone is* a retelling of the traditional Iñupiat tale, «Kunuuksaayuka,» which was first recorded by master storyteller Robert Nasruk Cleveland. The original Kunuuksaayuka was about a young boy and his journey to discover the source of a savage blizzard. In this game, however, you play as a young girl accompanied by an arctic fox to find and put an end to the blizzard. Playing through the tale is not the only focus of this game. The developers wanted to tell this story, but they also wanted the players to learn about the Iñupiat Native Alaskan people.

Scattered throughout the game are twenty-four owls, and upon locating them, each unlocks a cultural insight. Each cultural insight is a short documentary clip of actual people from the Iñupiat communities detailing different aspects of their lives and culture. We learn about how they hunt and their various sources of food. They talk about a particular drum they use in their music making. We are shown the importance of community and how important it is for everyone to work together in order for their community to thrive. They discuss the very real dangers that are often a moment away in such a harsh environment – dangers that are being exacerbated by climate change. Despite these threats, they cherish their environment and all the nature that surrounds them. As a culture, they recognize the importance of their entire ecosystem: the ice, temperature, animals, and even spirits. Best of all, we interact with all these aspects of their culture throughout the gameplay.

Popular media, while improving, still struggles to represent the vast diversity of our countries and world. Gaming is also increasingly becoming a larger part of many of our students' lives. Games like *Never Alone* are one way to meet our students where they are. We can take a medium they are familiar with and use it for the purpose of education.

Never Alone is not just a game. It is, at its heart, a documentary about the Iñupiat Alaskan people. It is narrated in their language, incorporates their music and their art, and was made by the very people represented in the game. Will this game be the perfect solution to get your students excited to learn? There is no perfect answer to that, but it will be successful in engaging students who are often disinterested in learning about topics that do not readily impact their lives.

DESCRIPTION OF ACTIVITY

- Amount of copies needed is at the discretion of the teacher
  - > The class can play together with the game can be projected in the front of the room
  - > Students can play in pairs/groups on computers - consoles - smartphones
  - > Or students can play individually on computers - consoles - smartphones
- *Never Alone* is a puzzle platformer that explores the cultural folklore of the Iñupiat Native Alaskan people. It is the first game developed in collaboration with the Cook Inlet Tribal Council, an Alaskan Native people.
  - > Play as both Nuna and Fox — Switch between the two companions at any time with one button, or play side-by-side in local co-op mode, as you rely on the unique skills of each character to succeed in your quest. Nuna can climb ladders and ropes, move heavy obstacles, and throw her bola at targets to solve puzzles. Fox can fit through small areas that Nuna can't reach, scramble up walls, and jump to great heights.
- *Never Alone is* based on the traditional Iñupiat tale, «Kunuuksaayuka,» which was first recorded by master storyteller Robert Nasruk Cleveland.
  - > The two characters set out to find the source of an eternal blizzard which threatens the survival of their people.
- "*Never Alone* is the product of an uncommon partnership of Alaska Native community members and game developers. Through all stages of development members of both communities met extensively to ensure that all creative and business decisions were appropriately considered and supported the goals of all stakeholders. Throughout the game and in supporting material, players will hear directly from members of both communities who were instrumental in shaping the game." - *Never Alone* Game Website

- There are documentary clips called "Cultural Insights" throughout that tie into the game's story. Students will watch these as they play.
  > In over 30 minutes of interviews, elders, storytellers, and other members of the Alaska Native community share stories and wisdom about their culture, values, and the amazing Arctic world encountered by players.
- Provide an accompanying handout before starting the game, as students will be answering questions as they play through the story.

OBJECTIVES

- Students will analyze the importance of the environment for a native/indigenous community.
- Students will determine why it is important that games about Native Americans are developed by Native Americans.
- Students will follow the Kunuuksaayuka story in *Never Alone*.

CORRELATION TO COMMON CORE STANDARDS

English Language Arts Anchor Standards

GRADES K-12

- College and Career Readiness Anchor Standards for Reading

  Key Ideas and Details

  > CCSS.ELA-LITERACY.CCRA.R.2

  Determine central ideas or themes of a text and analyze their development; summarize the key supporting details and ideas.

  > CCSS.ELA-LITERACY.CCRA.R.3

  Analyze how and why individuals, events, or ideas develop and interact over the course of a text.

- College and Career Readiness Anchor Standards for Writing

  Production and Distribution of Writing

  > CCSS.ELA-LITERACY.CCRA.W.4

  Produce clear and coherent writing in which the development, organization, and style are appropriate to task, purpose, and audience.

- College and Career Readiness Anchor Standards for Speaking and Listening

  Comprehension and Collaboration

  > CCSS.ELA-LITERACY.CCRA.SL.1

  Prepare for and participate effectively in a range of conversations and collaborations with diverse partners, building on others› ideas and expressing their own clearly and persuasively.

  > CCSS.ELA-LITERACY.CCRA.SL.2

  Integrate and evaluate information presented in diverse media and formats, including visually, quantitatively, and orally.

History – Social Studies

GRADES 6-8

Key Ideas and Details

> CCSS.ELA-LITERACY.RH.6-8.2

Determine the central ideas or information of a primary or secondary source; provide an accurate summary of the source distinct from prior knowledge or opinions.

Craft and Structure

> CCSS.ELA-LITERACY.RH.6-8.4

Determine the meaning of words and phrases as they are used in a text, including vocabulary specific to domains related to history/social studies.

Integration of Knowledge and Ideas

> CCSS.ELA-LITERACY.RH.6-8.9

Analyze the relationship between a primary and secondary source on the same topic.

GRADES 9-10

Key Ideas and Details

> CCSS.ELA-LITERACY.RH.9-10.2

Determine the central ideas or information of a primary or secondary source; provide an accurate summary of how key events or ideas develop over the course of the text.

Craft and Structure

> CCSS.ELA-LITERACY.RH.9-10.4

Determine the meaning of words and phrases as they are used in a text, including vocabulary describing political, social, or economic aspects of history/social science.

Integration of Knowledge and Ideas

> CCSS.ELA-LITERACY.RH.9-10.9

Compare and contrast treatments of the same topic in several primary and secondary sources.

GRADES 11-12

Key Ideas and Details

> CCSS.ELA-LITERACY.RH.11-12.2

Determine the central ideas or information of a primary or secondary source; provide an accurate summary that makes clear the relationships among the key details and ideas.

Craft and Structure

> CCSS.ELA-LITERACY.RH.11-12.4

Determine the meaning of words and phrases as they are used in a text, including analyzing how an author uses and refines the meaning of a key term over the course of a text (e.g., how Madison defines *faction* in *Federalist* No. 10).

Integration of Knowledge and Ideas

> CCSS.ELA-LITERACY.RH.11-12.9

Integrate information from diverse sources, both primary and secondary, into a coherent understanding of an idea or event, noting discrepancies among sources.

English Language Arts

Reading Literature

GRADE 6

Key Ideas and Details

> CCSS.ELA-LITERACY.RL.6.2

Determine a theme or central idea of a text and how it is conveyed through particular details; provide a summary of the text distinct from personal opinions or judgments.

Craft and Structure

> CCSS.ELA-LITERACY.RL.6.4

Determine the meaning of words and phrases as they are used in a text, including figurative and connotative meanings; analyze the impact of a specific word choice on meaning and tone

GRADE 7

Key Ideas and Details

> CCSS.ELA-LITERACY.RL.7.2

Determine a theme or central idea of a text and analyze its development over the course of the text; provide an objective summary of the text.

Craft and Structure

> CCSS.ELA-LITERACY.RL.7.4

Determine the meaning of words and phrases as they are used in a text, including figurative and connotative meanings; analyze the impact of rhymes and other repetitions of sounds (e.g., alliteration) on a specific verse or stanza of a poem or section of a story or drama.

GRADE 8

Key Ideas and Details

> CCSS.ELA-LITERACY.RL.8.2

Determine a theme or central idea of a text and analyze its development over the course of the text, including its relationship to the characters, setting, and plot; provide an objective summary of the text.

Craft and Structure

> CCSS.ELA-LITERACY.RL.8.4

Determine the meaning of words and phrases as they are used in a text, including figurative and connotative meanings; analyze the impact of specific word choices on meaning and tone, including analogies or allusions to other texts.

GRADES 9-10

Key Ideas and Details

> CCSS.ELA-LITERACY.RL.9-10.2

Determine a theme or central idea of a text and analyze in detail its development over the course of the text, including how it emerges and is shaped and refined by specific details; provide an objective summary of the text.

Craft and Structure

> CCSS.ELA-LITERACY.RL.9-10.4

Determine the meaning of words and phrases as they are used in the text, including figurative and connotative meanings; analyze the cumulative impact of specific word choices on meaning and tone (e.g., how the language evokes a sense of time and place; how it sets a formal or informal tone).

GRADES 11-12

Key Ideas and Details

> CCSS.ELA-LITERACY.RL.11-12.2

Determine two or more themes or central ideas of a text and analyze their development over the course of the text, including how they interact and build on one another to produce a complex account; provide an objective summary of the text.

Craft and Structure

> CCSS.ELA-LITERACY.RL.11-12.4

Determine the meaning of words and phrases as they are used in the text, including figurative and connotative meanings; analyze the impact of specific word choices on meaning and tone, including words with multiple meanings or language that is particularly fresh, engaging, or beautiful. (Include Shakespeare as well as other authors.)

Reading Informational Texts

GRADE 6

Key Ideas and Details

> CCSS.ELA-LITERACY.RI.6.2

Determine a central idea of a text and how it is conveyed through particular details; provide a summary of the text distinct from personal opinions or judgments.

> CCSS.ELA-LITERACY.RI.6.3

Analyze in detail how a key individual, event, or idea is introduced, illustrated, and elaborated in a text (e.g., through examples or anecdotes).

Craft and Structure

> CCSS.ELA-LITERACY.RI.6.4

Determine the meaning of words and phrases as they are used in a text, including figurative, connotative, and technical meanings.

GRADE 7

Key Ideas and Details

> CCSS.ELA-LITERACY.RI.7.2

Determine two or more central ideas in a text and analyze their development over the course of the text; provide an objective summary of the text.

> CCSS.ELA-LITERACY.RI.7.3

Analyze the interactions between individuals, events, and ideas in a text (e.g., how ideas influence individuals or events, or how individuals influence ideas or events).

Craft and Structure

> CCSS.ELA-LITERACY.RI.7.4

Determine the meaning of words and phrases as they are used in a text, including figurative, connotative, and technical meanings; analyze the impact of a specific word choice on meaning and tone.

GRADE 8

Key Ideas and Details

> CCSS.ELA-LITERACY.RI.8.2

Determine a central idea of a text and analyze its development over the course of the text, including its relationship to supporting ideas; provide an objective summary of the text.

> CCSS.ELA-LITERACY.RI.8.3

Analyze how a text makes connections among and distinctions between individuals, ideas, or events (e.g., through comparisons, analogies, or categories).

Craft and Structure

> CCSS.ELA-LITERACY.RI.8.4

Determine the meaning of words and phrases as they are used in a text, including figurative, connotative, and technical meanings; analyze the impact of specific word choices on meaning and tone, including analogies or allusions to other texts.

GRADES 9-10

Key Ideas and Details

> CCSS.ELA-LITERACY.RI.9-10.2

Determine a central idea of a text and analyze its development over the course of the text, including how it emerges and is shaped and refined by specific details; provide an objective summary of the text.

> CCSS.ELA-LITERACY.RI.9-10.3

Analyze how the author unfolds an analysis or series of ideas or events, including the order in which the points are made, how they are introduced and developed, and the connections that are drawn between them.

Craft and Structure

> CCSS.ELA-LITERACY.RI.9-10.4

Determine the meaning of words and phrases as they are used in a text, including figurative, connotative, and technical meanings; analyze the cumulative impact of specific word choices on meaning and tone (e.g., how the language of a court opinion differs from that of a newspaper).

Key Ideas and Details

> CCSS.ELA-LITERACY.RI.11-12.2

Determine two or more central ideas of a text and analyze their development over the course of the text, including how they interact and build on one another to provide a complex analysis; provide an objective summary of the text.

> CCSS.ELA-LITERACY.RI.11-12.3

Analyze a complex set of ideas or sequence of events and explain how specific individuals, ideas, or events interact and develop over the course of the text.

Craft and Structure

> CCSS.ELA-LITERACY.RI.11-12.4

Determine the meaning of words and phrases as they are used in a text, including figurative, connotative, and technical meanings; analyze how an author uses and refines the meaning of a key term or terms over the course of a text (e.g., how Madison defines faction in Federalist No. 10).

Speaking and Listening

GRADE 6

Comprehension and Collaboration

> CCSS.ELA-LITERACY.SL.6.1

Engage effectively in a range of collaborative discussions (one-on-one, in groups, and teacher-led) with diverse partners on grade 6 topics, texts, and issues, building on others› ideas and expressing their own clearly.

> CCSS.ELA-LITERACY.SL.6.2

Interpret information presented in diverse media and formats (e.g., visually, quantitatively, orally) and explain how it contributes to a topic, text, or issue under study.

GRADE 7

Comprehension and Collaboration

> CCSS.ELA-LITERACY.SL.7.1

Engage effectively in a range of collaborative discussions (one-on-one, in groups, and teacher-led) with diverse partners on grade 7 topics, texts, and issues, building on others› ideas and expressing their own clearly.

> CCSS.ELA-LITERACY.SL.7.2

Analyze the main ideas and supporting details presented in diverse media and formats (e.g., visually, quantitatively, orally) and explain how the ideas clarify a topic, text, or issue under study.

GRADE 8

Comprehension and Collaboration

> CCSS.ELA-LITERACY.SL.8.1

Engage effectively in a range of collaborative discussions (one-on-one, in groups, and teacher-led) with diverse partners on grade 8 topics, texts, and issues, building on others› ideas and expressing their own clearly.

Teaching with Video Games

> CCSS.ELA-LITERACY.SL.8.2

Analyze the purpose of information presented in diverse media and formats (e.g., visually, quantitatively, orally) and evaluate the motives (e.g., social, commercial, political) behind its presentation.

GRADES 9-10

Comprehension and Collaboration

> CCSS.ELA-LITERACY.SL.9-10.1

Initiate and participate effectively in a range of collaborative discussions (one-on-one, in groups, and teacher-led) with diverse partners on grades 9-10 topics, texts, and issues, building on others› ideas and expressing their own clearly and persuasively.

> CCSS.ELA-LITERACY.SL.9-10.2

Integrate multiple sources of information presented in diverse media or formats (e.g., visually, quantitatively, orally) evaluating the credibility and accuracy of each source.

GRADES 11-12

Comprehension and Collaboration

> CCSS.ELA-LITERACY.SL.11-12.1

Initiate and participate effectively in a range of collaborative discussions (one-on-one, in groups, and teacher-led) with diverse partners on grades 11-12 topics, texts, and issues, building on others› ideas and expressing their own clearly and persuasively.

> CCSS.ELA-LITERACY.SL.11-12.2

Integrate multiple sources of information presented in diverse formats and media (e.g., visually, quantitatively, orally) in order to make informed decisions and solve problems, evaluating the credibility and accuracy of each source and noting any discrepancies among the data.

TIME REQUIREMENTS

A single playthrough of *Never Alone* will take about three hours of gameplay. Consider teaching with this game over the course of a week in order to allow for sufficient discussion time.

SAFETY - TRIGGER WARNING

There is not much to prep here. Just make sure you are adequately prepared to speak on the behalf of minority groups and people of color.

Teaching Tolerance is a great resource for finding these strategies.

Beyond the Empathy Games 101: Digging Deep into Empathy, Ethics, and Design with Kelli Dunlap

An Introduction to Content Warnings and Trigger Warnings

Pandemic II

SEE PAGE 23 IN THE STUDENT PACKET

- Content Area/s: Science - Social Studies
- Developed by Dark Realm Studios
- Rated: 9+

WHERE TO PLAY

- Available on Web Browser

CONTEXT

This lesson should take place during a unit on

- Diseases
- Epidemics and Pandemics
- COVID-19

DO BEFORE - PREP

- Decide if you want to play together as a class, in pairs, groups, or individually
- Choose the texts that you want to teach alongside this game. Some examples are as follows
  > MPH Online: 10 of the Worst Pandemics in History
  > MPH Online: How to Survive a Pandemic
    CDC Centers for Disease Control and Prevention: Coronavirus (COVID-19)

OVERVIEW

Pandemic II is an online game where your goal is to create a disease that kills as many people as possible. You choose between a Virus, Bacteria, or Parasite and do your best to make sure the disease spreads as far and wide as it can. You want to create a pandemic. This game will get students thinking about different types of diseases, various symptoms of diseases, how diseases can spread, and how we can go about stopping the spread of the diseases. It allows students to interact with possible consequences if communities are not properly vaccinated, and to prepare to fend off a pandemic. It is also free to play in any web browser.

The aim of the lesson is for students to answer the question: how can both natural and human made factors lead to the spread, or suppression, of a disease? *Pandemic II* starts with your selected disease appearing in a single country. From there, it is your goal to kill as many people as possible by spreading your disease across the world. This isn›t the easiest process. Your success is heavily influenced by the disease›s starting point. If the game begins in Madagascar, an island, it can be challenging to spread the disease beyond the nation's borders. You might manage to kill every person in Madagascar, but other countries will probably be able to limit all travel in and out of Madagascar. Starting in the United States will lead to a very different result. This makes it very easy to spread to the rest of the Americas. Another aspect to take into account is how many people travel to, or through, the infected countries. The United States has many shipyards and airports which helped bring my disease to the continents across the Atlantic. The game will get students thinking about how the spread of diseases can be amplified by human-made factors.

Beyond human contributors, the game will also get students thinking about natural causes that can lead to epidemics and pandemics. The game provides you with an evolution chart where you can «buy» different symptoms, transmission methods, and different types of resistance. If your disease begins in Northern Africa, it makes sense to make your disease more heat resistant. There is also probably less water in Northern Africa so it would be wise to choose transmission methods like insects, rodents, or airborne. There is also a news-ticker on the main screen informing you about weather, climate, and natural disasters. If you see there is flooding somewhere, then it is time to make your disease transmit through water. You also need to think about your disease›s symptoms. Choosing symptoms like sweating or vomiting may help spread your disease, but it also makes your disease more noticeable. The more noticeable your disease is, the faster a cure/vaccine will be made to prevent it from spreading any further. That›s usually a good thing, but remember: in this game, we are the villains. We want to make sure that we can kill the entire human population before a vaccine can be generated and distributed.

Vaccines and the anti-vax movement are becoming a major concern in many parts of the United States and world. Despite extensive research and clear evidence that vaccines are not only effective, but necessary, many people still refuse to vaccinate themselves or their children. According to the Center for Disease Control and Protection (CDC), "Diseases that used to be common in this country and around the world, including polio, measles, diphtheria, pertussis (whooping cough), rubella (German measles), mumps, tetanus, rotavirus and Haemophilus Influenzae type b (Hib) can now be prevented by vaccination. Thanks to a vaccine, one of the most terrible diseases in history – smallpox – no longer exists outside the laboratory. Over the years vaccines have prevented countless cases of disease and saved millions of lives." If enough people begin refusing to take vaccines, more people will get sick and another pandemic becomes a possibility.

This is all amplified as the world moves into a post COVID-19 existence. COVID-19 has brought the world to its knees as countries across the globe have had to lock down their economies. As the world scrambles to make a vaccine (at the time of writing this book) it is important to analyze how and why this disease was able to spread so effectively. The fact that this game is also playable on any web browser is important as many schools are now operating online only. Schools will eventually return to normal operations, but COVID-19 has shown that there is a lot of existing technology that can be incorporated into their curriculum.

DESCRIPTION OF ACTIVITY

- Amount of copies needed is at the discretion of the teacher
  - > The game is free to play in web browsers
  - > The class can play together with the game can be projected in the front of the room
  - > Students can play in pairs/groups on computers
  - > Or students can play individually on computers
- There are two game modes: "Realistic" and "Relaxed". I recommend playing Relaxed

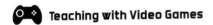

because it will only warrant 20-30 minutes of playtime. Realistic will require more.

> Realistic

While playing in realistic mode, you are able to save the progress of your disease. Games take longer to play since it takes longer to accumulate evolution points. Governments react more intelligently, and it is more difficult for your disease to spread effectively. This mode is recommended for intermediate or expert players.

> Relaxed

While playing in relaxed mode, you are unable to save the progress of your disease because most games should not last longer than 20 minutes. Governments react slower, making it easier to spread your disease. Some game events will not appear during Relaxed play. This mode is recommended for beginner players.

• *Pandemic II* is an online game where your goal is to create a disease that kills as many people as possible. You choose between a Virus, Bacteria, or Parasite and do your best to make sure the disease spreads as far and wide as it can. You want to create a pandemic.

> Virus Class

The virus class makes gaining evolution points easier than the other two classes. Virus classes also have a slight bonus to infectivity. However virus class diseases are more susceptible to environmental conditions.

> Bacteria Class

The bacteria class is the most well-rounded disease class to choose from and is recommended for beginners. Bacterial diseases benefit from an increased resistance to drugs.

> Parasite Class

The parasite class is slower than those other two classes at generating evolution points, but the parasite class is much more resistant to environmental conditions. It also is less visible than the other two classes.

• Objectives

> The objectives of *Pandemic II* are simple. Evolve your disease so that it can spread and kill everyone in the world. Make sure to keep visibility low so that governments are late to start enacting protections against your disease.

• Finishing the game.

> Completing the Game

There is only one way to beat *Pandemic II*: kill every last human on earth. It may take a while, and it may prove to be difficult, but it is possible.

> Losing the Game

Just like winning, there is only one way to lose in *Pandemic II*. If at any point during the game, not a single person is infected with your disease, you lose the game instantly.

OBJECTIVES

• How can both natural and human-made factors lead to the spread or suppression of a disease?

Teaching with Video Games

- Students will investigate the natural causes of pandemics and epidemics.
- Students will investigate the human-made causes of pandemics and epidemics.
- Students will investigate the importance of vaccines.

CORRELATION TO COMMON CORE STANDARDS

English Language Arts Anchor Standards

GRADES K-12

- College and Career Readiness Anchor Standards for Reading

  Key Ideas and Details

  > CCSS.ELA-LITERACY.CCRA.R.2

  Determine central ideas or themes of a text and analyze their development; summarize the key supporting details and ideas.

- College and Career Readiness Anchor Standards for Writing

  Production and Distribution of Writing

  > CCSS.ELA-LITERACY.CCRA.W.4

  Produce clear and coherent writing in which the development, organization, and style are appropriate to task, purpose, and audience.

- College and Career Readiness Anchor Standards for Speaking and Listening

  Comprehension and Collaboration

  > CCSS.ELA-LITERACY.CCRA.SL.1

  Prepare for and participate effectively in a range of conversations and collaborations with diverse partners, building on others› ideas and expressing their own clearly and persuasively.

  > CCSS.ELA-LITERACY.CCRA.SL.2

  Integrate and evaluate information presented in diverse media and formats, including visually, quantitatively, and orally.=

History - Social Studies

GRADES 6-8

Key Ideas and Details

> CCSS.ELA-LITERACY.RH.6-8.2

Determine the central ideas or information of a primary or secondary source; provide an accurate summary of the source distinct from prior knowledge or opinions.

Craft and Structure

> CCSS.ELA-LITERACY.RH.6-8.4

Determine the meaning of words and phrases as they are used in a text, including vocabulary specific to domains related to history/social studies.

Integration of Knowledge and Ideas

> CCSS.ELA-LITERACY.RH.6-8.9

Analyze the relationship between a primary and secondary source on the same topic.

GRADES 9-10

Key Ideas and Details

> CCSS.ELA-LITERACY.RH.9-10.2

Determine the central ideas or information of a primary or secondary source; provide an accurate summary of how key events or ideas develop over the course of the text.

Craft and Structure

> CCSS.ELA-LITERACY.RH.9-10.4

Determine the meaning of words and phrases as they are used in a text, including vocabulary describing political, social, or economic aspects of history/social science.

Integration of Knowledge and Ideas

> CCSS.ELA-LITERACY.RH.9-10.9

Compare and contrast treatments of the same topic in several primary and secondary sources.

GRADES 11-12

Key Ideas and Details

> CCSS.ELA-LITERACY.RH.11-12.2

Determine the central ideas or information of a primary or secondary source; provide an accurate summary that makes clear the relationships among the key details and ideas.

Craft and Structure

> CCSS.ELA-LITERACY.RH.11-12.4

Determine the meaning of words and phrases as they are used in a text, including analyzing how an author uses and refines the meaning of a key term over the course of a text (e.g., how Madison defines *faction* in *Federalist* No. 10).

Integration of Knowledge and Ideas

> CCSS.ELA-LITERACY.RH.11-12.9

Integrate information from diverse sources, both primary and secondary, into a coherent understanding of an idea or event, noting discrepancies among sources.

Science & Technical Subjects

GRADES 6-8

Key Ideas and Details

> CCSS.ELA-LITERACY.RST.6-8.2

Determine the central ideas or conclusions of a text; provide an accurate summary of the text distinct from prior knowledge or opinions.

Craft and Structure

> CCSS.ELA-LITERACY.RST.6-8.4

Determine the meaning of symbols, key terms, and other domain-specific words and phrases as they are used in a specific scientific or technical context relevant to *grades 6-8 texts and topics*.

GRADES 9-10

Key Ideas and Details

> CCSS.ELA-LITERACY.RST.9-10.2

Determine the central ideas or conclusions of a text; trace the text's explanation or depiction of a complex process, phenomenon, or concept; provide an accurate summary of the text.

Craft and Structure

> CCSS.ELA-LITERACY.RST.9-10.4

Determine the meaning of symbols, key terms, and other domain-specific words and phrases as they are used in a specific scientific or technical context relevant to *grades 9-10 texts and topics.*

GRADES 11-12

Key Ideas and Details

> CCSS.ELA-LITERACY.RST.11-12.2

Determine the central ideas or conclusions of a text; summarize complex concepts, processes, or information presented in a text by paraphrasing them in simpler but still accurate terms.

Craft and Structure

> CCSS.ELA-LITERACY.RST.11-12.4

Determine the meaning of symbols, key terms, and other domain-specific words and phrases as they are used in a specific scientific or technical context relevant to *grades 11-12 texts and topics.*

TIME REQUIREMENTS

The amount of time required for a single playthrough will vary. I recommend playing on the "Relaxed" game setting as those rounds will last no longer than twenty minutes. Plan to use this game over the course of two class periods. This will give most students the chance to play multiple times and try out different strategies to spread their disease.

SAFETY - TRIGGER WARNING

The game is about pandemics and puts the player in charge of infecting everyone in the world. COVID-19 is a real threat that has already affected the lives of so many students. Make sure to appropriately warn them beforehand about the content of the game. There may be students in your class that want to opt out of playing, in which case you can find an alternative activity.

- Beyond the Empathy Games 101: Digging Deep into Empathy, Ethics, and Design with Kelli Dunlap
- An Introduction to Content Warnings and Trigger Warnings

1979: Revolution Black Friday

SEE PAGE 26 IN THE STUDENT PACKET

- Content Area/s: Social Studies
- Developed by INK Stories
- Rated: 15+

WHERE TO PLAY

- Available on PlayStation 4, PlayStation 5, Nintendo Switch, Android, Xbox One, Xbox Series X/S, Microsoft Windows, iOS, Macintosh Operating Systems, macOS

CONTEXT

This lesson should take place during a unit on

- The Iranian/Islamic Revolution
- Protests and Political Movements

DO BEFORE - PREP

- Decide if you want to play together as a class, in pairs, groups, or individually
- Choose the texts that you want to teach alongside this game. Some examples are:
  > Persepolis: The Story of a Childhood
  > Argo

OVERVIEW

1979 Revolution: Black Friday tells a story of the Iranian Revolution through the perspective of a photographer. You play as Reza, a young man participating in the protests in Iran. Reza, however, is not a fighter. His weapon of choice is a camera, and it is your job to document various events of the Iranian Revolution.

War and conflict are often taught in a stereotypical fashion. Set up some context, go over the major players, teach some major events/battles, and move on to repercussions. Students might learn perfectly well, but there is often a disconnect between the events they are studying and their own personal experiences. It can be hard to feel empathetic when the events transpiring do not really have a tangible effect on their lives. Using *1979 Revolution: Black Friday* as a text can help resolve this disconnect. Reza is not a soldier. He is just an amateur photographer who worries about his family and friends. There is a constant tug of war between supporting his friends in the protest and supporting his brother, a police officer on the opposite side of the conflict. Even when he's among fellow protestors, he needs to choose between peaceful and violent forms of resistance.

One of the first choices you have in the game is whether or not to throw a rock at police officers. It is a heavy decision, and you are only given a moment to decide. This is in stark contrast to other games based on war or conflict where you shoot people without any real consideration

Teaching with Video Games

of what that means. Games set during a war often come in the form of first-person shooters and aren't created to be educational. *1979 Revolution: Black Friday* is not action packed like most other games set during wars. It has a clear intention of making these events in Iran feel real to the player. You cannot kill someone without second guessing yourself. Your decisions hold moral weight, and they will affect the outcome of the story.

Gameplay is simple and accessible. Most of the game involves cutscenes where the job of the player is to choose between a number of provided dialogue choices. These choices are often timed, forcing the player to think quickly (similar to games developed by Telltale Games). Other times you walk around, perhaps too slowly, and take pictures of your surroundings. When not taking pictures, you may be reading documents or listening to recordings. Very infrequently, there will be some quick-time events where you need to press a certain button at a precise moment.

One of the unique aspects of this game is that it blends fiction and non-fiction. The characters and story in the game are not real, but there are actual primary sources embedded throughout the game. Whenever you take a picture in-game, you are provided with a real-life image accompanied with a caption explaining what transpired. You gradually fill out a journal with photos, recordings of famous speeches, and other documents that you would find in any classroom or museum covering the Iranian Revolution.

This game would be perfect to pair with other texts the next time you teach about the Iranian Revolution. It is highly recommended to pair this alongside the graphic novel *Persepolis: The Story of a Childhood* by Marjane Satrapi. That novel also details the events of the revolution, but through the lens of a young girl. While the *1979 Revolution: Black Friday* is a great text, history is too often told through the perspective of men, so including a book like *Persepolis* is a must.

DESCRIPTION OF ACTIVITY

- Amount of copies needed is at the discretion of the teacher
  - > The class can play together with the game projected in the front of the room
  - > Students can play in pairs/groups on computers - consoles - smartphones
  - > Or students can play individually on computers - consoles - smartphones
- Go over the following vocabulary terms with the class:
  - > Iranian/Islamic Revolution

    A series of events that involved the overthrow of the last monarch of Iran, Mohammad Reza Pahlavi, and the replacement of his government with an Islamic republic under the Grand Ayatollah Ruhollah Khomeini, who was supported by the United States and was a leader of one of the factions in the revolt. The movement against the monarchy was supported by various leftist and Islamist organizations and student movements.
  - > Tehran

    Is the capital of Iran and Tehran Province. With a population of around 8.7 million in the city and 15 million in the larger metropolitan area of Greater Tehran, Tehran is the most populous city in Iran and Western Asia, and has the second-largest metropolitan area in the Middle East.
- Introduce the game *1979 Revolution: Black Friday*.

> *1979 Revolution: Black Friday is* an adventure interactive drama video game. Players control Reza Shirazi, a young photojournalist, documenting the events of the Iranian Revolution. As he becomes more involved, Reza is forced to make decisions in order to survive. These decisions will often come at a cost to his friends and family. The game has various outcomes that change depending on the player' decisions. Nonfiction texts and primary resources are embedded into the game. Find them by taking in-game photographs of the surroundings.

- Navid Khonsari

  > Director Navid Khonsari was a child in Iran at the time of the Iranian Revolution, witnessing many of the events that later inspired the game.

- Provide an accompanying handout before starting the game, as students will be answering questions as they play through the story.

OBJECTIVES

- Students will examine the role of the individual in the Iranian/Islamic Revolution.
- Students will investigate why people protest and why governments often try to silence them.

CORRELATION TO COMMON CORE STANDARDS

English Language Arts Anchor Standards

GRADES K-12

- College and Career Readiness Anchor Standards for Reading

  Key Ideas and Details

  > CCSS.ELA-LITERACY.CCRA.R.2

  Determine central ideas or themes of a text and analyze their development; summarize the key supporting details and ideas.

  > CCSS.ELA-LITERACY.CCRA.R.3

  Analyze how and why individuals, events, or ideas develop and interact over the course of a text.

- College and Career Readiness Anchor Standards for Writing

  Production and Distribution of Writing

  > CCSS.ELA-LITERACY.CCRA.W.4

  Produce clear and coherent writing in which the development, organization, and style are appropriate to task, purpose, and audience.

- College and Career Readiness Anchor Standards for Speaking and Listening

  Comprehension and Collaboration

  > CCSS.ELA-LITERACY.CCRA.SL.1

  Prepare for and participate effectively in a range of conversations and collaborations with diverse partners, building on others› ideas and expressing their own clearly and persuasively.

> CCSS.ELA-LITERACY.CCRA.SL.2

Integrate and evaluate information presented in diverse media and formats, including visually, quantitatively, and orally.

History - Social Studies

GRADES 6-8

Key Ideas and Details

> CCSS.ELA-LITERACY.RH.6-8.2

Determine the central ideas or information of a primary or secondary source; provide an accurate summary of the source distinct from prior knowledge or opinions.

Craft and Structure

> CCSS.ELA-LITERACY.RH.6-8.4

Determine the meaning of words and phrases as they are used in a text, including vocabulary specific to domains related to history/social studies.

Integration of Knowledge and Ideas

> CCSS.ELA-LITERACY.RH.6-8.9

Analyze the relationship between a primary and secondary source on the same topic.

GRADES 9-10

Key Ideas and Details

> CCSS.ELA-LITERACY.RH.9-10.2

Determine the central ideas or information of a primary or secondary source; provide an accurate summary of how key events or ideas develop over the course of the text.

Craft and Structure

> CCSS.ELA-LITERACY.RH.9-10.4

Determine the meaning of words and phrases as they are used in a text, including vocabulary describing political, social, or economic aspects of history/social science.

Integration of Knowledge and Ideas

> CCSS.ELA-LITERACY.RH.9-10.9

Compare and contrast treatments of the same topic in several primary and secondary sources.

GRADES 11-12

Key Ideas and Details

> CCSS.ELA-LITERACY.RH.11-12.2

Determine the central ideas or information of a primary or secondary source; provide an accurate summary that makes clear the relationships among the key details and ideas.

Craft and Structure

> CCSS.ELA-LITERACY.RH.11-12.4

Determine the meaning of words and phrases as they are used in a text, including analyzing how an author uses and refines the meaning of a key term over the course of a text (e.g., how Madison defines *faction* in *Federalist* No. 10).

Integration of Knowledge and Ideas

> CCSS.ELA-LITERACY.RH.11-12.9

Integrate information from diverse sources, both primary and secondary, into a coherent understanding of an idea or event, noting discrepancies among sources.

TIME REQUIREMENTS

A full playthrough of *1979 Revolution: Black Friday* will take about two-three hours of playtime. Spending two or three class periods of the game will allow for enough time to play and discuss during each session.

SAFETY - TRIGGER WARNING

1979 Revolution: Black Friday leans on the mature side. While there is nothing in the game that is overly grotesque, there are depictions of death and torture. Prepare your students for these themes adequately beforehand.

- Beyond the Empathy Games 101: Digging Deep into Empathy, Ethics, and Design with Kelli Dunlap

- An Introduction to Content Warnings and Trigger Warnings

Donut County

SEE PAGE 29 IN THE STUDENT PACKET

- Content Area/s: Social Studies
- Developed by Ben Esposito
- Rated: 8+

WHERE TO PLAY

- Available on PlayStation 4, PlayStation 5, Xbox One, Xbox Series X/S, Nintendo Switch, iOS, Microsoft Windows, macOS, Classic Mac OS

CONTEXT

This lesson should take place during a unit on

- Housing Issues
- Gentrification

DO BEFORE - PREP

- Decide if you want to play together as a class, in pairs, groups, or individually
- This game is not meant to introduce gentrification as a topic to students. This game should be utilized after students already have a solid understanding of what gentrification is and how it affects people before playing this game.
- Choose the texts that you want to teach alongside this game. Some examples are as follows
    - > Venture Beat: Donut County Doesn't Glaze over Gentrification
    - > The Atlantic: This is What Happens After a Neighborhood Gets Gentrified
    - > Vox: Is it Time for American Cities to Stop Growing?

OVERVIEW

Gentrification is the process of changing the character of a neighborhood through the influx of more affluent residents and businesses; this process typically displaces current inhabitants in the process. Most major metropolitan areas are well aware of this phenomenon and the effects it can have on disadvantaged communities. There is a decent chance that a lot of people reading this might be doing so from a neighborhood that fell victim to gentrification because their families were looking for cheaper rent, or even by those who have been pushed out of neighborhoods themselves. *Donut County* presents this very complex issue as a simple, fun, and intuitive puzzle game.

At first glance *Donut County* seems like a simplistic puzzle game: the player controls a hole that gradually gets bigger as it eats up more items throughout various locations. As the game progresses however, it becomes clear that *Donut County* is actually a metaphor for gentrification. The hole the player controls symbolizes the influx of more affluent residents who move in and drastically change the neighborhood. As it gets bigger, it gradually displaces the people who were originally living in the game's levels. Using video games to teach concepts like gentrification can be tricky. The last thing a teacher wants to do is gamify trauma, especially if the content directly impacts the students in the classroom. *Donut County* works because it acts as an analytical piece. It is a fun game that only reflects gentrification when observed with a more critical eye. Students will have the opportunity to play the game and decide for themselves if the game adequately or fairly depicts gentrification.

The developer of the game, Ben Esposito, deliberately created this game as a means of discussing gentrification and one›s role in the process. Many of us are perfectly aware that this is something that happens, but it can be more challenging for someone to take ownership of their own contributions and enabling of gentrification at large. These conversations are especially important as gentrification, by and large, is caused by more affluent white residents moving into communities that are predominately people of color. This inevitably causes rent to increase, likely closing business and forcing people of color to move out of their homes and migrate elsewhere. Ben Esposito was inspired to create *Donut County* after moving to Los Angeles and discovering numerous mom-and-pop donut shops throughout the city. They were independent businesses that had not yet been eaten up by larger chains. In the game, donut shops and other restaurants and businesses serve as hubs where community members gather. The hole that the player controls is the destruction brought in by gentrification and mass consumption caused by capitalism.

In *Donut County*, those responsible for gentrification are not affluent white people, but snarky and selfish raccoons. They move in and use the hole in the ground to steal other people›s «trash,» as a means of building funds in order to buy themselves silly toys. The player takes on the role of BK, one of the newly arrived raccoons. BK has a complete and total disregard for the well-being of the local residents whom he is displacing. All he cares about is earning enough money to buy a new drone. He dubs anyone and anything in his way as «trash.» He does have a soft spot for one local, Mira, one of his employees. Mira wants BK to become a better person/ raccoon and takes it upon herself to teach him why what he is doing is wrong. This complicates the situation even further because Mira recognizes that she is also somewhat complicit in the gentrification process due to her role as BK's employee. The situation is not always so black and white. Even good people may unintentionally cause harm to others. By putting the player in the shoes of BK, the player has to reconcile their own enabling of gentrification. We aren›t playing as a hero. We are playing as the gentrifier. And for most of the game, our avatar is completely dismissive of the concerns of the people he is actively harming.

This game is rated for people ages eight and up. It is a game perfectly suitable for children. It›s cute, funny, and a blast to play. The dialogue is funny and cheesy but carries real meaning. We know what it really means every time BK calls a local or their belongings «trash,» or when he claims that he is actually saving the town. We know the significance of Mira feeling guilty for being an employee for BK›s business despite seeing first-hand the negative effects on the community. Gentrification is an extraordinarily complex subject and *Donut County* does a remarkable job presenting it in such a simple fashion. Obviously, the concept of gentrification cannot just be taught using this game. It needs to be paired with a number of other texts. Your students should know what gentrification is before even touching this game. From there, students can play the game and discuss how the game presents the material. They can make connections between the game and the content they already learned in class.

DESCRIPTION OF ACTIVITY

- Amount of copies needed is at the discretion of the teacher
  > The class can play together with the game projected in the front of the room
  > Students can play in pairs/groups on computers - consoles - smartphones
  > Or students can play individually on computers - consoles - smartphones
- Go over the following vocabulary terms with the class:
  > Gentrification: a process of changing the character of a neighborhood through the influx of more affluent residents and businesses. This process typically displaces current inhabitants in the process.
  > Mom and Pop Shop: a colloquial term used to describe a small, family-owned or independent business. Mom-and-pop stores are often operations that struggle to compete with larger establishments, such as big-box retailers, who generally boast more buying power than smaller players.
- *Donut County* is a video game developed by designer Ben Esposito and published by Annapurna Interactive. In the game, the player moves a hole to swallow objects, which makes the hole increase in size.
- In *Donut County*, the players control a "donut hole" that cuts across several different game levels, each of which is self-contained but includes several smaller areas that open up as the player progresses. The goal of the game is to swallow every object to essentially clear out the level. As players move the hole to swallow objects, the hole increases in size. The player literally controls a hole in the ground that swallows up its surroundings.
- Human Mira works for her friend BK, a raccoon, at the local donut shop in Donut County. BK's job is to schedule the delivery of donuts to the residents of Donut County. However, Mira discovers that he is not actually sending donuts to the Donut County residents. He is instead actual holes which have been consuming the homes and residents of the place.
- Provide an accompanying handout before starting the game, as students will be answering questions as they play through the story.

OBJECTIVES

- Students will investigate the effects of gentrification.
- Students will critique *Donut County*'s portrayal of gentrification.
  > Students will compare how gentrification is portrayed in the game with gentrification in real life.

CORRELATION TO COMMON CORE STANDARDS

English Language Arts Anchor Standards

GRADES K-12

- College and Career Readiness Anchor Standards for Reading

  Key Ideas and Details

> CCSS.ELA-LITERACY.CCRA.R.2

Determine central ideas or themes of a text and analyze their development; summarize the key supporting details and ideas.

> CCSS.ELA-LITERACY.CCRA.R.3

Analyze how and why individuals, events, or ideas develop and interact over the course of a text.

- College and Career Readiness Anchor Standards for Writing

Production and Distribution of Writing

> CCSS.ELA-LITERACY.CCRA.W.4

Produce clear and coherent writing in which the development, organization, and style are appropriate to task, purpose, and audience.

- College and Career Readiness Anchor Standards for Speaking and Listening

Comprehension and Collaboration

> CCSS.ELA-LITERACY.CCRA.SL.1

Prepare for and participate effectively in a range of conversations and collaborations with diverse partners, building on others› ideas and expressing their own clearly and persuasively.

> CCSS.ELA-LITERACY.CCRA.SL.2

Integrate and evaluate information presented in diverse media and formats, including visually, quantitatively, and orally.

History - Social Studies

GRADES 6-8

Key Ideas and Details

> CCSS.ELA-LITERACY.RH.6-8.2

Determine the central ideas or information of a primary or secondary source; provide an accurate summary of the source distinct from prior knowledge or opinions.

Craft and Structure

> CCSS.ELA-LITERACY.RH.6-8.4

Determine the meaning of words and phrases as they are used in a text, including vocabulary specific to domains related to history/social studies.

Integration of Knowledge and Ideas

> CCSS.ELA-LITERACY.RH.6-8.9

Analyze the relationship between a primary and secondary source on the same topic.

GRADES 9-10

Key Ideas and Details

> CCSS.ELA-LITERACY.RH.9-10.2

Determine the central ideas or information of a primary or secondary source; provide an accurate summary of how key events or ideas develop over the course of the text.

Teaching with Video Games

Craft and Structure

> CCSS.ELA-LITERACY.RH.9-10.4

Determine the meaning of words and phrases as they are used in a text, including vocabulary describing political, social, or economic aspects of history/social science.

Integration of Knowledge and Ideas

> CCSS.ELA-LITERACY.RH.9-10.9

Compare and contrast treatments of the same topic in several primary and secondary sources.

GRADES 11-12

Key Ideas and Details

> CCSS.ELA-LITERACY.RH.11-12.2

Determine the central ideas or information of a primary or secondary source; provide an accurate summary that makes clear the relationships among the key details and ideas.

Craft and Structure

> CCSS.ELA-LITERACY.RH.11-12.4

Determine the meaning of words and phrases as they are used in a text, including analyzing how an author uses and refines the meaning of a key term over the course of a text (e.g., how Madison defines *faction* in *Federalist* No. 10).

Integration of Knowledge and Ideas

> CCSS.ELA-LITERACY.RH.11-12.9

Integrate information from diverse sources, both primary and secondary, into a coherent understanding of an idea or event, noting discrepancies among sources.

TIME REQUIREMENTS

Donut County takes about two hours to play in its entirety. Do note that this game should not be taught on its own. It needs to be taught alongside other texts. Students should have an understanding of what gentrification is before playing.

SAFETY - TRIGGER WARNING

This game is rated for ages eight and up, so accessible to all students. You probably do not need to do much extra prep in terms of trigger warning, beyond teaching about gentrification.

- Teaching Tolerance is a great resource for finding these strategies.
- Beyond the Empathy Games 101: Digging Deep into Empathy, Ethics, and Design with Kelli Dunlap
- An Introduction to Content Warnings and Trigger Warnin

Super Mario Odyssey

SEE PAGE 34 IN THE STUDENT PACKET

- Content Area/s: Social Studies
- Developed by Nintendo
- Rated: 10+

WHERE TO PLAY

- Available on Nintendo Switch

CONTEXT

This lesson should take place during a unit on

- Cultural Representation
- Stereotypes
- Media Literacy

DO BEFORE - PREP

- Complete the game beforehand. The game has a number of different levels available, but they are not all accessible from the start. The levels can only be played in order on an initial play-through. The option to select specific levels becomes available after you beat them. after you beat the game. This lesson requires the teacher to be able to freely select between different levels. This therefore requires that the game has been completed before brining teaching this specific activity.

- Choose the texts that you want to teach alongside this game. Some examples are:

  > Nerdmuch: Super Mario Odyssey: Mario's Mexican Outfit Is a Tired Stereotype

  > NewsELA: Why Stereotypes should be avoided

  > Super Mario Odyssey, Like Nintendo›s Best Games, Is a Surrealist Triumph

OVERVIEW

Mario is one of the most popular characters in the world. He is an icon of video game culture that has shaped the industry. One thing Mario games have historically done well is to capture the fun and unique qualities of various cultures without (usually) degrading them with offensive stereotypes – although this is subjective and different people will have different opinions on the matter. In *Super Mario Odyssey* we see Mario, an Italian plumber, travel to worlds that borrow cultural aspects from Mexico, Japan, New York, and more.

The purpose of this lesson is to analyze how there is a hidden curriculum in life that is constantly educating us and shaping our understanding of the world. This includes how one views people and cultures different from their own. Many of our own assumptions are based on how people are portrayed in popular media, including video games. Students can observe the various representations of culture in *Super Mario Odyssey* and then decide for themselves if the game was being respectful or offensive. Beyond that, they can reflect on how their own preconceived notions of other countries might have been shaped by pieces of entertainment like Mario. This will get them thinking of other examples of how they might be learning in unexpected places.

Media and entertainment are not always successful at depicting various cultures without tapping into some kind of stereotype. *Super Mario Odyssey* does dip into some stereotypical aspects of each culture represented in the game. It is fun, enjoyable, and a perfect example to show students appropriate ways to have fun with culture. That being said, the game does not always do this perfectly. The Aim for the lesson is, «How are we often learning without even realizing?» This lesson consists of playing through three of the game›s levels: The Sand Kingdom Tostarena, the Metro Kingdom New Donk City, and the Bowser Kingdom Bowser's Castle. Each of the levels are inspired by different real-world locations. Tostarena is inspired by various parts of Mexico, New Donk City is a sprawling cityscape modeled after New York City, and Bowser›s Castle is heavily influenced by traditional Japanese castle architecture. Each level has characters wearing each culture›s respective clothing and music from their respective cultures plays in the background. It is Mario›s job to engage with each new culture in order to reach the end of the level. The objective of each level is to collect a certain amount of moons in order to advance to the next world. In some cases, Mario needs to perform in a Mariachi band in Tostarena, or attend a jazz fest in New Donk City. One downside of this lesson is that the game needs to be completed beforehand in order to travel freely between the three levels. This is one challenge of using larger games in general.

There are a million different choices that go into the creation of a video game, which are by and large influenced by aspects of real life that make their way into each game›s development. Those involved in the creation of *Super Mario Odyssey* made very intentional choices to create each level as they did. Recognizing those decisions is an important part of having a critical eye. It is also important to have dialogue about cultural representation because what may seem offensive to one person may not be to another. A lot of what we learn comes from the media we consume. That media, however, has always been created by people who have a specific goal in mind – goals that can have unintentional consequences. The developers of *Super Mario Odyssey* may claim that their intention was only to create a fun experience, but the sheer nature of placing the players in locations that look like real places has an effect. It may teach someone that NYC is full of yellow taxis, or accidentally reinforce a negative stereotype that Mexico is all desert. This is the hidden curriculum that is ever-present in our lives. Playing a video game is by no means the only way to teach this concept to your students, but it is definitely a fun and engaging method.

DESCRIPTION OF ACTIVITY

- Only one copy of the game is necessary. Project in the front of the class and have one student play at a time.
- Even in video games, we are often learning something without even realizing. Learning does not always need to be explicit.
- Unlike other types of media, in video games we can actually be a part of the story. Here we play as Mario and help him make his way through various worlds.
- While the game is critically acclaimed, the ways that it represents various cultures can be problematic.

- Mario is himself a stereotype of Italians, as Italians do not actually look or speak like Mario. He is usually not outright offensive. Yes, he borrows some stereotypical qualities of Italians, but he is a genuine person in his own right and he never depicts people from Italy in a negative light.
- As the name of the game implies, Mario embarks on an odyssey across many different worlds. Many of these worlds are inspired by actual locations.
- Provide some screenshots on the board to show the various worlds within the game. In my slides, I will have photos of the real-life places that inspired them.
  > Sand Kingdom (Influenced by Mexico and Mesoamerica)
  > Wooded Kingdom (Influenced by Redwood National Park)
  > Metro Kingdom (Influenced by New York City)
  > Snow Kingdom (Influenced by Siberia and Scandinavia)
  > Seaside Kingdom (Influenced by the French Riviera)
  > Bowser's Kingdom (Influenced by Japanese Architecture)
- For the sake of this lesson, we will be using the Sand, Metro, and Bowser's Kingdoms.
- Provide an accompanying handout before starting the game, as students will be answering questions as they play through the story.

OBJECTIVES

- Students will discuss different types of stereotypes (positive, negative, caricatures).
- Students will connect what they learn to various stereotypes they observe in popular media.

CORRELATION TO COMMON CORE STANDARDS

English Language Arts Anchor Standards

GRADES K-12

- College and Career Readiness Anchor Standards for Reading

  Key Ideas and Details
  > CCSS.ELA-LITERACY.CCRA.R.2

    Determine central ideas or themes of a text and analyze their development; summarize the key supporting details and ideas.
  > CCSS.ELA-LITERACY.CCRA.R.3

    Analyze how and why individuals, events, or ideas develop and interact over the course of a text.
- College and Career Readiness Anchor Standards for Writing

  Production and Distribution of Writing
  > CCSS.ELA-LITERACY.CCRA.W.4

    Produce clear and coherent writing in which the development, organization, and style are appropriate to task, purpose, and audience.
- College and Career Readiness Anchor Standards for Speaking and Listening

Teaching with Video Games

Comprehension and Collaboration

> CCSS.ELA-LITERACY.CCRA.SL.1

Prepare for and participate effectively in a range of conversations and collaborations with diverse partners, building on others› ideas and expressing their own clearly and persuasively.

> CCSS.ELA-LITERACY.CCRA.SL.2

Integrate and evaluate information presented in diverse media and formats, including visually, quantitatively, and orally.

History - Social Studies

GRADES 6-8

Key Ideas and Details

> CCSS.ELA-LITERACY.RH.6-8.2

Determine the central ideas or information of a primary or secondary source; provide an accurate summary of the source distinct from prior knowledge or opinions.

Craft and Structure

> CCSS.ELA-LITERACY.RH.6-8.4

Determine the meaning of words and phrases as they are used in a text, including vocabulary specific to domains related to history/social studies.

Integration of Knowledge and Ideas

> CCSS.ELA-LITERACY.RH.6-8.9

Analyze the relationship between a primary and secondary source on the same topic.

GRADES 9-10

Key Ideas and Details

> CCSS.ELA-LITERACY.RH.9-10.2

Determine the central ideas or information of a primary or secondary source; provide an accurate summary of how key events or ideas develop over the course of the text.

Craft and Structure

> CCSS.ELA-LITERACY.RH.9-10.4

Determine the meaning of words and phrases as they are used in a text, including vocabulary describing political, social, or economic aspects of history/social science.

Integration of Knowledge and Ideas

> CCSS.ELA-LITERACY.RH.9-10.9

Compare and contrast treatments of the same topic in several primary and secondary sources.

GRADES 11-12

Key Ideas and Details

> CCSS.ELA-LITERACY.RH.11-12.2

 **Teaching with Video Games**

Determine the central ideas or information of a primary or secondary source; provide an accurate summary that makes clear the relationships among the key details and ideas.

Craft and Structure

> CCSS.ELA-LITERACY.RH.11-12.4

Determine the meaning of words and phrases as they are used in a text, including analyzing how an author uses and refines the meaning of a key term over the course of a text (e.g., how Madison defines *faction* in *Federalist* No. 10).

Integration of Knowledge and Ideas

> CCSS.ELA-LITERACY.RH.11-12.9

Integrate information from diverse sources, both primary and secondary, into a coherent understanding of an idea or event, noting discrepancies among sources.

TIME REQUIREMENTS

This lesson will only take one hour. Plan to spend one to two class periods depending on how long your class is. Make sure to give about thirty minutes of playtime total: ten minutes for each of the three levels explored. This will leave the remainder of the class for discussion and work.

SAFETY - TRIGGER WARNING

Super Mario Odyssey is classroom- and age-appropriate. The discussion around cultural representation and stereotypes could lead to difficult conversation and tension. Prepare for these conversations as needed.

- Teaching Tolerance
- Beyond the Empathy Games 101: Digging Deep into Empathy, Ethics, and Design with Kelli Dunlap
- An Introduction to Content Warnings and Trigger Warnings

Teaching with Video Games

Bury Me, My Love

SEE PAGE 36 IN THE STUDENT PACKET

- Content Area/s: Social Studies
- Developed by The Pixel Hunt, Figs, and ARTE France
- Rated: 10+

WHERE TO PLAY

- Available on iOS, Android, Microsoft Windows, Nintendo Switch

CONTEXT

This lesson should take place during a unit on:

- The Syrian Refugee Crisis
- Migration/Immigration

DO BEFORE - PREP

- Decide if you want to play together as a class, in pairs, groups, or individually.
- Choose the texts that you want to teach alongside this game. Some examples are:
    > Gamasutra - What Reality Inspired Games Are
    > Le Monde - The journey of a Syrian migrant through her WhatsApp thread

OVERVIEW

Whenever we learn about war, there is always talk how to help refugees from these conflicts. It can often be hard to convey their experiences because most teachers and students have not experienced war first-hand. *Bury Me, My Love* tells the story of Nour, a Syrian refugee, as she makes her way to safety in Europe. It is unique in that the story is told entirely through text messages. The player acts as Nour's husband Majd, and it is his job to help guide Nour on her travels towards Europe. While it is playable in several different mediums, it actually makes most sense to play this on a smartphone. Students can play their own copies of the game if they want, but it also makes sense to have students play in groups. That way they can make decisions together. The narrative will also drastically change depending on your guidance of Nour. This can lead to each group in the class coming up with a different ending.

The game is best played with some background knowledge of the Syrian Refugee Crisis. Without that information it can be challenging to understand why Nour, a middle-class woman, would leave her family and literally risk her life to escape to another country. It also helps to have a general understanding of what happens to refugees and asylum seekers once they cross the border into another country. Nour will travel through many countries on her journey to Western Europe, and each provides a new set of challenges. The game does not have a defined length. The journey may end after a couple of days, or it can last more than a year. This all depends on how the player advises her. You can do your best to guide her and give advice, but at the end of the day it is very likely that Nour will stop responding and you will be left to wonder why. With nineteen different endings, this game will provide students with realistic consequences for the choices they make.

While the characters of *Bury Me, My Love* are fictional, the stories are very real. The game is based on the real-life experiences of many Syrian refugees and how millions of people have been separated from their families due to the civil war in their country. For so many of them, a smartphone was the only way to remain in contact. The game was even directly inspired by a Le Monde article that detailed the way two migrants used WhatsApp to chat with their families in order to ask for advice and find information during their journey. WhatsApp has over 1.5 billion active users. There are students in each of your classrooms that are familiar with this messaging service. As always, it is important to tap into students' prior knowledge and skills when putting together a lesson. A game like *Bury Me, My Love* is told through an interface nearly everyone knows how to navigate. There is no learning curve. No one needs to learn how to use a controller or play with a keyboard and mouse. And this is more than just a game. It is great storytelling, in a medium that all students will be able to utilize.

DESCRIPTION OF ACTIVITY

- Amount of copies needed is at the discretion of the teacher
  - > The class can play together with the game projected in the front of the room
  - > Students can play in pairs/groups on computers - consoles - smartphones
  - > Or students can play individually on computers - consoles - smartphones
- *Bury Me, My Love* tells the story of Nour, a Syrian refugee trying to escape her war-torn home to Europe. Students play as Majd, her husband. The entire game is told through text messages as you try to remain in contact and help your wife make it to safety.
- *Bury Me, My Love* is a "reality-inspired game," a documented fiction that draws inspiration directly from real-world events. The original idea stems from an article written by *Le Monde* journalist, Lucie Soullier, telling the story of Dana, a young Syrian woman who fled her country and is now living in Germany.
  - > "In Arabic, '*Bury Me, My Love*' is an expression that means ,'Take care,' or 'Don't even think about dying before I do.' You might say it to a loved one, before going separate ways. They are the last words Dana's mother told her to wish her good luck, as the young Syrian girl left her country. It was on September the 19th, 2015, when Dana had decided she would reach Germany at any cost." *Bury Me, My Love* is historical fiction. Every detail and plot point is directly inspired by something the developers saw, read, or heard. The game is based on real-life events. Bury Me, My Love features: 40 different locations, 19 different endings, 110,000 words in total."
- There are two ways to play. In the first, the game shows Nour texting you in real time. So if she does not respond to you for 14 hours in-game, it would take 14 hours in real life to receive that text message. This is the most fruitful way to play the game, as it is more realistic, but unfortunately that doesn't work well for a classroom setting.
  - > Instead, you can play in a fast-paced mode. There will be no time in between messages, so keep an eye on what time all messages are received because some of them may have actually been many "in-game" hours apart.
- Provide an accompanying handout before starting the game, as students will be answering questions as they play through the story.

Teaching with Video Games

OBJECTIVES

- Students will examine one refugee's story and use it to map her experiences.
- Students will analyze how the story of an individual refugee (microcosm) during war is different from that of a society (macrocosm)?
- Students will consider challenges facing the international community and weigh responses to the crisis.

CORRELATION TO COMMON CORE STANDARDS

English Language Arts Anchor Standards

GRADES K-12

- College and Career Readiness Anchor Standards for Reading

  ### Key Ideas and Details

  > CCSS.ELA-LITERACY.CCRA.R.2

  Determine central ideas or themes of a text and analyze their development; summarize the key supporting details and ideas.

  > CCSS.ELA-LITERACY.CCRA.R.3

  Analyze how and why individuals, events, or ideas develop and interact over the course of a text.

- College and Career Readiness Anchor Standards for Writing

  ### Production and Distribution of Writing

  > CCSS.ELA-LITERACY.CCRA.W.4

  Produce clear and coherent writing in which the development, organization, and style are appropriate to task, purpose, and audience.

- College and Career Readiness Anchor Standards for Speaking and Listening

  ### Comprehension and Collaboration

  > CCSS.ELA-LITERACY.CCRA.SL.1

  Prepare for and participate effectively in a range of conversations and collaborations with diverse partners, building on others› ideas and expressing their own clearly and persuasively.

  > CCSS.ELA-LITERACY.CCRA.SL.2

  Integrate and evaluate information presented in diverse media and formats, including visually, quantitatively, and orally.

History - Social Studies

GRADES 6-8

  ### Key Ideas and Details

  > CCSS.ELA-LITERACY.RH.6-8.2

  Determine the central ideas or information of a primary or secondary source; provide an accurate summary of the source distinct from prior knowledge or opinions.

Craft and Structure

> CCSS.ELA-LITERACY.RH.6-8.4

Determine the meaning of words and phrases as they are used in a text, including vocabulary specific to domains related to history/social studies.

Integration of Knowledge and Ideas

> CCSS.ELA-LITERACY.RH.6-8.9

Analyze the relationship between a primary and secondary source on the same topic.

GRADES 9-10

Key Ideas and Details

> CCSS.ELA-LITERACY.RH.9-10.2

Determine the central ideas or information of a primary or secondary source; provide an accurate summary of how key events or ideas develop over the course of the text.

Craft and Structure

> CCSS.ELA-LITERACY.RH.9-10.4

Determine the meaning of words and phrases as they are used in a text, including vocabulary describing political, social, or economic aspects of history/social science.

Integration of Knowledge and Ideas

> CCSS.ELA-LITERACY.RH.9-10.9

Compare and contrast treatments of the same topic in several primary and secondary sources.

GRADES 11-12

Key Ideas and Details

> CCSS.ELA-LITERACY.RH.11-12.2

Determine the central ideas or information of a primary or secondary source; provide an accurate summary that makes clear the relationships among the key details and ideas.

Craft and Structure

> CCSS.ELA-LITERACY.RH.11-12.4

Determine the meaning of words and phrases as they are used in a text, including analyzing how an author uses and refines the meaning of a key term over the course of a text (e.g., how Madison defines *faction* in *Federalist* No. 10).

Integration of Knowledge and Ideas

> CCSS.ELA-LITERACY.RH.11-12.9

Integrate information from diverse sources, both primary and secondary, into a coherent understanding of an idea or event, noting discrepancies among sources.

Teaching with Video Games

TIME REQUIREMENTS

Bury Me, My Love only takes two hours at most to finish one playthrough. There are, however, nineteen different ends. Some of these narrative threads will last longer than others. If a student's story ends very quickly, it is up to the discretion of the teacher to let them play through a second time. Between playtime and worktime, it will probably take two to three days to complete this activity.

SAFETY - TRIGGER WARNING

Bury Me, My Love is a very accessible text. The nature of gameplay through texting means that there are not going to be many triggering images. The game does, however, deal with a refugee making a very dangerous journey. If there are refugees in your classroom, this can be upsetting. The game also often ends with a recording that can be emotionally difficult to listen to, especially since there is very little sound at all during the game.

- Beyond the Empathy Games 101: Digging Deep into Empathy, Ethics, and Design with Kelli Dunlap
- An Introduction to Content Warnings and Trigger Warnings

Journey

SEE PAGE 40 IN THE STUDENT PACKET

- Content Area/s: English Language Arts
- Developed by thatgamecompany
- Rated: 10+

WHERE TO PLAY

- Available on iOS, PlayStation 3, PlayStation 4, Playstation 5, Microsoft Windows

CONTEXT

This lesson should take place during a unit on The Hero's Journey

DO BEFORE - PREP

- Decide if you want to play together as a class, in pairs, groups, or individually
- Choose the texts that you want to teach alongside this game. Some examples are:
    - > AmbiGamingCorner: The Interesting Case of the Hero's Journey
    - > Hero's Journey 101: Definition and Step-by-Step Guide (With Checklist!)

OVERVIEW

The Hero's Journey is one of the most popular storytelling tropes out there. It is an archetypal story pattern where a character embarks, often reluctantly, on an adventure. The character needs to overcome a conflict and eventually return home with a better understanding of the world they inhabit. Some of the biggest franchises across popular media utilize the Hero's Journey as their mechanism for telling a story. *Harry Potter, The Hunger Games*, the Marvel Cinematic Universe, and nearly every video game in history are about someone setting off on a journey. *Pokémon*, the largest media franchise in the world, was originally the story of a young kid named Red starting his journey to become a Pokémon master.

Journey is a very simple story. A robed figure departs on an adventure to reach the top of a mountain. The journey will not be an easy one, but in the end, the robed figure returns with more knowledge of the world. What is fascinating is that it does all of this without saying a word. The game communicates solely through its visuals, as there is zero dialogue. *Journey* is a great game to teach the Hero's Journey trope. Not everyone will agree that the robed figure is a hero, but it will force the students to focus on the protagonist's actions since the robed figure never speaks with another character.

Joseph Campbell, an American mythological researcher, broke the Hero›s Journey into three acts: departure, initiation, and return. Within those three acts are seventeen stages. They can be described as:

Teaching with Video Games

ACT	STAGE	DEFINITION
1) The Departure	*1) The call to adventure*	The hero starts off as an ordinary person living a completely normal life. There is an inciting incident that forces them to begin a new journey.
	2) Refusal of the call	The hero is often reluctant to set off on this new adventure. They did not ask to be thrust into the unknown. They might be afraid to leave their comfort zone in order to become a hero. They may, after all, not come back.
	3) Supernatural aid	Many heroes are accompanied by a magical helper or guide, someone who aids them on this new adventure.
	4) Crossing the threshold	The hero officially leaves the world they have known all their life. They venture out into the unknown. ready to face the dangers that await them.
	5) Belly of the whale	The belly of the whale represents the final separation from the hero›s home. They are too far gone and can never return to the life they once had. They have accepted their fate and the trials ahead.
2) The Initiation	*6) The road of trials*	Every hero will face challenges that test them on their new journey. This could be a test of new powers they have acquired or a test of their will to move forward. The hero must overcome these trials.
	7) The meeting with the goddess	Every hero acquires items and gifts that aid them on their quest. This is the stage the hero gains something they need in order to continue.
	8) The temptress	Leaving on a life changing journey can be very challenging. The hero will face temptations that make them consider abandoning their journey and giving up their powers. It can be a physical or mental temptation.
	9) Atonement	This is the center point of the Hero's Journey. The hero must forgive themselves for any faults or failures they may have.
	10) Apotheosis	The hero learns something that provides them with a better understanding of themselves and the world they inhabit. With this new knowledge the hero is ready to continue their journey.
	11) The ultimate boon	The ultimate boon is the end goal of the journey. What exactly did the hero acquire or accomplish?

3) The Return	*12) Refusal of the return*	Just as a hero might have initially refused the call to be a hero, they may refuse the call to return home. They may not want to return to normal life.
	13) The magic flight	This might be a final fight or boss. Sometimes in order to accomplish the task at hand, the hero will need to face off against some adversarial entity.
	14) Rescue from without	The hero may have needed help form a guide to set off on their journey. They may equally need help to guide them back home.
	15) The crossing of the return threshold	The hero returns home a different person than when they set out. Ideally, the hero should be able to use the knowledge and wisdom they gained in order to make their world a better place than when they left it.
	16) Master of two worlds	The hero is not the same person they were when they left. They have grown and are now a part of two different worlds. They can act as a mediary between these two aspects of life.
	17) Freedom to live	The hero now lives in the moment. They no longer worry about the mistakes of their past or about the uncertainty of the future.

The robed figure may not seem like the heroic type when the game starts, but as you progress it becomes clear that this character is one of the archetypal heroes. Each of the above seventeen stages can all be applied to the robed figure at some point during their story. Christopher Reeve defined being a hero as «an ordinary individual who finds the strength to persevere and endure in spite of overwhelming obstacles." A hero does not need to be a superhero, nor a savior. As Joseph Campbell put it, "A hero is someone who has given his or her life to something bigger than oneself."

This game is a one of a kind. It is broken up into eight distinct sections with a playtime of a little under three hours. It is an experience without any spoken dialogue. *Journey* focuses solely on visuals and sounds to tell this story. The moments in between the eight levels are opportune moments to have discussion about the narrative. These are also ideal times to switch out which student is playing. But students who are not playing will remain engaged because the game is so visually engaging and the music is top-notch, as well. As a game, it is pretty simple. As a story, however, it is much more complex. It gets the players to think about this world and want to learn more. It makes you feel for a character who does not speak and whose face you never see.

The game would probably best be taught after having already taught a traditional text. Use a more standard Hero's Journey to lay the foundation for an understanding of the archetype and then use this game to help cement that understanding and get students thinking critically about what it actually means to be a «hero.»

DESCRIPTION OF ACTIVITY

- Amount of copies needed is at the discretion of the teacher
  - > The class can play together with the game projected in the front of the room
  - > Students can play in pairs/groups on computers - consoles - smartphones
  - > Or students can play individually on computers - consoles - smartphones
- In narratology and comparative mythology, the monomyth, or the Hero›s Journey, is the common template of a broad category of tales and lore that involve a hero who goes on an adventure, and in a decisive crisis, wins a victory and comes home changed or transformed. - Wikipedia
- The Hero's Journey can be found across many different mediums and pieces of literature.
- In *Journey*, the players take the role of a robed figure traveling through a desert towards a large mountain. The player is not given any instructions on how to play the game or what the game›s goal is, nor any map of the game›s world.
- There is no spoken dialogue besides the chirping call of the player, and the cutscenes are shown without any words. It is up to the player to interpret the storyline of *Journey*, leading to many theories as to what exactly is taking place.
- The Robed Figure will go through many of the stages in the Hero's Journey, but it will be up to you to decide if the Figure is a hero.
- Have students take turns playing the game. There are eight levels in the game that students can rotate through. Each level ends with the screen fading to white. This is when students should switch turns.
- The game has optional collectables.
  - > Symbols will increase the length of the Robed Figure's scarf, which will let the player jump further.

    The symbols help with gameplay, but they aren't necessary.
  - > Ancient Glyphs add to the lore.

    Not necessary for this lesson.
- Provide an accompanying handout before starting the game, as students will be answering questions as they play through the story.
  - > There is an attached handout detailing the parts of a Hero's Journey that can be provided to students during the activity.

OBJECTIVES

- Students will define what makes a person/character a hero.
- Students will follow the Hero's Journey in Journey.
- Students will create their own definitions of "hero."

CORRELATION TO COMMON CORE STANDARDS

English Language Arts Anchor Standards

GRADES K-12

- College and Career Readiness Anchor Standards for Reading

  Key Ideas and Details

  > CCSS.ELA-LITERACY.CCRA.R.2

  Determine central ideas or themes of a text and analyze their development; summarize the key supporting details and ideas.

  > CCSS.ELA-LITERACY.CCRA.R.3

  Analyze how and why individuals, events, or ideas develop and interact over the course of a text.

- College and Career Readiness Anchor Standards for Writing

  Production and Distribution of Writing

  > CCSS.ELA-LITERACY.CCRA.W.4

  Produce clear and coherent writing in which the development, organization, and style are appropriate to task, purpose, and audience.

- College and Career Readiness Anchor Standards for Speaking and Listening

  Comprehension and Collaboration

  > CCSS.ELA-LITERACY.CCRA.SL.1

  Prepare for and participate effectively in a range of conversations and collaborations with diverse partners, building on others› ideas and expressing their own clearly and persuasively.

  > CCSS.ELA-LITERACY.CCRA.SL.2

  Integrate and evaluate information presented in diverse media and formats, including visually, quantitatively, and orally.

English Language Arts

Reading Literature

GRADE 6

Key Ideas and Details

> CCSS.ELA-LITERACY.RL.6.2

Determine a theme or central idea of a text and how it is conveyed through particular details; provide a summary of the text distinct from personal opinions or judgments.

Craft and Structure

> CCSS.ELA-LITERACY.RL.6.4

Determine the meaning of words and phrases as they are used in a text, including figurative and connotative meanings; analyze the impact of a specific word choice on meaning and tone

GRADE 7

Key Ideas and Details

> CCSS.ELA-LITERACY.RL.7.2

Determine a theme or central idea of a text and analyze its development over the course of the text; provide an objective summary of the text.

Craft and Structure

> CCSS.ELA-LITERACY.RL.7.4

Determine the meaning of words and phrases as they are used in a text, including figurative and connotative meanings; analyze the impact of rhymes and other repetitions of sounds (e.g., alliteration) on a specific verse or stanza of a poem or section of a story or drama.

GRADE 8

Key Ideas and Details

> CCSS.ELA-LITERACY.RL.8.2

Determine a theme or central idea of a text and analyze its development over the course of the text, including its relationship to the characters, setting, and plot; provide an objective summary of the text.

Craft and Structure

> CCSS.ELA-LITERACY.RL.8.4

Determine the meaning of words and phrases as they are used in a text, including figurative and connotative meanings; analyze the impact of specific word choices on meaning and tone, including analogies or allusions to other texts.

GRADES 9-10

Key Ideas and Details

> CCSS.ELA-LITERACY.RL.9-10.2

Determine a theme or central idea of a text and analyze in detail its development over the course of the text, including how it emerges and is shaped and refined by specific details; provide an objective summary of the text.

Craft and Structure

> CCSS.ELA-LITERACY.RL.9-10.4

Determine the meaning of words and phrases as they are used in the text, including figurative and connotative meanings; analyze the cumulative impact of specific word choices on meaning and tone (e.g., how the language evokes a sense of time and place; how it sets a formal or informal tone).

GRADES 11-12

Key Ideas and Details

> CCSS.ELA-LITERACY.RL.11-12.2

Determine two or more themes or central ideas of a text and analyze their development over the course of the text, including how they interact and build on one another to produce a complex account; provide an objective summary of the text.

Craft and Structure

> CCSS.ELA-LITERACY.RL.11-12.4

Determine the meaning of words and phrases as they are used in the text, including figurative and connotative meanings; analyze the impact of specific word choices on meaning and tone, including words with multiple meanings or language that is particularly fresh, engaging, or beautiful. (Include Shakespeare as well as other authors.)

Reading Informational Texts

GRADE 6

Key Ideas and Details

> CCSS.ELA-LITERACY.RI.6.2

Determine a central idea of a text and how it is conveyed through particular details; provide a summary of the text distinct from personal opinions or judgments.

> CCSS.ELA-LITERACY.RI.6.3

Analyze in detail how a key individual, event, or idea is introduced, illustrated, and elaborated in a text (e.g., through examples or anecdotes).

Craft and Structure

> CCSS.ELA-LITERACY.RI.6.4

Determine the meaning of words and phrases as they are used in a text, including figurative, connotative, and technical meanings.

GRADE 7

Key Ideas and Details

> CCSS.ELA-LITERACY.RI.7.2

Determine two or more central ideas in a text and analyze their development over the course of the text; provide an objective summary of the text.

> CCSS.ELA-LITERACY.RI.7.3

Analyze the interactions between individuals, events, and ideas in a text (e.g., how ideas influence individuals or events, or how individuals influence ideas or events).

Craft and Structure

> CCSS.ELA-LITERACY.RI.7.4

Determine the meaning of words and phrases as they are used in a text, including figurative, connotative, and technical meanings; analyze the impact of a specific word choice on meaning and tone.

GRADE 8

Key Ideas and Details

> CCSS.ELA-LITERACY.RI.8.2

Determine a central idea of a text and analyze its development over the course of the text, including its relationship to supporting ideas; provide an objective summary of the text.

> CCSS.ELA-LITERACY.RI.8.3

Teaching with Video Games

Analyze how a text makes connections among and distinctions between individuals, ideas, or events (e.g., through comparisons, analogies, or categories).

Craft and Structure

> CCSS.ELA-LITERACY.RI.8.4

Determine the meaning of words and phrases as they are used in a text, including figurative, connotative, and technical meanings; analyze the impact of specific word choices on meaning and tone, including analogies or allusions to other texts.

GRADES 9-10

Key Ideas and Details

> CCSS.ELA-LITERACY.RI.9-10.2

Determine a central idea of a text and analyze its development over the course of the text, including how it emerges and is shaped and refined by specific details; provide an objective summary of the text.

> CCSS.ELA-LITERACY.RI.9-10.3

Analyze how the author unfolds an analysis or series of ideas or events, including the order in which the points are made, how they are introduced and developed, and the connections that are drawn between them.

Craft and Structure

> CCSS.ELA-LITERACY.RI.9-10.4

Determine the meaning of words and phrases as they are used in a text, including figurative, connotative, and technical meanings; analyze the cumulative impact of specific word choices on meaning and tone (e.g., how the language of a court opinion differs from that of a newspaper).

GRADES 11-12

Key Ideas and Details

> CCSS.ELA-LITERACY.RI.11-12.2

Determine two or more central ideas of a text and analyze their development over the course of the text, including how they interact and build on one another to provide a complex analysis; provide an objective summary of the text.

> CCSS.ELA-LITERACY.RI.11-12.3

Analyze a complex set of ideas or sequence of events and explain how specific individuals, ideas, or events interact and develop over the course of the text.

Craft and Structure

> CCSS.ELA-LITERACY.RI.11-12.4

Determine the meaning of words and phrases as they are used in a text, including figurative, connotative, and technical meanings; analyze how an author uses and refines the meaning of a key term or terms over the course of a text (e.g., how Madison defines faction in Federalist No. 10).

Speaking and Listening

GRADE 6

Comprehension and Collaboration

> CCSS.ELA-LITERACY.SL.6.1

Engage effectively in a range of collaborative discussions (one-on-one, in groups, and teacher-led) with diverse partners on grade 6 topics, texts, and issues, building on others› ideas and expressing their own clearly.

> CCSS.ELA-LITERACY.SL.6.2

Interpret information presented in diverse media and formats (e.g., visually, quantitatively, orally) and explain how it contributes to a topic, text, or issue under study.

GRADE 7

Comprehension and Collaboration

> CCSS.ELA-LITERACY.SL.7.1

Engage effectively in a range of collaborative discussions (one-on-one, in groups, and teacher-led) with diverse partners on grade 7 topics, texts, and issues, building on others› ideas and expressing their own clearly.

> CCSS.ELA-LITERACY.SL.7.2

Analyze the main ideas and supporting details presented in diverse media and formats (e.g., visually, quantitatively, orally) and explain how the ideas clarify a topic, text, or issue under study.

GRADE 8

Comprehension and Collaboration

> CCSS.ELA-LITERACY.SL.8.1

Engage effectively in a range of collaborative discussions (one-on-one, in groups, and teacher-led) with diverse partners on grade 8 topics, texts, and issues, building on others› ideas and expressing their own clearly.

> CCSS.ELA-LITERACY.SL.8.2

Analyze the purpose of information presented in diverse media and formats (e.g., visually, quantitatively, orally) and evaluate the motives (e.g., social, commercial, political) behind its presentation.

GRADES 9-10

Comprehension and Collaboration

> CCSS.ELA-LITERACY.SL.9-10.1

Initiate and participate effectively in a range of collaborative discussions (one-on-one, in groups, and teacher-led) with diverse partners on grades 9-10 topics, texts, and issues, building on others› ideas and expressing their own clearly and persuasively.

> CCSS.ELA-LITERACY.SL.9-10.2

Integrate multiple sources of information presented in diverse media or formats (e.g., visually, quantitatively, orally) evaluating the credibility and accuracy of each source.

GRADES 11-12

Comprehension and Collaboration

> CCSS.ELA-LITERACY.SL.11-12.1

Teaching with Video Games

Initiate and participate effectively in a range of collaborative discussions (one-on-one, in groups, and teacher-led) with diverse partners on grades 11-12 topics, texts, and issues, building on others› ideas and expressing their own clearly and persuasively.

> CCSS.ELA-LITERACY.SL.11-12.2

Integrate multiple sources of information presented in diverse formats and media (e.g., visually, quantitatively, orally) in order to make informed decisions and solve problems, evaluating the credibility and accuracy of each source and noting any discrepancies among the data.

TIME REQUIREMENTS

Journey takes about two hours to play. This is under the assumption that the player is not wasting too much time searching for all of the collectables. Plan to spend three to four class periods with the game in order to provide adequate play time and work time.

SAFETY - TRIGGER WARNING

There is nothing about this game that should be triggering for your students.

Life is Strange 2: Episode 1

SEE PAGE 46 IN THE STUDENT PACKET

- Content Area/s: English Language Arts - Social Studies
- Developed by Dontnod
- Rated: 16+

WHERE TO PLAY

- Available on PlayStation 4, PlayStation 5, Xbox One, Xbox Series X/S, Microsoft Windows, macOS, Linux

CONTEXT

This lesson should take place during a unit on

- Racism/discrimination in the United States
- The Hero's Journey

DO BEFORE - PREP

- Important to note is that this game is broken up into five episodes. You could theoretically play all five with your students, but if time is an issue then it is perfectly fine to only play through the first episode, which acts as a self-contained story. This activity only utilizes the first episode of the game.
- Choose the texts that you want to teach alongside this game. Some examples are as follows
  > Engadget: 'Life is Strange 2' and the reality of gun violence in games
  > Polygon: Life is Strange 2 is an intimate portrait of the Trump era
  > The Washington Post: Fatal Force
  > Universal Declaration of Human Rights

OVERVIEW

Another game that utilizes the Hero's Journey is *Life is Strange 2*. *Life is Strange 2* offers a different take on heroism, in the form of a sixteen-year-old trying to protect his little brother. You will notice that this lesson is very similar to the previous one based on the video game *Journey*. Here, you play as Sean Diaz, a Mexican American teenager who is thrust on a journey with his younger brother Daniel. The two of them need to make their way from Seattle to Mexico. After a confrontation with a neighbor, a policeman arrives and shoots down Sean and Daniel›s father, seemingly out of fear. In this moment Daniel unwillingly uses his newfound telekinetic powers to accidentally harm the police officer.

Fearing retribution, Sean and Daniel are forced to run away from home. The brothers set off towards Mexico, with the police on their tail, in hopes of finding safety. Sixteen-year-old Sean has responsibility thrust upon him as he is now responsible for Daniel's safety and shelter in

Teaching with Video Games

addition to teaching him how to live with his newfound telekinetic abilities. Not an easy task for a teenager. The player's choices will not only shape the fates of the Diaz brothers, but also those of everyone they come in contact with. Some people will be there to aid in your journey while others will do what they can to stop you. Mexico is a long way from Seattle, and it will not be easy to get there.

Dontnod is known for bringing real world issues of discrimination into their games. It is made very clear that the police officer who killed Sean and Daniel's father responded out of bias due to the color of their skin. Throughout the game, the brothers encounter characters who casually make racist comments; one even brings up how President Trump›s border wall is necessary. It can be challenging to tackle heavy topics like this with your students, but it is still a conversation that needs to take place in an educational setting. Social Studies and ELA teachers would not be doing their job right if they never pushed boundaries. Yes, we want students to feel safe, but everyone will sooner or later but put in an uncomfortable situation in order to teach certain content.

While you do walk around, there is less «playing» than in traditional games. This game is similar to *1979 Revolution: Black Friday* in that you can interact with your environment, but the gameplay is mostly just triggering dialogue. There are dialogue choices implemented into every conversation. This gives the players some control over how the story plays out. Your choices can shape Sean as an empathetic and considerate kid, or you can turn him into a boorish rebel. It is ultimately your choice. You wander highways, campsites, gas stations, and motels while trying to figure out how to get to Mexico. The everyday people you interact with, become a constant threat since you are wanted by the police. This is only heightened by the added effect of racism. Whether or not you agree with Sean›s decision to run away, it is clear that he is doing everything he can to protect his brother. He is being heroic.

Life is Strange 2 is a unique take on the Hero›s Journey. He is not a superhero or anyone with special powers and abilities. Daniel, the one with telekinetic powers, is not the hero of this story. Think of Sean as the Sam to Daniel's Frodo. Sean is just a teenager, a kid who does not properly think through all his actions. He acts impulsively, but at the end of the day it is difficult to argue that his actions are not those of a hero. The dialogue can be clunky and is often way too on the nose (the developers may not be the best at writing edgy dialogue for teenagers), but the game still gets the players to care about its two protagonists. The overall plot and the amount of choice the player is provided in directing the dialogue really helps forge a connection with Sean and Daniel. Empathy should be a part of every teacher's curriculum and this game can help get students to empathize with two kids in circumstances very different from their own.

DESCRIPTION OF ACTIVITY

- Only one copy of the game is necessary. Project in the front of the class and have one student play at a time.
- In narratology and comparative mythology, the monomyth, or the hero›s journey, is the common template of a broad category of tales and lore that involve a hero who goes on an adventure, and in a decisive crisis, wins a victory and comes home changed or transformed. - Wikipedia
- The Hero's Journey can be found across many different mediums and pieces of literature.
- *Life is Strange 2* offers a different take on heroism in the form of a sixteen-year-old

trying to protect his little brother.

- "After a tragic incident, brothers Sean and Daniel Diaz run away from home. Fearing the police, and dealing with Daniel›s new telekinetic power, the boys flee to Mexico for safety. Suddenly, sixteen-year-old Sean is responsible for Daniel's safety, shelter, and teaching him right from wrong. As Sean, your choices shape the fates of the Diaz brothers, and the lives of everyone they meet. The road to Mexico is long and filled with danger. This is the trip that could bond Sean and Daniel forever... or tear their brotherhood apart" (<u>Square Enix, Dontnod Entertainment</u>)

- We will only be playing through the first episode of *Life is Strange 2*. There are five chapters in total that you can finish on your own at a later time.

- Provide an accompanying handouts before starting the game, as students will be answering questions as they play through the story.
  - > There is an attached handout detailing the parts of a Hero's Journey that can be provided to students during the activity.

OBJECTIVES

- Students will define what makes a person a hero.
- Students will follow the Hero's Journey in *Life is Strange 2*
- Students will create their own definition of "hero."

CORRELATION TO COMMON CORE STANDARDS

English Language Arts Anchor Standards

GRADES K-12

- College and Career Readiness Anchor Standards for Reading
  Key Ideas and Details
  - > CCSS.ELA-LITERACY.CCRA.R.2
    Determine central ideas or themes of a text and analyze their development; summarize the key supporting details and ideas.
  - > CCSS.ELA-LITERACY.CCRA.R.3
    Analyze how and why individuals, events, or ideas develop and interact over the course of a text.
- College and Career Readiness Anchor Standards for Writing
  Production and Distribution of Writing
  - > CCSS.ELA-LITERACY.CCRA.W.4
    Produce clear and coherent writing in which the development, organization, and style are appropriate to task, purpose, and audience.
- College and Career Readiness Anchor Standards for Speaking and Listening
  Comprehension and Collaboration
  - > CCSS.ELA-LITERACY.CCRA.SL.1

Prepare for and participate effectively in a range of conversations and collaborations with diverse partners, building on others› ideas and expressing their own clearly and persuasively.

> CCSS.ELA-LITERACY.CCRA.SL.2

Integrate and evaluate information presented in diverse media and formats, including visually, quantitatively, and orally.

History - Social Studies

GRADES 9-10

Key Ideas and Details

> CCSS.ELA-LITERACY.RH.9-10.2

Determine the central ideas or information of a primary or secondary source; provide an accurate summary of how key events or ideas develop over the course of the text.

Craft and Structure

> CCSS.ELA-LITERACY.RH.9-10.4

Determine the meaning of words and phrases as they are used in a text, including vocabulary describing political, social, or economic aspects of history/social science.

Integration of Knowledge and Ideas

> CCSS.ELA-LITERACY.RH.9-10.9

Compare and contrast treatments of the same topic in several primary and secondary sources.

GRADES 11-12

Key Ideas and Details

> CCSS.ELA-LITERACY.RH.11-12.2

Determine the central ideas or information of a primary or secondary source; provide an accurate summary that makes clear the relationships among the key details and ideas.

Craft and Structure

> CCSS.ELA-LITERACY.RH.11-12.4

Determine the meaning of words and phrases as they are used in a text, including analyzing how an author uses and refines the meaning of a key term over the course of a text (e.g., how Madison defines *faction* in *Federalist* No. 10).

Integration of Knowledge and Ideas

> CCSS.ELA-LITERACY.RH.11-12.9

Integrate information from diverse sources, both primary and secondary, into a coherent understanding of an idea or event, noting discrepancies among sources.

English Language Arts

Reading Literature

GRADES 9-10

Key Ideas and Details

> CCSS.ELA-LITERACY.RL.9-10.2

Determine a theme or central idea of a text and analyze in detail its development over the course of the text, including how it emerges and is shaped and refined by specific details; provide an objective summary of the text.

Craft and Structure

> CCSS.ELA-LITERACY.RL.9-10.4

Determine the meaning of words and phrases as they are used in the text, including figurative and connotative meanings; analyze the cumulative impact of specific word choices on meaning and tone (e.g., how the language evokes a sense of time and place; how it sets a formal or informal tone).

GRADES 11-12

Key Ideas and Details

> CCSS.ELA-LITERACY.RL.11-12.2

Determine two or more themes or central ideas of a text and analyze their development over the course of the text, including how they interact and build on one another to produce a complex account; provide an objective summary of the text.

Craft and Structure

> CCSS.ELA-LITERACY.RL.11-12.4

Determine the meaning of words and phrases as they are used in the text, including figurative and connotative meanings; analyze the impact of specific word choices on meaning and tone, including words with multiple meanings or language that is particularly fresh, engaging, or beautiful. (Include Shakespeare as well as other authors.)

Reading Informational Texts

GRADES 9-10

Key Ideas and Details

> CCSS.ELA-LITERACY.RI.9-10.2

Determine a central idea of a text and analyze its development over the course of the text, including how it emerges and is shaped and refined by specific details; provide an objective summary of the text.

> CCSS.ELA-LITERACY.RI.9-10.3

Analyze how the author unfolds an analysis or series of ideas or events, including the order in which the points are made, how they are introduced and developed, and the connections that are drawn between them.

Craft and Structure

> CCSS.ELA-LITERACY.RI.9-10.4

Teaching with Video Games

Determine the meaning of words and phrases as they are used in a text, including figurative, connotative, and technical meanings; analyze the cumulative impact of specific word choices on meaning and tone (e.g., how the language of a court opinion differs from that of a newspaper).

GRADES 11-12

Key Ideas and Details

> CCSS.ELA-LITERACY.RI.11-12.2

Determine two or more central ideas of a text and analyze their development over the course of the text, including how they interact and build on one another to provide a complex analysis; provide an objective summary of the text.

> CCSS.ELA-LITERACY.RI.11-12.3

Analyze a complex set of ideas or sequence of events and explain how specific individuals, ideas, or events interact and develop over the course of the text.

Craft and Structure

> CCSS.ELA-LITERACY.RI.11-12.4

Determine the meaning of words and phrases as they are used in a text, including figurative, connotative, and technical meanings; analyze how an author uses and refines the meaning of a key term or terms over the course of a text (e.g., how Madison defines faction in Federalist No. 10).

Speaking and Listening

GRADES 9-10

Comprehension and Collaboration

> CCSS.ELA-LITERACY.SL.9-10.1

Initiate and participate effectively in a range of collaborative discussions (one-on-one, in groups, and teacher-led) with diverse partners on grades 9-10 topics, texts, and issues, building on others› ideas and expressing their own clearly and persuasively.

> CCSS.ELA-LITERACY.SL.9-10.2

Integrate multiple sources of information presented in diverse media or formats (e.g., visually, quantitatively, orally) evaluating the credibility and accuracy of each source.

GRADES 11-12

Comprehension and Collaboration

> CCSS.ELA-LITERACY.SL.11-12.1

Initiate and participate effectively in a range of collaborative discussions (one-on-one, in groups, and teacher-led) with diverse partners on grades 11-12 topics, texts, and issues, building on others› ideas and expressing their own clearly and persuasively.

> CCSS.ELA-LITERACY.SL.11-12.2

Integrate multiple sources of information presented in diverse formats and media (e.g., visually, quantitatively, orally) in order to make informed decisions and solve problems, evaluating the credibility and accuracy of each source and noting any discrepancies among the data.

TIME REQUIREMENTS

This first episode of *Life is Strange 2* will take approximately three hours of playtime to complete. This does vary slightly depending on how much the students decide to explore in game. The game will proceed at the pace of the player. Play ahead of time and plan accordingly. It is okay to push students to move a little more quickly if they are spending too much time in one area.

SAFETY - TRIGGER WARNING

The *Life is Strange* franchise is no stranger to depicting violent and triggering moments. Very early in this game is a depiction of an innocent man of color (Latino) being killed by a police officer, an image often at the forefront of American politics and protests. This game will deal with death and the impact this has on people (specifically teenagers) of color.

- Teaching Tolerance
- Beyond the Empathy Games 101: Digging Deep into Empathy, Ethics, and Design with Kelli Dunlap
- An Introduction to Content Warnings and Trigger Warnings

Teaching with Video Games

What Remains of Edith Finch

SEE PAGE 52 IN THE STUDENT PACKET

- Content Area/s: English Language Arts
- Developed by Giant Sparrow
- Rated: 13+

WHERE TO PLAY

- Available on Playstation 4, PlayStation 5, Xbox One, Xbox Series X/S, Nintendo Switch, Microsoft Windows

CONTEXT

This lesson should take place during a unit on

> Creative Writing
> Literary Elements

DO BEFORE - PREP

- Choose the texts that you want to teach alongside this game. Some examples are as follows
  > What is Creative Writing: Definition, Types, & Examples
  > How to Get Started With Creative Writing

OVERVIEW

What Remains of Edith Finch is the perfect game if you need examples of creative writing. Some students can naturally write beautiful and unique stories without much thought, but it can be difficult for other students to be "creative." We can tell them to use their imagination, but sometimes students need visual examples of what creative means. In *What Remains of Edith Finch*, students play as Edith, who explores her family estate to discover why she is the last remaining member in her family. The entire game consists of slowly navigating through the house as you learn more about your family and investigate secrets and knowledge.

This game is very similar to *Gone Home*. It is a walking simulator that focuses on story over action. It is a narrative driven game, where even the dialogue interacts with the environment. Seriously, there are subtitles on screen that will actually move as the player or their surroundings touch them. The story of the game focuses on the Finch family curse. Every person in the Finch family is bound to meet an untimely and potentially unnatural end. With each new generation of the family, only one person survives to carry on the Finch name.

Where the game shines is when you learn about each death in the family. When you enter each respective family member's bedroom, you are transported to the moment they died. Each story, however, is told through a completely unique perspective and uses completely different storytelling devices. One story is told like in a comic book, another through the lens of a camera, or from the eyes of a baby. The main narrative even interacts with the environment of the game. It's a wonderfully unique game to inspire students' creative writing.

DESCRIPTION OF ACTIVITY

- Only one copy of the game is needed.
    - > The game can be projected in the front of the class with one student playing at a time.
- In *What Remains of Edith Finch*, you play as a girl, Edith, the last remaining member of her family. You investigate her home trying to discover how each member of her family died.
- The Finch family has a curse that causes all but one member of each generation to die.
    - > As you progress through the story you will learn of each death and the various social/emotional issues that plague the Finch family.
    - > The game deals with themes of neglect, trauma, obsession, denial, drug abuse, escapism, and depression.
    - > Each of these stories will be told using different storytelling mediums.

        You can tell students this ahead of time, but don't tell them the types of storytelling devices used.

        The stories in the game are told in the form of hallucinations, comic books, through the lens of a photograph camera, daydreams/imagination, the first-person perspective of a baby and toddler, a flip book, letters, poetry, and flashbacks.
- The main narrative is even written across the screen as the game progresses, and the text almost always interacts with the environment around the letters.
- With each new family member, we are provided with a unique style of storytelling, which can be utilized in our own work.
- Provide an accompanying handout before starting the game, as students will be answering questions as they play through the story.

OBJECTIVES

- Students will examine multiple methods of storytelling.
- Students will determine which type of storytelling method most resonates with them.

CORRELATION TO COMMON CORE STANDARDS

English Language Arts Anchor Standards

GRADES K-12

> College and Career Readiness Anchor Standards for Reading

> Key Ideas and Details

> > CCSS.ELA-LITERACY.CCRA.R.2

Teaching with Video Games

Determine central ideas or themes of a text and analyze their development; summarize the key supporting details and ideas.

> CCSS.ELA-LITERACY.CCRA.R.3

Analyze how and why individuals, events, or ideas develop and interact over the course of a text.

College and Career Readiness Anchor Standards for Writing

Production and Distribution of Writing

> CCSS.ELA-LITERACY.CCRA.W.4

Produce clear and coherent writing in which the development, organization, and style are appropriate to task, purpose, and audience.

- College and Career Readiness Anchor Standards for Speaking and Listening

Comprehension and Collaboration

> CCSS.ELA-LITERACY.CCRA.SL.1

Prepare for and participate effectively in a range of conversations and collaborations with diverse partners, building on others› ideas and expressing their own clearly and persuasively.

> CCSS.ELA-LITERACY.CCRA.SL.2

Integrate and evaluate information presented in diverse media and formats, including visually, quantitatively, and orally.

English Language Arts

Reading Literature

GRADE 6

Key Ideas and Details

> CCSS.ELA-LITERACY.RL.6.2

Determine a theme or central idea of a text and how it is conveyed through particular details; provide a summary of the text distinct from personal opinions or judgments.

Craft and Structure

> CCSS.ELA-LITERACY.RL.6.4

Determine the meaning of words and phrases as they are used in a text, including figurative and connotative meanings; analyze the impact of a specific word choice on meaning and tone

GRADE 7

Key Ideas and Details

> CCSS.ELA-LITERACY.RL.7.2

Determine a theme or central idea of a text and analyze its development over the course of the text; provide an objective summary of the text.

Craft and Structure

> CCSS.ELA-LITERACY.RL.7.4

Determine the meaning of words and phrases as they are used in a text, including figurative and connotative meanings; analyze the impact of rhymes and other repetitions of sounds (e.g., alliteration) on a specific verse or stanza of a poem or section of a story or drama.

GRADE 8

Key Ideas and Details

> CCSS.ELA-LITERACY.RL.8.2

Determine a theme or central idea of a text and analyze its development over the course of the text, including its relationship to the characters, setting, and plot; provide an objective summary of the text.

Craft and Structure

> CCSS.ELA-LITERACY.RL.8.4

Determine the meaning of words and phrases as they are used in a text, including figurative and connotative meanings; analyze the impact of specific word choices on meaning and tone, including analogies or allusions to other texts.

GRADES 9-10

Key Ideas and Details

> CCSS.ELA-LITERACY.RL.9-10.2

Determine a theme or central idea of a text and analyze in detail its development over the course of the text, including how it emerges and is shaped and refined by specific details; provide an objective summary of the text.

Craft and Structure

> CCSS.ELA-LITERACY.RL.9-10.4

Determine the meaning of words and phrases as they are used in the text, including figurative and connotative meanings; analyze the cumulative impact of specific word choices on meaning and tone (e.g., how the language evokes a sense of time and place; how it sets a formal or informal tone).

GRADES 11-12

Key Ideas and Details

> CCSS.ELA-LITERACY.RL.11-12.2

Determine two or more themes or central ideas of a text and analyze their development over the course of the text, including how they interact and build on one another to produce a complex account; provide an objective summary of the text.

Craft and Structure

> CCSS.ELA-LITERACY.RL.11-12.4

Determine the meaning of words and phrases as they are used in the text, including figurative and connotative meanings; analyze the impact of specific word choices on meaning and tone, including words with multiple meanings or language that is particularly fresh, engaging, or beautiful. (Include Shakespeare as well as other authors.)

Reading Informational Texts

GRADE 6

Key Ideas and Details

Teaching with Video Games

> CCSS.ELA-LITERACY.RI.6.2

Determine a central idea of a text and how it is conveyed through particular details; provide a summary of the text distinct from personal opinions or judgments.

> CCSS.ELA-LITERACY.RI.6.3

Analyze in detail how a key individual, event, or idea is introduced, illustrated, and elaborated in a text (e.g., through examples or anecdotes).

Craft and Structure

> CCSS.ELA-LITERACY.RI.6.4

Determine the meaning of words and phrases as they are used in a text, including figurative, connotative, and technical meanings.

GRADE 7

Key Ideas and Details

> CCSS.ELA-LITERACY.RI.7.2

Determine two or more central ideas in a text and analyze their development over the course of the text; provide an objective summary of the text.

> CCSS.ELA-LITERACY.RI.7.3

Analyze the interactions between individuals, events, and ideas in a text (e.g., how ideas influence individuals or events, or how individuals influence ideas or events).

Craft and Structure

Determine the meaning of words and phrases as they are used in a text, including figurative, connotative, and technical meanings; analyze the impact of a specific word choice on meaning and tone.

GRADE 8

Key Ideas and Details

> CCSS.ELA-LITERACY.RI.8.2

Determine a central idea of a text and analyze its development over the course of the text, including its relationship to supporting ideas; provide an objective summary of the text.

> CCSS.ELA-LITERACY.RI.8.3

Analyze how a text makes connections among and distinctions between individuals, ideas, or events (e.g., through comparisons, analogies, or categories).

Craft and Structure

> CCSS.ELA-LITERACY.RI.8.4

Determine the meaning of words and phrases as they are used in a text, including figurative, connotative, and technical meanings; analyze the impact of specific word choices on meaning and tone, including analogies or allusions to other texts.

GRADES 9-10

Key Ideas and Details

> CCSS.ELA-LITERACY.RI.9-10.2

Determine a central idea of a text and analyze its development over the course of the text, including how it emerges and is shaped and refined by specific details; provide an objective summary of the text.

> **CCSS.ELA-LITERACY.RI.9-10.3**

Analyze how the author unfolds an analysis or series of ideas or events, including the order in which the points are made, how they are introduced and developed, and the connections that are drawn between them.

Craft and Structure

> **CCSS.ELA-LITERACY.RI.9-10.4**

Determine the meaning of words and phrases as they are used in a text, including figurative, connotative, and technical meanings; analyze the cumulative impact of specific word choices on meaning and tone (e.g., how the language of a court opinion differs from that of a newspaper).

GRADES 11-12

Key Ideas and Details

> **CCSS.ELA-LITERACY.RI.11-12.2**

Determine two or more central ideas of a text and analyze their development over the course of the text, including how they interact and build on one another to provide a complex analysis; provide an objective summary of the text.

> **CCSS.ELA-LITERACY.RI.11-12.3**

Analyze a complex set of ideas or sequence of events and explain how specific individuals, ideas, or events interact and develop over the course of the text.

Craft and Structure

CCSS.ELA-LITERACY.RI.11-12.4

Determine the meaning of words and phrases as they are used in a text, including figurative, connotative, and technical meanings; analyze how an author uses and refines the meaning of a key term or terms over the course of a text (e.g., how Madison defines faction in Federalist No. 10).

Speaking and Listening

GRADE 6

Comprehension and Collaboration

> **CCSS.ELA-LITERACY.SL.6.1**

Engage effectively in a range of collaborative discussions (one-on-one, in groups, and teacher-led) with diverse partners on grade 6 topics, texts, and issues, building on others› ideas and expressing their own clearly.

> **CCSS.ELA-LITERACY.SL.6.2**

Interpret information presented in diverse media and formats (e.g., visually, quantitatively, orally) and explain how it contributes to a topic, text, or issue under study.

GRADE 7

Comprehension and Collaboration

> **CCSS.ELA-LITERACY.SL.7.1**

Engage effectively in a range of collaborative discussions (one-on-one, in groups, and teacher-led) with diverse partners on grade 7 topics, texts, and issues, building on others› ideas and expressing their own clearly.

> CCSS.ELA-LITERACY.SL.7.2

Analyze the main ideas and supporting details presented in diverse media and formats (e.g., visually, quantitatively, orally) and explain how the ideas clarify a topic, text, or issue under study.

GRADE 8

Comprehension and Collaboration

> CCSS.ELA-LITERACY.SL.8.1

Engage effectively in a range of collaborative discussions (one-on-one, in groups, and teacher-led) with diverse partners on grade 8 topics, texts, and issues, building on others› ideas and expressing their own clearly.

> CCSS.ELA-LITERACY.SL.8.2

Analyze the purpose of information presented in diverse media and formats (e.g., visually, quantitatively, orally) and evaluate the motives (e.g., social, commercial, political) behind its presentation.

GRADES 9-10

Comprehension and Collaboration

> CCSS.ELA-LITERACY.SL.9-10.1

Initiate and participate effectively in a range of collaborative discussions (one-on-one, in groups, and teacher-led) with diverse partners on grades 9-10 topics, texts, and issues, building on others› ideas and expressing their own clearly and persuasively.

> CCSS.ELA-LITERACY.SL.9-10.2

Integrate multiple sources of information presented in diverse media or formats (e.g., visually, quantitatively, orally) evaluating the credibility and accuracy of each source.

GRADES 11-12

Comprehension and Collaboration

> CCSS.ELA-LITERACY.SL.11-12.1

Initiate and participate effectively in a range of collaborative discussions (one-on-one, in groups, and teacher-led) with diverse partners on grades 11-12 topics, texts, and issues, building on others› ideas and expressing their own clearly and persuasively.

> CCSS.ELA-LITERACY.SL.11-12.2

Integrate multiple sources of information presented in diverse formats and media (e.g., visually, quantitatively, orally) in order to make informed decisions and solve problems, evaluating the credibility and accuracy of each source and noting any discrepancies among the data.

TIME REQUIREMENTS

What Remains of Edith Finch will take between two and three hours to finish. A large portion of the attached handout can be completed while the game is being played, so it will probably only take three class periods to finish this lesson.

SAFETY - TRIGGER WARNING

This game can be very mature at times. The theme of death is prevalent throughout. There is also a specific story within the game that will deal with suicide. This part of the game in particular needs to be prepared beforehand. Allow students the option to opt out of this scene because you never know who might have lost a loved one to suicide.

- Teaching Tolerance
- Beyond the Empathy Games 101: Digging Deep into Empathy, Ethics, and Design with Kelli Dunlap
- An Introduction to Content Warnings and Trigger Warnings

Flower

SEE PAGE 55 IN THE STUDENT PACKET

- Content Area/s: English Language Arts
- Developed by thatgamecompany
- Rated: 7+

WHERE TO PLAY

- Available on PlayStation 3, PlayStation 4, PlayStation 5, PlayStation Vita, iOS, Microsoft Windows

CONTEXT

- This lesson should take place during a unit on
  - > Theme
  - > Literary Elements

DO BEFORE - PREP

- Decide if you want to play together as a class, in pairs, groups, or individually
- Choose the texts that you want to teach alongside this game. Some examples are as follows
  - > Brainpop: Theme
  - > Literary Terms: Theme

OVERVIEW

Theme is often one of the first concepts taught in an English Language Arts class. The theme is the central idea of a book or another piece of writing. It is an idea that recurs or pervades a work of art or literature that can often be summed up in one word. That may seem simple, but simple topics are often complicated to teach. Thatgamecompany is known for their beautiful, short, and simplistic games, like *Journey*. *Flower* is no exception. The developers intended for the game to be a meditative experience that allows the players to «be in complete zen.» The player utilizes motion controllers with their controllers or smartphone, depending on how they are playing, to guide a petal of a flower in the wind. It is also the perfect game to use as a text for teaching students how to identify a theme.

You enter the dreams of six different flowers on a windowsill in a bustling city. In the beginning of the game, the city seems heavily industrialized. It is bleak and full of steel, with a sweeping gray skyline. Playing through a flower›s dream gradually brings color and life back to this depressed environment. Even the flower›s home gradually becomes more lively. The theme of *Flower* is very clear as you progress through the game: balance. It is about finding a balance between urbanization and nature. We are all aware of how the natural environments around us are being destroyed for the sake of development, but many of us are apathetic to its consequences. There will come a time when we will need to fundamentally change how we treat nature and our environmental surroundings, but that does not mean that cities are bad. This game is all about showing us that balance can be attainable if we put in the effort.

In *Flower*, you control a petal and the speed of the wind on which it travels. You move to other clusters of flowers in order to create a longer trail of petals. As you travel through the first level, you bring color back to a grassland that was once devoid of any life. Eventually you start activating windmills and street lamps, and you bring color back to a colorless cityscape. Cities can be beautiful, but the game wants us to remember that there must always be a balance between cities and nature in order for each to thrive. For every New York City, there must be a Central Park. This is a theme that we have seen across countless pieces of media, whether video games, movies, or television. Balance is a trope that we are all familiar with but do not necessarily take seriously enough to implement it in our own lives. *Flower* is a wonderful resource for teaching this theme.

The controls are simple and intuitive, the game is gorgeous, and it clocks in at just under an hour of gameplay. This is a great place to start if you have never used a video game in class - and an even better place if you are an ELA teacher looking for a lesson on theme.

DESCRIPTION OF ACTIVITY

- Amount of copies needed is at the discretion of the teacher
  - > The class can play together with the game projected in the front of the room
  - > Students can play in pairs/groups on computers - consoles - smartphones
  - > Or students can play individually on computers - consoles - smartphones
- *Theme* is incorporated into most books, movies, TV, and even video games.
  - > Most writers or creators want their work to convey a message to their audience.
  - > Theme is the focus of the lesson based on the video game *Flower*.
- *Flower* is divided up into six main levels and one credits level. Each level is represented by a flower in a pot on a city apartment windowsill, and upon selecting a flower, the player is taken into the «dream» of that flower.
- Once inside a level, the player controls the wind as it blows a single flower petal through the air. Changes in the pitch and roll of the floating petal are accomplished by tilting the controller. Pressing any button blows the wind harder, which in turn moves the petal faster.
- Groups and lines of flowers are present in each level; approaching these with the petal causes them to bloom and a new petal to trail the first. When the player approaches certain flowers or groups of flowers, changes are made to the game world. These include opening new areas, transforming dead grassy areas to bright green fields, or activating wind turbines. These changes generally result in new flowers sprouting for the player to interact with.
- A musical chime that harmonizes with the background music plays as the player guides the flower pedal through each level. The music will adjust to the changes taking place within that world. The more flower petals the player has, for example, the faster the petals will move and the fast the music plays.
- It is impossible for the player to lose a level or any progress. The game features no enemies, hit points, or time limits.

- Provide an accompanying handout before starting the game, as students will be answering questions as they play through the story.

OBJECTIVES

- Students will determine the theme or central idea of *Flower*.
- Students will explore how the theme is directly incorporated into the gameplay of *Flower*.

CORRELATION TO COMMON CORE STANDARDS

English Language Arts Anchor Standards

GRADES K-12

- College and Career Readiness Anchor Standards for Reading

  Key Ideas and Details

  > CCSS.ELA-LITERACY.CCRA.R.2

  Determine central ideas or themes of a text and analyze their development; summarize the key supporting details and ideas.

  > CCSS.ELA-LITERACY.CCRA.R.3

  Analyze how and why individuals, events, or ideas develop and interact over the course of a text.

- College and Career Readiness Anchor Standards for Writing

  Production and Distribution of Writing

  > CCSS.ELA-LITERACY.CCRA.W.4

  Produce clear and coherent writing in which the development, organization, and style are appropriate to task, purpose, and audience.

- College and Career Readiness Anchor Standards for Speaking and Listening

  Comprehension and Collaboration

  > CCSS.ELA-LITERACY.CCRA.SL.1

  Prepare for and participate effectively in a range of conversations and collaborations with diverse partners, building on others› ideas and expressing their own clearly and persuasively.

  > CCSS.ELA-LITERACY.CCRA.SL.2

  Integrate and evaluate information presented in diverse media and formats, including visually, quantitatively, and orally.

English Language Arts

Reading Literature

GRADE 6

  Key Ideas and Details

  > CCSS.ELA-LITERACY.RL.6.2

Determine a theme or central idea of a text and how it is conveyed through particular details; provide a summary of the text distinct from personal opinions or judgments.

Craft and Structure

> CCSS.ELA-LITERACY.RL.6.4

Determine the meaning of words and phrases as they are used in a text, including figurative and connotative meanings; analyze the impact of a specific word choice on meaning and tone

GRADE 7

Key Ideas and Details

> CCSS.ELA-LITERACY.RL.7.2

Determine a theme or central idea of a text and analyze its development over the course of the text; provide an objective summary of the text.

Craft and Structure

> CCSS.ELA-LITERACY.RL.7.4

Determine the meaning of words and phrases as they are used in a text, including figurative and connotative meanings; analyze the impact of rhymes and other repetitions of sounds (e.g., alliteration) on a specific verse or stanza of a poem or section of a story or drama.

GRADE 8

Key Ideas and Details

> CCSS.ELA-LITERACY.RL.8.2

Determine a theme or central idea of a text and analyze its development over the course of the text, including its relationship to the characters, setting, and plot; provide an objective summary of the text.

Craft and Structure

> CCSS.ELA-LITERACY.RL.8.4

Determine the meaning of words and phrases as they are used in a text, including figurative and connotative meanings; analyze the impact of specific word choices on meaning and tone, including analogies or allusions to other texts.

GRADES 9-10

Key Ideas and Details

> CCSS.ELA-LITERACY.RL.9-10.2

Determine a theme or central idea of a text and analyze in detail its development over the course of the text, including how it emerges and is shaped and refined by specific details; provide an objective summary of the text.

Craft and Structure

> CCSS.ELA-LITERACY.RL.9-10.4

Determine the meaning of words and phrases as they are used in the text, including figurative and connotative meanings; analyze the cumulative impact of specific word choices on meaning and tone (e.g., how the language evokes a sense of time

Teaching with Video Games

and place; how it sets a formal or informal tone).

GRADES 11-12

Key Ideas and Details

> CCSS.ELA-LITERACY.RL.11-12.2

Determine two or more themes or central ideas of a text and analyze their development over the course of the text, including how they interact and build on one another to produce a complex account; provide an objective summary of the text.

Craft and Structure

> CCSS.ELA-LITERACY.RL.11-12.4

Determine the meaning of words and phrases as they are used in the text, including figurative and connotative meanings; analyze the impact of specific word choices on meaning and tone, including words with multiple meanings or language that is particularly fresh, engaging, or beautiful. (Include Shakespeare as well as other authors.)

Reading Informational Texts

GRADE 6

Key Ideas and Details

> CCSS.ELA-LITERACY.RI.6.2

Determine a central idea of a text and how it is conveyed through particular details; provide a summary of the text distinct from personal opinions or judgments.

> CCSS.ELA-LITERACY.RI.6.3

Analyze in detail how a key individual, event, or idea is introduced, illustrated, and elaborated in a text (e.g., through examples or anecdotes).

Craft and Structure

> CCSS.ELA-LITERACY.RI.6.4

Determine the meaning of words and phrases as they are used in a text, including figurative, connotative, and technical meanings.

GRADE 7

Key Ideas and Details

> CCSS.ELA-LITERACY.RI.7.2

Determine two or more central ideas in a text and analyze their development over the course of the text; provide an objective summary of the text.

> CCSS.ELA-LITERACY.RI.7.3

Analyze the interactions between individuals, events, and ideas in a text (e.g., how ideas influence individuals or events, or how individuals influence ideas or events).

Craft and Structure

> CCSS.ELA-LITERACY.RI.7.4

Determine the meaning of words and phrases as they are used in a text, including figurative, connotative, and technical meanings; analyze the impact of a specific word choice on meaning and tone.

GRADE 8

Key Ideas and Details

> CCSS.ELA-LITERACY.RI.8.2

Determine a central idea of a text and analyze its development over the course of the text, including its relationship to supporting ideas; provide an objective summary of the text.

> CCSS.ELA-LITERACY.RI.8.3

Analyze how a text makes connections among and distinctions between individuals, ideas, or events (e.g., through comparisons, analogies, or categories).

Craft and Structure

> CCSS.ELA-LITERACY.RI.8.4

Determine the meaning of words and phrases as they are used in a text, including figurative, connotative, and technical meanings; analyze the impact of specific word choices on meaning and tone, including analogies or allusions to other texts.

GRADES 9-10

Key Ideas and Details

> CCSS.ELA-LITERACY.RI.9-10.2

Determine a central idea of a text and analyze its development over the course of the text, including how it emerges and is shaped and refined by specific details; provide an objective summary of the text.

> CCSS.ELA-LITERACY.RI.9-10.3

Analyze how the author unfolds an analysis or series of ideas or events, including the order in which the points are made, how they are introduced and developed, and the connections that are drawn between them.

Craft and Structure

> CCSS.ELA-LITERACY.RI.9-10.4

Determine the meaning of words and phrases as they are used in a text, including figurative, connotative, and technical meanings; analyze the cumulative impact of specific word choices on meaning and tone (e.g., how the language of a court opinion differs from that of a newspaper).

GRADES 11-12

Key Ideas and Details

> CCSS.ELA-LITERACY.RI.11-12.2

Determine two or more central ideas of a text and analyze their development over the course of the text, including how they interact and build on one another to provide a complex analysis; provide an objective summary of the text.

> CCSS.ELA-LITERACY.RI.11-12.3

Analyze a complex set of ideas or sequence of events and explain how specific individuals, ideas, or events interact and develop over the course of the text.

Craft and Structure

> CCSS.ELA-LITERACY.RI.12.4-11

Determine the meaning of words and phrases as they are used in a text, including figurative, connotative, and technical meanings; analyze how an author uses and refines the meaning of a key term or terms over the course of a text (e.g., how Madison defines faction in Federalist No. 10).

Speaking and Listening

GRADE 6

Comprehension and Collaboration

> CCSS.ELA-LITERACY.SL.6.1

Engage effectively in a range of collaborative discussions (one-on-one, in groups, and teacher-led) with diverse partners on grade 6 topics, texts, and issues, building on others› ideas and expressing their own clearly.

> CCSS.ELA-LITERACY.SL.6.2

Interpret information presented in diverse media and formats (e.g., visually, quantitatively, orally) and explain how it contributes to a topic, text, or issue under study.

GRADE 7

Comprehension and Collaboration

> CCSS.ELA-LITERACY.SL.7.1

Engage effectively in a range of collaborative discussions (one-on-one, in groups, and teacher-led) with diverse partners on grade 7 topics, texts, and issues, building on others› ideas and expressing their own clearly.

> CCSS.ELA-LITERACY.SL.7.2

Analyze the main ideas and supporting details presented in diverse media and formats (e.g., visually, quantitatively, orally) and explain how the ideas clarify a topic, text, or issue under study.

GRADE 8

Comprehension and Collaboration

> CCSS.ELA-LITERACY.SL.8.1

Engage effectively in a range of collaborative discussions (one-on-one, in groups, and teacher-led) with diverse partners on grade 8 topics, texts, and issues, building on others› ideas and expressing their own clearly.

> CCSS.ELA-LITERACY.SL.8.2

Analyze the purpose of information presented in diverse media and formats (e.g., visually, quantitatively, orally) and evaluate the motives (e.g., social, commercial, political) behind its presentation.

GRADES 9-10

Comprehension and Collaboration

> CCSS.ELA-LITERACY.SL.9-10.1

Initiate and participate effectively in a range of collaborative discussions (one-on-one, in groups, and teacher-led) with diverse partners on grades 9-10 topics, texts, and issues, building on others› ideas and expressing their own clearly and persuasively.

> CCSS.ELA-LITERACY.SL.9-10.2

Integrate multiple sources of information presented in diverse media or formats (e.g., visually, quantitatively, orally) evaluating the credibility and accuracy of each source.

GRADES 11-12

Comprehension and Collaboration

> CCSS.ELA-LITERACY.SL.11-12.1

Initiate and participate effectively in a range of collaborative discussions (one-on-one, in groups, and teacher-led) with diverse partners on grades 11-12 topics, texts, and issues, building on others› ideas and expressing their own clearly and persuasively.

> CCSS.ELA-LITERACY.SL.11-12.2

Integrate multiple sources of information presented in diverse formats and media (e.g., visually, quantitatively, orally) in order to make informed decisions and solve problems, evaluating the credibility and accuracy of each source and noting any discrepancies among the data.

TIME REQUIREMENTS

Flower will take under two hours to play start to finish. Depending on the length of your class, it is possible to finish the game in one sitting. For most classes, however, it would make sense to pace this lesson over the course of two days.

SAFETY - TRIGGER WARNING

There is nothing about this game that should be triggering for your students.

Teaching with Video Games

Emily is Away

SEE PAGE 58 IN THE STUDENT PACKET

- Content Area/s: English Language Arts - Social Emotional Health
- Developed by Kyle Seeley
- Rated: 15+

WHERE TO PLAY

- Available for free on Microsoft Windows, macOS, Linux

CONTEXT

This lesson should take place during a unit on

- Writing Strategies
- Short Stories
- Literary Elements

DO BEFORE - PREP

- Decide if you want to play together as a class, in pairs, groups, or individually
  > Free to play on computers
- Choose the texts that you want to teach alongside this game. Some examples are:
  > TV Tropes: Dialogue Tree
  > Game Maker›s Toolkit: Can We Make Talking as Much Fund as Shooting?

OVERVIEW

Sometimes teachers need games that are short, accessible, and free in order to give beginners a way to «dip their toes in the water» before investing time and money into bigger games. Enter: *Emily is Away*. *Emily is Away* is an interactive story set in a retro chat-client. The game is free to play and only takes about 30 to 40 minutes to complete. It can be taught in one or two lessons, and is a fun and unique way to encourage students to read.

AIM (AOL Instant Messenger) radically changed how people communicated with each other. It was the first widespread way that people communicated in real time over the internet. Email existed, but that was a much slower form of engagement during the 1990s. With AIM, your friends could actually see if you were online and a chat would automatically open if someone started a conversation with you. The telephone made is so every day people no longer needed to be face-to-face in order to converse with one another. Instant messaging made it so that we could talk live while also taking the time to think before saying anything. It laid the foundation for texting, which is currently the most prevalent form of communication between adults in many countries.

Emily is Away takes this medium and turns it into a short story. It is a visual novel where the player can interact with the story. While the plot of the game is mostly linear, the player does get to choose various dialogue options that will directly affect the relationship between the player and their friend Emily. The Aim for this lesson is for the students to examine how the dialogue choices in *Emily is Away* strengthen the overall narrative of the game. It is a very poignant game that exemplifies just how people, especially teenagers, have learned to communicate differently than previous generations. It is also a story that cannot be told as a traditional text. The dialogue choices are necessary to help the players project themselves into the game›s story. There are visual cues that add to the story in ways that simple text cannot accomplish. And it's fun for teens to interact with a technology that is now considered ancient by their standards.

When you enter the game, you are greeted by that familiar sign-in tone from AIM. The basic plot of the game is about how the player interacts with their high school crush from their senior year through their college years. Each chapter pushes you forward another year in school. You get to create a screenname, read your friends personal profiles, and choose icons that were popular during that year. Anyone who engaged in any type of instant messaging as a kid will most definitely be reminded of the many awkward conversations their teenage selves had over the platform. The type of conversations that randomly keep you up at night because you know you could have said something so much better than what you had ultimately decided to say.

The Aim of the lesson is, «How do the dialogue choices in *Emily is Away* strengthen the overall narrative of the game?» The purpose of choosing this game was to show how inserting player choice in a narrative-heavy game gives the «readers» more autonomy than a typical book. It lets the players connect more with the story because they actually have some choice in how it plays out. While this is generally the case for most video games, games like *Emily is Away* are unique in that the player actually has a say in the dialogue. Your first major choice in the game is to choose whether or not to attend a party with your friend Emily.

The game is broken up into five chapters told over the course of five years. It begins in your senior year of high school and continues through college graduation. Your relationship with Emily gets more and more complicated every year she reaches out to you. You attend different colleges, and it is clear that this friendship is struggling to stay afloat. You can attempt to remain friends, or you can choose to try and have a romantic relationship with Emily. Emily often reaches out looking for advice and instead of helping her, you may make choices that are in your own best interest. This is the fun of role playing. One might make choices that they would never have done in real life simply to see how a situation plays out.

What the player begins to realize is that no matter what choices you make, your relationship with Emily eventually deteriorates. There is nothing you can do to save it. This is especially true for those who went off to college before social media was available. People change with time and it can be extraordinarily difficult to maintain relationships with people who are physically distant from you. While the way the game ends may vary, you are still unable to salvage your friendship.

This game leans hard into how teenagers speak and interact with each other. So while it may make you feel uncomfortable as a teacher, it is very realistic. *Emily is Away* is a great game to start with if you have never taught with a video game before. The only difficulty is in choosing dialogue you will not regret. It is short and free to play which makes it a lot more accessible than some of the other video games mentioned here in this book. Plus, there are two sequels (although you need to pay for them) that build upon the idea of telling a story through older means of instant messaging.

DESCRIPTION OF ACTIVITY

- Amount of copies needed is at the discretion of the teacher
    - > The class can play together with the game projected in the front of the room
    - > Students can play in pairs/groups on computers
    - > Or students can play individually on computers
- Go over the following vocabulary terms with the class:
    - > AIM (AOL Instant Messenger)

        An instant messaging and presence computer program created by AOL.

        AIM was popular from the late 1990s to the late 2000s in North America and was the leading instant messaging application in that region. AIM›s popularity declined steeply in the early 2010s as Internet social networks like Facebook and Twitter gained popularity.
    - > Visual Novel

        A term to distinguish itself from a «Game» because there is usually no gameplay involved, and the only interaction that the player can make with the game is making certain choices at specific points in the game that decides which branch of the storyline that the player will take.
- Go over the basic premise of *Emily is Away*.
    - > "*Emily is Away* is an interactive story set in a retro chat-client. Create a screenname and choose your path through the branching narrative."
    - > *Emily Is Away* is a visual novel by game developer Kyle Seeley. Set in the early-to-mid-2000s, *Emily Is Away* tells the story of the protagonist›s relationship with a girl, Emily, over the course of five years, from the senior year of high school to the senior year of college.
    - > The game is presented through a chat client styled after AOL Instant Messenger.
    - > You will be provided dialogue choices throughout the game in order for you to progress in a way that connects with you most.
    - > There are no wrong decisions.
- Provide an accompanying handout before starting the game, as students will be answering questions as they play through the story.

OBJECTIVES

- Students will analyze the effectiveness of dialogue choices in *Emily is Away*.
- Students will interpret the meaning of visual cues as used in *Emily is Away*.
- Students will explore the different mediums in which a story can be told.

CORRELATION TO COMMON CORE STANDARDS

English Language Arts Anchor Standards

GRADES K-12

- College and Career Readiness Anchor Standards for Reading

Key Ideas and Details

> ### CCSS.ELA-LITERACY.CCRA.R.2

Determine central ideas or themes of a text and analyze their development; summarize the key supporting details and ideas.

> ### CCSS.ELA-LITERACY.CCRA.R.3

Analyze how and why individuals, events, or ideas develop and interact over the course of a text.

- College and Career Readiness Anchor Standards for Writing

Production and Distribution of Writing

> ### CCSS.ELA-LITERACY.CCRA.W.4

Produce clear and coherent writing in which the development, organization, and style are appropriate to task, purpose, and audience.

- College and Career Readiness Anchor Standards for Speaking and Listening

Comprehension and Collaboration

> ### CCSS.ELA-LITERACY.CCRA.SL.1

Prepare for and participate effectively in a range of conversations and collaborations with diverse partners, building on others› ideas and expressing their own clearly and persuasively.

> ### CCSS.ELA-LITERACY.CCRA.SL.2

Integrate and evaluate information presented in diverse media and formats, including visually, quantitatively, and orally.

English Language Arts

Reading Literature

GRADE 6

Key Ideas and Details

> ### CCSS.ELA-LITERACY.RL.6.2

Determine a theme or central idea of a text and how it is conveyed through particular details; provide a summary of the text distinct from personal opinions or judgments.

Craft and Structure

> ### CCSS.ELA-LITERACY.RL.6.4

Determine the meaning of words and phrases as they are used in a text, including figurative and connotative meanings; analyze the impact of a specific word choice on meaning and tone

GRADE 7

Key Ideas and Details

> ### CCSS.ELA-LITERACY.RL.7.2

Determine a theme or central idea of a text and analyze its development over the course of the text; provide an objective summary of the text.

Craft and Structure

> CCSS.ELA-LITERACY.RL.7.4

Determine the meaning of words and phrases as they are used in a text, including figurative and connotative meanings; analyze the impact of rhymes and other repetitions of sounds (e.g., alliteration) on a specific verse or stanza of a poem or section of a story or drama.

GRADE 8

Key Ideas and Details

> CCSS.ELA-LITERACY.RL.8.2

Determine a theme or central idea of a text and analyze its development over the course of the text, including its relationship to the characters, setting, and plot; provide an objective summary of the text.

Craft and Structure

> CCSS.ELA-LITERACY.RL.8.4

Determine the meaning of words and phrases as they are used in a text, including figurative and connotative meanings; analyze the impact of specific word choices on meaning and tone, including analogies or allusions to other texts.

GRADES 9-10

Key Ideas and Details

> CCSS.ELA-LITERACY.RL.9-10.2

Determine a theme or central idea of a text and analyze in detail its development over the course of the text, including how it emerges and is shaped and refined by specific details; provide an objective summary of the text.

Craft and Structure

> CCSS.ELA-LITERACY.RL.9-10.4

Determine the meaning of words and phrases as they are used in the text, including figurative and connotative meanings; analyze the cumulative impact of specific word choices on meaning and tone (e.g., how the language evokes a sense of time and place; how it sets a formal or informal tone).

GRADES 11-12

Key Ideas and Details

> CCSS.ELA-LITERACY.RL.11-12.2

Determine two or more themes or central ideas of a text and analyze their development over the course of the text, including how they interact and build on one another to produce a complex account; provide an objective summary of the text.

Craft and Structure

> CCSS.ELA-LITERACY.RL.11-12.4

Determine the meaning of words and phrases as they are used in the text, including figurative and connotative meanings; analyze the impact of specific word choices on meaning and tone, including words with multiple meanings or language that is particularly fresh, engaging, or beautiful. (Include Shakespeare as well as other authors.)

Reading Informational Texts

GRADE 6

Key Ideas and Details

> CCSS.ELA-LITERACY.RI.6.2

Determine a central idea of a text and how it is conveyed through particular details; provide a summary of the text distinct from personal opinions or judgments.

> CCSS.ELA-LITERACY.RI.6.3

Analyze in detail how a key individual, event, or idea is introduced, illustrated, and elaborated in a text (e.g., through examples or anecdotes).

Craft and Structure

> CCSS.ELA-LITERACY.RI.6.4

Determine the meaning of words and phrases as they are used in a text, including figurative, connotative, and technical meanings.

GRADE 7

Key Ideas and Details

> CCSS.ELA-LITERACY.RI.7.2

Determine two or more central ideas in a text and analyze their development over the course of the text; provide an objective summary of the text.

> CCSS.ELA-LITERACY.RI.7.3

Analyze the interactions between individuals, events, and ideas in a text (e.g., how ideas influence individuals or events, or how individuals influence ideas or events).

Craft and Structure

> CCSS.ELA-LITERACY.RI.7.4

Determine the meaning of words and phrases as they are used in a text, including figurative, connotative, and technical meanings; analyze the impact of a specific word choice on meaning and tone.

GRADE 8

Key Ideas and Details

> CCSS.ELA-LITERACY.RI.8.2

Determine a central idea of a text and analyze its development over the course of the text, including its relationship to supporting ideas; provide an objective summary of the text.

> CCSS.ELA-LITERACY.RI.8.3

Analyze how a text makes connections among and distinctions between individuals, ideas, or events (e.g., through comparisons, analogies, or categories).

Craft and Structure

> CCSS.ELA-LITERACY.RI.8.4

Determine the meaning of words and phrases as they are used in a text, including figurative, connotative, and technical meanings; analyze the impact of specific word choices on meaning and tone, including analogies or allusions to other texts.

GRADES 9-10

Key Ideas and Details

> CCSS.ELA-LITERACY.RI.9-10.2

Determine a central idea of a text and analyze its development over the course of the text, including how it emerges and is shaped and refined by specific details; provide an objective summary of the text.

> CCSS.ELA-LITERACY.RI.9-10.3

Analyze how the author unfolds an analysis or series of ideas or events, including the order in which the points are made, how they are introduced and developed, and the connections that are drawn between them.

Craft and Structure

> CCSS.ELA-LITERACY.RI.9-10.4

Determine the meaning of words and phrases as they are used in a text, including figurative, connotative, and technical meanings; analyze the cumulative impact of specific word choices on meaning and tone (e.g., how the language of a court opinion differs from that of a newspaper).

GRADES 11-12

Key Ideas and Details

> CCSS.ELA-LITERACY.RI.11-12.2

Determine two or more central ideas of a text and analyze their development over the course of the text, including how they interact and build on one another to provide a complex analysis; provide an objective summary of the text.

> CCSS.ELA-LITERACY.RI.11-12.3

Analyze a complex set of ideas or sequence of events and explain how specific individuals, ideas, or events interact and develop over the course of the text.

Craft and Structure

> CCSS.ELA-LITERACY.RI.11-12.4

Determine the meaning of words and phrases as they are used in a text, including figurative, connotative, and technical meanings; analyze how an author uses and refines the meaning of a key term or terms over the course of a text (e.g., how Madison defines faction in Federalist No. 10).

Speaking and Listening

GRADE 6

Comprehension and Collaboration

> CCSS.ELA-LITERACY.SL.6.1

Engage effectively in a range of collaborative discussions (one-on-one, in groups, and teacher-led) with diverse partners on grade 6 topics, texts, and issues, building on others› ideas and expressing their own clearly.

> CCSS.ELA-LITERACY.SL.6.2

Interpret information presented in diverse media and formats (e.g., visually, quantitatively, orally) and explain how it contributes to a topic, text, or issue under study.

GRADE 7

Comprehension and Collaboration

> ### CCSS.ELA-LITERACY.SL.7.1

Engage effectively in a range of collaborative discussions (one-on-one, in groups, and teacher-led) with diverse partners on grade 7 topics, texts, and issues, building on others› ideas and expressing their own clearly.

> ### CCSS.ELA-LITERACY.SL.7.2

Analyze the main ideas and supporting details presented in diverse media and formats (e.g., visually, quantitatively, orally) and explain how the ideas clarify a topic, text, or issue under study.

GRADE 8

Comprehension and Collaboration

> ### CCSS.ELA-LITERACY.SL.8.1

Engage effectively in a range of collaborative discussions (one-on-one, in groups, and teacher-led) with diverse partners on grade 8 topics, texts, and issues, building on others› ideas and expressing their own clearly.

> ### CCSS.ELA-LITERACY.SL.8.2

Analyze the purpose of information presented in diverse media and formats (e.g., visually, quantitatively, orally) and evaluate the motives (e.g., social, commercial, political) behind its presentation.

GRADES 9-10

Comprehension and Collaboration

> ### CCSS.ELA-LITERACY.SL.9-10.1

Initiate and participate effectively in a range of collaborative discussions (one-on-one, in groups, and teacher-led) with diverse partners on grades 9-10 topics, texts, and issues, building on others› ideas and expressing their own clearly and persuasively.

> ### CCSS.ELA-LITERACY.SL.9-10.2

Integrate multiple sources of information presented in diverse media or formats (e.g., visually, quantitatively, orally) evaluating the credibility and accuracy of each source.

GRADES 11-12

Comprehension and Collaboration

> ### CCSS.ELA-LITERACY.SL.11-12.1

Initiate and participate effectively in a range of collaborative discussions (one-on-one, in groups, and teacher-led) with diverse partners on grades 11-12 topics, texts, and issues, building on others› ideas and expressing their own clearly and persuasively.

> ### CCSS.ELA-LITERACY.SL.11-12.2

Integrate multiple sources of information presented in diverse formats and media (e.g., visually, quantitatively, orally) in order to make informed decisions and solve problems, evaluating the credibility and accuracy of each source and noting any discrepancies among the data.

Teaching with Video Games

Writing

GRADE 6

Text Types and Purposes

> CCSS.ELA-LITERACY.W.6.1

  Write arguments to support claims with clear reasons and relevant evidence.

> CCSS.ELA-LITERACY.W.6.1.A

  Introduce claim(s) and organize the reasons and evidence clearly.

GRADE 7

Text Types and Purposes

> CCSS.ELA-LITERACY.W.7.1

  Write arguments to support claims with clear reasons and relevant evidence.

> CCSS.ELA-LITERACY.W.7.1.A

  Introduce claim(s), acknowledge alternate or opposing claims, and organize the reasons and evidence logically.

GRADE 8

Text Types and Purposes

> CCSS.ELA-LITERACY.W.8.1

  Write arguments to support claims with clear reasons and relevant evidence

> CCSS.ELA-LITERACY.W.8.1.A

  Introduce claim(s), acknowledge and distinguish the claim(s) from alternate or opposing claims, and organize the reasons and evidence logically.

GRADES 9-10

Text Types and Purposes

> CCSS.ELA-LITERACY.W.9-10.1

  Write arguments to support claims in an analysis of substantive topics or texts, using valid reasoning and relevant and sufficient evidence.

> CCSS.ELA-LITERACY.W.9-10.1.A

  Introduce precise claim(s), distinguish the claim(s) from alternate or opposing claims, and create an organization that establishes clear relationships among claim(s), counterclaims, reasons, and evidence.

GRADES 11-12

Text Types and Purposes

> CCSS.ELA-LITERACY.W.11-12.1

  Write arguments to support claims in an analysis of substantive topics or texts, using valid reasoning and relevant and sufficient evidence.

> CCSS.ELA-LITERACY.W.11-12.1.A

  Introduce precise, knowledgeable claim(s), establish the significance of the claim(s), distinguish the claim(s) from alternate or opposing claims, and create an organization that logically sequences claim(s), counterclaims, reasons, and evidence.

TIME REQUIREMENTS

Emily is Away is short and sweet. The game can be completed in 45-50 minutes. Depending on the length of your class period, this lesson can be completed in one to two days.

SAFETY - TRIGGER WARNING

While the game is fairly tame, it does deal with some sexual themes and utilizes some profanity. It should be perfectly acceptable for high school-aged students, and for middle school, it should be used at the discretion of the teacher.

- Beyond the Empathy Games 101: Digging Deep into Empathy, Ethics, and Design with Kelli Dunlap
- An Introduction to Content Warnings and Trigger Warnings

Batman: The Telltale Series

SEE PAGE 60 IN THE STUDENT PACKET

- Content Area/s: English Language Arts
- Developed by Telltale Games
- Rated: 16+

WHERE TO PLAY

- Available on Microsoft Windows, PlayStation 3, PlayStation 4, PlayStation 5, Xbox 360, Xbox One, Xbox Series X/S, iOS, Android, Nintendo Switch

CONTEXT

This lesson should take place during a unit on

- Writing Strategies
- Short Stories
- Literary Elements

DO BEFORE - PREP

- Decide if you want to play together as a class, in pairs, groups, or individually
- Choose the texts that you want to teach alongside this game. Some examples are:

  > TV Tropes: Dialogue Tree
  > Game Maker›s Toolkit: Can We Make Talking as Much Fund as Shooting?

OVERVIEW

Yes, Superhero games can have a place in schools, as well. Telltale Games is known for their interactive, narrative-based games. Instead of focusing on fighting and action, the core gameplay in their games lies in the decisions the player makes as a character. The player gets to choose the dialogue for the protagonist in every scene. These decisions even have consequences that shape the course of the story. Characters will remember and notice what you say, leading to different outcomes. This allows the player to form the protagonist as they see fit. They can be mild or aggressive. This makes it easy for the player to project their own personality traits onto a protagonist, or role play as someone completely different. It is a type of storytelling unique to video games. Yes, there are quicktime events during action scenes, but the focus of the game is more about choosing dialogue and anticipating the consequences of your choices.

Batman: The Telltale Series takes this gaming style and applies it to the titular Batman. Batman's story has been told a million times across different mediums, but this game is different because the player gets to choose what kind of person and hero Batman will be. Through its use of dialogue choices, it allows our students to take an active role in crafting a story with one of the most popular characters ever made. As Telltale Games puts it, "Enter the fractured psyche of Bruce Wayne and discover the powerful and far-reaching consequences of your choices as the Dark Knight. In this gritty and violent story, you'll make discoveries that will shatter Bruce Wayne's world, and the already fragile stability of a corrupt Gotham City. Your actions and your choices will determine the fate of the Batman."

The game balances the story between Batman and his secret identity as Bruce Wayne. The player is even offered the option to address problems as either Bruce Wayne or Batman during important moments in the story. This helps the player drive the narrative and make decisions that have consequences that shape the course of the story. Characters will remember and notice what you say, leading to potentially different outcomes.

The Aim of the lesson is: «How do the dialogue choices in *Batman: The Telltale Series* strengthen or weaken the overall narrative of the game?» Students will need to keep track of the decisions made by the player and analyze the significance of the their dialogue choices. This can be done individually, if each student has a copy of the game, or together as a class. The game even has a unique feature where those who are watching can use their phones to vote for their preferred decisions in the game.

While analyzing the effectiveness of dialogue choices in the game will be the focus of this mini unit, the game also offers chances to talk about morality. This is especially true since the player gets to ultimately decide what kind of hero Batman will be, spurring conversations about whether the ends justify the means and whether it would actually be a good thing to act as vigilantes in our societies.

DESCRIPTION OF ACTIVITY

- Amount of copies needed is at the discretion of the teacher
  > The class can play together with the game projected in the front of the room
  > Students can play in pairs/groups on computers - consoles - smartphone
  > Or students can play individually on computers - consoles - smartphone
- The story of *Batman: The Telltale Series* happens across five episodes:
  > Episode 1: Realm of Shadows
  > Episode 2: Children of Arkham
  > Episode 3: New World Order
  > Episode 4: Guardian of Gotham
  > Episode 5: City of Light
- Go over the following vocabulary terms with the class.
  > Visual Novel
    A term to distinguish itself from a «Game» because there is usually no gameplay involved, and the only interaction that the player can make with the game is making certain choices at specific points in the game that decide which branch of the storyline that the player will take.
- Go over the basic premise of *Batman: The Telltale Series*.
  > In *Batman: The Telltale Series* you get to choose what Bruce Wayne/Batman says. You have an active role in telling the story.

> Keeping Track of Your Actions

The game will keep track of your choices and compare your decisions with other people who played the game.

> This game is just as much a Bruce Wayne game as it is a Batman game. You will need to make choices for both parts of Bruce's identity.

- You will be provided dialogue choices throughout the game in order for you to progress in a way that connects with you most.

> There are no wrong decisions.

- Provide an accompanying handout before starting the game, as students will be answering questions as they play through the story.

OBJECTIVES

- Students will analyze the effectiveness of dialogue choices in *Batman: The Telltale Series*
- Students will interpret the meaning of visual cues as used in *Batman: The Telltale Series*
- Students will explore the different mediums in which a story can be told

CORRELATION TO COMMON CORE STANDARDS

English Language Arts Anchor Standards

GRADES K-12

- College and Career Readiness Anchor Standards for Reading

  Key Ideas and Details

  > CCSS.ELA-LITERACY.CCRA.R.2

  Determine central ideas or themes of a text and analyze their development; summarize the key supporting details and ideas.

  > CCSS.ELA-LITERACY.CCRA.R.3

  Analyze how and why individuals, events, or ideas develop and interact over the course of a text.

- College and Career Readiness Anchor Standards for Writing

  Production and Distribution of Writing

  > CCSS.ELA-LITERACY.CCRA.W.4

  Produce clear and coherent writing in which the development, organization, and style are appropriate to task, purpose, and audience.

- College and Career Readiness Anchor Standards for Speaking and Listening

  Comprehension and Collaboration

  > CCSS.ELA-LITERACY.CCRA.SL.1

  Prepare for and participate effectively in a range of conversations and collaborations with diverse partners, building on others› ideas and expressing their own clearly and persuasively.

  > CCSS.ELA-LITERACY.CCRA.SL.2

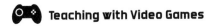

Integrate and evaluate information presented in diverse media and formats, including visually, quantitatively, and orally.

English Language Arts

Reading Literature

GRADES 9-10

Key Ideas and Details

> CCSS.ELA-LITERACY.RL.9-10.2

Determine a theme or central idea of a text and analyze in detail its development over the course of the text, including how it emerges and is shaped and refined by specific details; provide an objective summary of the text.

Craft and Structure

> CCSS.ELA-LITERACY.RL.9-10.4

Determine the meaning of words and phrases as they are used in the text, including figurative and connotative meanings; analyze the cumulative impact of specific word choices on meaning and tone (e.g., how the language evokes a sense of time and place; how it sets a formal or informal tone).

GRADES 11-12

Key Ideas and Details

> CCSS.ELA-LITERACY.RL.11-12.2

Determine two or more themes or central ideas of a text and analyze their development over the course of the text, including how they interact and build on one another to produce a complex account; provide an objective summary of the text.

Craft and Structure

> CCSS.ELA-LITERACY.RL.11-12.4

Determine the meaning of words and phrases as they are used in the text, including figurative and connotative meanings; analyze the impact of specific word choices on meaning and tone, including words with multiple meanings or language that is particularly fresh, engaging, or beautiful. (Include Shakespeare as well as other authors.)

Reading Informational Texts

GRADES 9-10

Key Ideas and Details

> CCSS.ELA-LITERACY.RI.9-10.2

Determine a central idea of a text and analyze its development over the course of the text, including how it emerges and is shaped and refined by specific details; provide an objective summary of the text.

> CCSS.ELA-LITERACY.RI.9-10.3

Analyze how the author unfolds an analysis or series of ideas or events, including the order in which the points are made, how they are introduced and developed, and the connections that are drawn between them.

Craft and Structure

> **CCSS.ELA-LITERACY.RI.9-10.4**

Determine the meaning of words and phrases as they are used in a text, including figurative, connotative, and technical meanings; analyze the cumulative impact of specific word choices on meaning and tone (e.g., how the language of a court opinion differs from that of a newspaper).

GRADES 11-12

Key Ideas and Details

> **CCSS.ELA-LITERACY.RI.11-12.2**

Determine two or more central ideas of a text and analyze their development over the course of the text, including how they interact and build on one another to provide a complex analysis; provide an objective summary of the text.

> **CCSS.ELA-LITERACY.RI.11-12.3**

Analyze a complex set of ideas or sequence of events and explain how specific individuals, ideas, or events interact and develop over the course of the text.

Craft and Structure

CCSS.ELA-LITERACY.RI.11-12.4

Determine the meaning of words and phrases as they are used in a text, including figurative, connotative, and technical meanings; analyze how an author uses and refines the meaning of a key term or terms over the course of a text (e.g., how Madison defines faction in Federalist No. 10).

Speaking and Listening

GRADES 9-10

Comprehension and Collaboration

> **CCSS.ELA-LITERACY.SL.9-10.1**

Initiate and participate effectively in a range of collaborative discussions (one-on-one, in groups, and teacher-led) with diverse partners on grades 9-10 topics, texts, and issues, building on others› ideas and expressing their own clearly and persuasively.

> **CCSS.ELA-LITERACY.SL.9-10.2**

Integrate multiple sources of information presented in diverse media or formats (e.g., visually, quantitatively, orally) evaluating the credibility and accuracy of each source.

GRADES 11-12

Comprehension and Collaboration

> **CCSS.ELA-LITERACY.SL.11-12.1**

Initiate and participate effectively in a range of collaborative discussions (one-on-one, in groups, and teacher-led) with diverse partners on grades 11-12 topics, texts, and issues, building on others› ideas and expressing their own clearly and persuasively.

> **CCSS.ELA-LITERACY.SL.11-12.2**

Integrate multiple sources of information presented in diverse formats and media (e.g., visually, quantitatively, orally) in order to make informed decisions and solve problems, evaluating the credibility and accuracy of each source and noting any discrepancies among the data.

Writing

GRADES 9-10

Text Types and Purposes

> CCSS.ELA-LITERACY.W.9-10.1

Write arguments to support claims in an analysis of substantive topics or texts, using valid reasoning and relevant and sufficient evidence.

> CCSS.ELA-LITERACY.W.9-10.1.A

Introduce precise claim(s), distinguish the claim(s) from alternate or opposing claims, and create an organization that establishes clear relationships among claim(s), counterclaims, reasons, and evidence.

GRADES 11-12

Text Types and Purposes

> CCSS.ELA-LITERACY.W.11-12.1

Write arguments to support claims in an analysis of substantive topics or texts, using valid reasoning and relevant and sufficient evidence.

> CCSS.ELA-LITERACY.W.11-12.1.A

Introduce precise, knowledgeable claim(s), establish the significance of the claim(s), distinguish the claim(s) from alternate or opposing claims, and create an organization that logically sequences claim(s), counterclaims, reasons, and evidence.

TIME REQUIREMENTS

This game is on the longer side. Playing through all five episodes will take between eight and ten hours. It would be wise to allocate two weeks' worth of class time to this activity in order for it to be beneficial for the students.

SAFETY - TRIGGER WARNING

Do not let the fact that this is a Batman video› game fool you. It is a mature game that can be quite graphic at times in its depiction of violence. In that regard, this game is not recommended for middle school students. It should be perfectly acceptable for high school students, but it would be best to play first yourself to make sure that it is something you can use in your class.

- Beyond the Empathy Games 101: Digging Deep into Empathy, Ethics, and Design with Kelli Dunlap

- An Introduction to Content Warnings and Trigger Warnings

Teaching with Video Games

Her Story

SEE PAGE 66 IN THE STUDENT PACKET

- Content Area/s: English Language Arts
- Developed by Sam Barlow
- Rated: 16+

WHERE TO PLAY

- Available on Microsoft Windows, macOS, iOS, Android

CONTEXT

This lesson should take place during a unit on

- Writing Strategies
- Foreshadowing
- Literary Elements

DO BEFORE - PREP

- Decide if you want to play together as a class, in pairs, groups, or individually.
- Choose the texts that you want to teach alongside this game. Some examples are:
  > The game is a murder mystery, so consider pairing it without one of your favorite murder mystery texts!
  > Literary Devices: Foreshadowing
  > Game Maker's Toolkit: How Her Story Works

OVERVIEW

Her Story is a crime fiction game with nonlinear storytelling. It revolves around a police database full of live action video footage that the player must navigate through in order to discover why a man was murdered and who killed him. After playing through the game, you will notice that this was the perfect opportunity to teach about foreshadowing and nonlinear storytelling. One of the jobs of ELA teachers is to teach students how to identify and use various writing strategies. This includes analyzing an author's use of literary elements and rhetorical devices, such as *foreshadowing*. Foreshadowing is a literary technique in which the writer gives an advance hint of what is to come later in the story.

Her Story is constructed around this technique. You watch clips of an interview, searching for breadcrumbs that will inevitably solve the mystery. The catch is that the video clips are not in any order, and there is no way to watch the full interviews as originally recorded. You instead search for words that you think are important and any video that contains those key words. You end up watching seven different interviews completely out of order and intertwined with one another. This encourages you to take notes as if you were really a detective trying to solve the case. The developers of the game describe it like this:

Her Story lets the player act as a detective. A crime fiction game with non-linear storytelling, *Her Story* revolves around a police database full of live action video footage. The players are granted access to a police database of archived video footage that covers seven interviews from 1994 in which a British woman is interviewed by detectives about her missing husband. Players take on the role of the person sat before a police computer terminal, their own computer or device playing the part of the fictional computer. They type search queries and the database returns clips of the answers where the woman speaks those words.

This is where the creator›s use of foreshadowing shines. You never want the player to feel helpless when playing your game. Sam Barlow accomplishes this by using three strategies to foreshadow its ending while also making sure to not give too much away. There are occasional reflections in a computer screen, flashing red and blue lights with a siren in the background, and music changes whenever something of note is said in one of the interviews. These little moments indicate to the player that what they just heard was important, but it's never clear why. Learning why a moment was important is the player›s responsibility.

This game will help students learn how authors incorporate foreshadowing into their work. Of course a video game that uses visual cues to foreshadow events is different from a novel or short story, but understanding an author›s thought process will help them across all mediums. *Her Story* also provides a chance to talk about narrative styles overall, since this game has such an unorthodox way of presenting its story.

DESCRIPTION OF ACTIVITY

- Foreshadowing is incorporated into most books, movies, TV, and even video games.
  > Most well-written stories foreshadow their endings in some capacity. The author leaves us hints to keep us thinking about how the character's story will end. Sometimes they are blatant, while other times they are subtle.
  > *Her Story* incorporates foreshadowing in different ways.
- *Her Story* lets the player act as a detective. A crime fiction game with non-linear storytelling, *Her Story* revolves around a police database full of live action video footage.
  > The players are granted access to a police database of archived video footage that covers seven interviews from 1994 in which a British woman is interviewed by detectives about her missing husband.
  > Players take on the role of the person sitting before a police computer terminal, their own computer or device playing the part of the fictional computer. They type search queries and the database returns clips of the answers where the woman speaks the words that the player inputted into the database.

    1) The player searches for a keyword. The game starts with the word murder.

    2) After watching the videos that pop up, you can search for a new word that you think is important based on the information you learned.

    3) The player can also tag videos as "important."
- *Her Story* uses three strategies to foreshadow the ending of the game:
  > Reflections in a computer screen
  > Flashing red and blue lights with a siren in the background

> Music changes

- Someone has been murdered and it is up to you to figure out who. Use these moments of foreshadowing to help solve the case.

- SPOILERS - Do not mention these points to the students until they notice it themselves.

  > Reflections in a computer screen

    A reflection in the computer screen appears whenever Eve mentions her pregnancy. At the end of the game it is revealed that the person accessing the police database is actually Eve's child.

    Sirens occur whenever Simon's murder is mentioned. The woman is being interviewed because she is a suspect of this murder.

    Music changes depending on who is being interviewed. It is revealed that there are actually two women being interviewed. They are identical twin sisters.

- When you turn on the game you will notice a couple of "read me" text files on the desktop. These are the instructions of the game. Open these and read them together as a class.

- Have students watch the video Game Maker's Toolkit: How Her Story Works after finishing the game.

- Provide an accompanying handout before starting the game, as students will be answering questions as they play through the story.

OBJECTIVES

- Students will identify examples of foreshadowing in *Her Story*.
- Students will break down the meaning of narrative.
- Students will explore how narrative does not always need to be chronological.

CORRELATION TO COMMON CORE STANDARDS

English Language Arts Anchor Standards

GRADES K-12

- College and Career Readiness Anchor Standards for Reading

  Key Ideas and Details

  > CCSS.ELA-LITERACY.CCRA.R.2

    Determine central ideas or themes of a text and analyze their development; summarize the key supporting details and ideas.

  > CCSS.ELA-LITERACY.CCRA.R.3

    Analyze how and why individuals, events, or ideas develop and interact over the course of a text.

- College and Career Readiness Anchor Standards for Writing

  Production and Distribution of Writing

  > CCSS.ELA-LITERACY.CCRA.W.4

Produce clear and coherent writing in which the development, organization, and style are appropriate to task, purpose, and audience.

- College and Career Readiness Anchor Standards for Speaking and Listening

Comprehension and Collaboration

> CCSS.ELA-LITERACY.CCRA.SL.1

Prepare for and participate effectively in a range of conversations and collaborations with diverse partners, building on others› ideas and expressing their own clearly and persuasively.

> CCSS.ELA-LITERACY.CCRA.SL.2

Integrate and evaluate information presented in diverse media and formats, including visually, quantitatively, and orally.

English Language Arts

Reading Literature

GRADES 9-10

Key Ideas and Details

> CCSS.ELA-LITERACY.RL.9-10.2

Determine a theme or central idea of a text and analyze in detail its development over the course of the text, including how it emerges and is shaped and refined by specific details; provide an objective summary of the text.

Craft and Structure

> CCSS.ELA-LITERACY.RL.9-10.4

Determine the meaning of words and phrases as they are used in the text, including figurative and connotative meanings; analyze the cumulative impact of specific word choices on meaning and tone (e.g., how the language evokes a sense of time and place; how it sets a formal or informal tone).

GRADES 11-12

Key Ideas and Details

> CCSS.ELA-LITERACY.RL.11-12.2

Determine two or more themes or central ideas of a text and analyze their development over the course of the text, including how they interact and build on one another to produce a complex account; provide an objective summary of the text.

Craft and Structure

> CCSS.ELA-LITERACY.RL.11-12.4

Determine the meaning of words and phrases as they are used in the text, including figurative and connotative meanings; analyze the impact of specific word choices on meaning and tone, including words with multiple meanings or language that is particularly fresh, engaging, or beautiful. (Include Shakespeare as well as other authors.)

Reading Informational Texts

GRADES 9-10

Teaching with Video Games

Key Ideas and Details

> CCSS.ELA-LITERACY.RI.9-10.2

Determine a central idea of a text and analyze its development over the course of the text, including how it emerges and is shaped and refined by specific details; provide an objective summary of the text.

> CCSS.ELA-LITERACY.RI.9-10.3

Analyze how the author unfolds an analysis or series of ideas or events, including the order in which the points are made, how they are introduced and developed, and the connections that are drawn between them.

Craft and Structure

> CCSS.ELA-LITERACY.RI.9-10.4

Determine the meaning of words and phrases as they are used in a text, including figurative, connotative, and technical meanings; analyze the cumulative impact of specific word choices on meaning and tone (e.g., how the language of a court opinion differs from that of a newspaper).

GRADES 11-12

Key Ideas and Details

> CCSS.ELA-LITERACY.RI.11-12.2

Determine two or more central ideas of a text and analyze their development over the course of the text, including how they interact and build on one another to provide a complex analysis; provide an objective summary of the text.

> CCSS.ELA-LITERACY.RI.11-12.3

Analyze a complex set of ideas or sequence of events and explain how specific individuals, ideas, or events interact and develop over the course of the text.

Craft and Structure

CCSS.ELA-LITERACY.RI.11-12.4

Determine the meaning of words and phrases as they are used in a text, including figurative, connotative, and technical meanings; analyze how an author uses and refines the meaning of a key term or terms over the course of a text (e.g., how Madison defines faction in Federalist No. 10).

Speaking and Listening

GRADES 9-10

Comprehension and Collaboration

> CCSS.ELA-LITERACY.SL.9-10.1

Initiate and participate effectively in a range of collaborative discussions (one-on-one, in groups, and teacher-led) with diverse partners on grades 9-10 topics, texts, and issues, building on others› ideas and expressing their own clearly and persuasively.

> CCSS.ELA-LITERACY.SL.9-10.2

Integrate multiple sources of information presented in diverse media or formats (e.g., visually, quantitatively, orally) evaluating the credibility and accuracy of each source.

Comprehension and Collaboration

> CCSS.ELA-LITERACY.SL.11-12.1

Initiate and participate effectively in a range of collaborative discussions (one-on-one, in groups, and teacher-led) with diverse partners on grades 11-12 topics, texts, and issues, building on others› ideas and expressing their own clearly and persuasively.

> CCSS.ELA-LITERACY.SL.11-12.2

Integrate multiple sources of information presented in diverse formats and media (e.g., visually, quantitatively, orally) in order to make informed decisions and solve problems, evaluating the credibility and accuracy of each source and noting any discrepancies among the data.

Writing

GRADES 9-10

Text Types and Purposes

> CCSS.ELA-LITERACY.W.9-10.1

Write arguments to support claims in an analysis of substantive topics or texts, using valid reasoning and relevant and sufficient evidence.

> CCSS.ELA-LITERACY.W.9-10.1.A

Introduce precise claim(s), distinguish the claim(s) from alternate or opposing claims, and create an organization that establishes clear relationships among claim(s), counterclaims, reasons, and evidence.

GRADES 11-12

Text Types and Purposes

> CCSS.ELA-LITERACY.W.11-12.1

Write arguments to support claims in an analysis of substantive topics or texts, using valid reasoning and relevant and sufficient evidence.

> CCSS.ELA-LITERACY.W.11-12.1.A

Introduce precise, knowledgeable claim(s), establish the significance of the claim(s), distinguish the claim(s) from alternate or opposing claims, and create an organization that logically sequences claim(s), counterclaims, reasons, and evidence.

TIME REQUIREMENTS

Her Story is interesting in that the game will be as long as it needs to be. It is a mystery story that some people may solve far more quickly than others. Gameplay could last as little as 45 minutes, or as long as four hours. Plan for two to three hours of playtime to figure everything out.

SAFETY - TRIGGER WARNING

Her Story is not a violent game. All the player ever sees or hears are interview clips of a single character. That being said, the game is very mature in its use of language and profanity. For this reason, it is probably not suited well for middle school classes, but it works in most high school classes.

- Beyond the Empathy Games 101: Digging Deep into Empathy, Ethics, and Design with Kelli Dunlap
- An Introduction to Content Warnings and Trigger Warnings

Tacoma

SEE PAGE 69 IN THE STUDENT PACKET

- Content Area/s: English Language Arts
- Developed by The Fullbright Company
- Rated: 13+

WHERE TO PLAY

- Available on PlayStation 4, PlayStation 5, Xbox One, Xbox Series X/S, Microsoft Windows, macOS, and Linux

CONTEXT

This lesson should take place during a unit on

- Nonlinear Storytelling
- Literary Elements
- Plot

DO BEFORE - PREP

- Choose the texts that you want to teach alongside this game. Some examples are:
  - > What is Creative Writing: Definition, Types, & Examples
  - > How to Get Started With Creative Writing

OVERVIEW

Another game that would be perfect to teach nonlinear storytelling is *Tacoma*, developed by The Fullbright Company. They are the same group that made the critically acclaimed *Gone Home* (which we will get to in Part III of this book). *Tacoma* falls into the walking simulator genre. The gameplay focuses solely on telling a story. *Tacoma* is a sci-fi narrative adventure set aboard a high-tech space station in the year 2088. You explore every detail of how the station's crew lives and works. Ultimately, you must learn the fate of the crew after disaster strikes the station.

You travel through various sections of this space station watching augmented reality recordings of what had previously transpired. You can pause, fast forward, and rewind every conversation that has taken place. The game lets the player choose the order in which the events are revealed. The crew may all be talking together at one moment, but then scatter across the ship a minute later. You get to decide which crew members to follow around and who to eavesdrop on during their conversations. Once you are all caught up, you can reset the recording back to the beginning to learn about the other characters. Each new recording also notes how many days have passed since the footage was captured. It is the player›s job to keep chronological track of each moment in the game. It›s a mechanic I have never encountered elsewhere and I believe this is a completely unique experience that really needs to be played to fully understand.

Telling a story nonlinearly can be tricky. Think of media like the movies like *Memento*, TV shows

Teaching with Video Games

like *Westworld*, and video games like *Her Story*. While all three are fantastic, they can often be difficult to follow. *Her Story* is a wonderful game that you should consider teaching with, but it will demand a lot of thinking on your students' part, which can be frustrating at times. *Tacoma* does not seem to have this issue. You can pause every recording and replay it as needed. It is a super accessible game with simple controls that almost anyone can pick up quickly.

Plus, the content in your classroom should be as diverse as the students in the room, and in *Tacoma*, we learn and connect with people of various backgrounds, ethnicities, and sexualities. But the game is written so naturally, without drawing attention to the theme of diversity. One could only hope that by the time we reach 2088, the year *Tacoma* is set, the world will be as accepting of each other as the characters are in the game.

It is a quick story with likable characters and could serve as a great addition to any classroom. The mechanics are unique but simple. It is a game that could easily be played together as a class instead of each student needing their own copy.

DESCRIPTION OF ACTIVITY

- Only one copy of the game is needed.
    - > The game can be projected in the front of the class with one student playing at a time.
- Go over the following vocabulary terms with the class:
    - > Walking Simulator

        A walking simulator is an adventure game focused on gradual exploration and discovery through observation, with little in the way of action. The gameplay focuses solely on telling a story.

    - > Plot

        The main events of a play, novel, movie, or similar work, devised and presented by the writer as an interrelated sequence.

    - > Nonlinear Storytelling

        Is a narrative technique where events are portrayed out of order or in other ways where the narrative does not follow the direct causality pattern of the events featured.

    - > Augmented Reality

        Augmented reality is an interactive experience of a real-world environment where the objects that reside in the real world are enhanced by computer-generated perceptual information, sometimes across multiple sensory modalities, including visual, auditory, haptic, somatosensory, and olfactory.

- *Tacoma* is a sci-fi narrative adventure. Set aboard a high-tech space station in the year 2088, explore every detail of how the station's crew lived and worked, finding the clues that add up to a gripping story of trust, fear, and resolve in the face of disaster.
- The crew is missing, and it is up to you to discover what happened to them.
- You travel through various sections of this space station watching Augmented Reality recordings of what has previously transpired. You can pause, fast forward, and rewind everything recorded in order to listen to every conversation that has taken place.

- The game lets you choose the order in which the events are revealed.
- Provide an accompanying handout before starting the game, as students will be answering questions as they play through the story.

OBJECTIVES

- Students will analyze the plot of *Tacoma*.
- Students will determine whether or not nonlinear storytelling is an effective way to tell a story.

CORRELATION TO COMMON CORE STANDARDS

English Language Arts Anchor Standards

GRADES K-12

- College and Career Readiness Anchor Standards for Reading

  Key Ideas and Details

  > CCSS.ELA-LITERACY.CCRA.R.2

  Determine central ideas or themes of a text and analyze their development; summarize the key supporting details and ideas.

  > CCSS.ELA-LITERACY.CCRA.R.3

  Analyze how and why individuals, events, or ideas develop and interact over the course of a text.

- College and Career Readiness Anchor Standards for Writing

  Production and Distribution of Writing

  > CCSS.ELA-LITERACY.CCRA.W.4

  Produce clear and coherent writing in which the development, organization, and style are appropriate to task, purpose, and audience.

- College and Career Readiness Anchor Standards for Speaking and Listening

  Comprehension and Collaboration

  > CCSS.ELA-LITERACY.CCRA.SL.1

  Prepare for and participate effectively in a range of conversations and collaborations with diverse partners, building on others› ideas and expressing their own clearly and persuasively.

  > CCSS.ELA-LITERACY.CCRA.SL.2

  Integrate and evaluate information presented in diverse media and formats, including visually, quantitatively, and orally.

English Language Arts

Reading Literature

GRADE 6

Key Ideas and Details

> CCSS.ELA-LITERACY.RL.6.2

Determine a theme or central idea of a text and how it is conveyed through particular details; provide a summary of the text distinct from personal opinions or judgments.

Craft and Structure

> CCSS.ELA-LITERACY.RL.6.4

Determine the meaning of words and phrases as they are used in a text, including figurative and connotative meanings; analyze the impact of a specific word choice on meaning and tone

GRADE 7

Key Ideas and Details

> CCSS.ELA-LITERACY.RL.7.2

Determine a theme or central idea of a text and analyze its development over the course of the text; provide an objective summary of the text.

Craft and Structure

> CCSS.ELA-LITERACY.RL.7.4

Determine the meaning of words and phrases as they are used in a text, including figurative and connotative meanings; analyze the impact of rhymes and other repetitions of sounds (e.g., alliteration) on a specific verse or stanza of a poem or section of a story or drama.

GRADE 8

Key Ideas and Details

> CCSS.ELA-LITERACY.RL.8.2

Determine a theme or central idea of a text and analyze its development over the course of the text, including its relationship to the characters, setting, and plot; provide an objective summary of the text.

Craft and Structure

> CCSS.ELA-LITERACY.RL.8.4

Determine the meaning of words and phrases as they are used in a text, including figurative and connotative meanings; analyze the impact of specific word choices on meaning and tone, including analogies or allusions to other texts.

GRADES 9-10

Key Ideas and Details

> CCSS.ELA-LITERACY.RL.9-10.2

Determine a theme or central idea of a text and analyze in detail its development over the course of the text, including how it emerges and is shaped and refined by specific details; provide an objective summary of the text.

Craft and Structure

> CCSS.ELA-LITERACY.RL.9-10.4

Determine the meaning of words and phrases as they are used in the text, including figurative and connotative meanings; analyze the cumulative impact of specific word choices on meaning and tone (e.g., how the language evokes a sense of time and place; how it sets a formal or informal tone).

GRADES 11–12

Key Ideas and Details

> CCSS.ELA-LITERACY.RL.11-12.2

Determine two or more themes or central ideas of a text and analyze their development over the course of the text, including how they interact and build on one another to produce a complex account; provide an objective summary of the text.

Craft and Structure

> CCSS.ELA-LITERACY.RL.11-12.4

Determine the meaning of words and phrases as they are used in the text, including figurative and connotative meanings; analyze the impact of specific word choices on meaning and tone, including words with multiple meanings or language that is particularly fresh, engaging, or beautiful. (Include Shakespeare as well as other authors.)

Reading Informational Texts

GRADE 6

Key Ideas and Details

> CCSS.ELA-LITERACY.RI.6.2

Determine a central idea of a text and how it is conveyed through particular details; provide a summary of the text distinct from personal opinions or judgments.

> CCSS.ELA-LITERACY.RI.6.3

Analyze in detail how a key individual, event, or idea is introduced, illustrated, and elaborated in a text (e.g., through examples or anecdotes).

Craft and Structure

> CCSS.ELA-LITERACY.RI.6.4

Determine the meaning of words and phrases as they are used in a text, including figurative, connotative, and technical meanings.

GRADE 7

Key Ideas and Details

> CCSS.ELA-LITERACY.RI.7.2

Determine two or more central ideas in a text and analyze their development over the course of the text; provide an objective summary of the text.

> CCSS.ELA-LITERACY.RI.7.3

Analyze the interactions between individuals, events, and ideas in a text (e.g., how ideas influence individuals or events, or how individuals influence ideas or events).

Craft and Structure

> CCSS.ELA-LITERACY.RI.7.4

Determine the meaning of words and phrases as they are used in a text, including figurative, connotative, and technical meanings; analyze the impact of a specific word choice on meaning and tone.

GRADE 8

Key Ideas and Details

> CCSS.ELA-LITERACY.RI.8.2

Determine a central idea of a text and analyze its development over the course of the text, including its relationship to supporting ideas; provide an objective summary of the text.

> CCSS.ELA-LITERACY.RI.8.3

Analyze how a text makes connections among and distinctions between individuals, ideas, or events (e.g., through comparisons, analogies, or categories).

Craft and Structure

> CCSS.ELA-LITERACY.RI.8.4

Determine the meaning of words and phrases as they are used in a text, including figurative, connotative, and technical meanings; analyze the impact of specific word choices on meaning and tone, including analogies or allusions to other texts.

GRADES 9-10

Key Ideas and Details

> CCSS.ELA-LITERACY.RI.9-10.2

Determine a central idea of a text and analyze its development over the course of the text, including how it emerges and is shaped and refined by specific details; provide an objective summary of the text.

> CCSS.ELA-LITERACY.RI.9-10.3

Analyze how the author unfolds an analysis or series of ideas or events, including the order in which the points are made, how they are introduced and developed, and the connections that are drawn between them.

Craft and Structure

> CCSS.ELA-LITERACY.RI.9-10.4

Determine the meaning of words and phrases as they are used in a text, including figurative, connotative, and technical meanings; analyze the cumulative impact of specific word choices on meaning and tone (e.g., how the language of a court opinion differs from that of a newspaper).

GRADES 11-12

Key Ideas and Details

> CCSS.ELA-LITERACY.RI.11-12.2

Determine two or more central ideas of a text and analyze their development over the course of the text, including how they interact and build on one another to provide a complex analysis; provide an objective summary of the text.

> CCSS.ELA-LITERACY.RI.11-12.3

Analyze a complex set of ideas or sequence of events and explain how specific individuals, ideas, or events interact and develop over the course of the text.

Craft and Structure

> CCSS.ELA-LITERACY.RI.12.4-11

Determine the meaning of words and phrases as they are used in a text, including figurative, connotative, and technical meanings; analyze how an author uses and refines the meaning of a key term or terms over the course of a text (e.g., how Madison defines faction in Federalist No. 10).

Speaking and Listening

GRADE 6

Comprehension and Collaboration

> CCSS.ELA-LITERACY.SL.6.1

Engage effectively in a range of collaborative discussions (one-on-one, in groups, and teacher-led) with diverse partners on grade 6 topics, texts, and issues, building on others› ideas and expressing their own clearly.

> CCSS.ELA-LITERACY.SL.6.2

Interpret information presented in diverse media and formats (e.g., visually, quantitatively, orally) and explain how it contributes to a topic, text, or issue under study.

GRADE 7

Comprehension and Collaboration

> CCSS.ELA-LITERACY.SL.7.1

Engage effectively in a range of collaborative discussions (one-on-one, in groups, and teacher-led) with diverse partners on grade 7 topics, texts, and issues, building on others› ideas and expressing their own clearly.

> CCSS.ELA-LITERACY.SL.7.2

Analyze the main ideas and supporting details presented in diverse media and formats (e.g., visually, quantitatively, orally) and explain how the ideas clarify a topic, text, or issue under study.

GRADE 8

Comprehension and Collaboration

> CCSS.ELA-LITERACY.SL.8.1

Engage effectively in a range of collaborative discussions (one-on-one, in groups, and teacher-led) with diverse partners on grade 8 topics, texts, and issues, building on others› ideas and expressing their own clearly.

> CCSS.ELA-LITERACY.SL.8.2

Analyze the purpose of information presented in diverse media and formats (e.g., visually, quantitatively, orally) and evaluate the motives (e.g., social, commercial, political) behind its presentation.

GRADES 9-10

Comprehension and Collaboration

> CCSS.ELA-LITERACY.SL.9-10.1

Initiate and participate effectively in a range of collaborative discussions (one-on-one, in groups, and teacher-led) with diverse partners on grades 9-10 topics, texts, and issues, building on others› ideas and expressing their own clearly and persuasively.

Teaching with Video Games

> CCSS.ELA-LITERACY.SL.9-10.2

Integrate multiple sources of information presented in diverse media or formats (e.g., visually, quantitatively, orally) evaluating the credibility and accuracy of each source.

GRADES 11-12

Comprehension and Collaboration

> CCSS.ELA-LITERACY.SL.11-12.1

Initiate and participate effectively in a range of collaborative discussions (one-on-one, in groups, and teacher-led) with diverse partners on grades 11-12 topics, texts, and issues, building on others› ideas and expressing their own clearly and persuasively.

> CCSS.ELA-LITERACY.SL.11-12.2

Integrate multiple sources of information presented in diverse formats and media (e.g., visually, quantitatively, orally) in order to make informed decisions and solve problems, evaluating the credibility and accuracy of each source and noting any discrepancies among the data.

TIME REQUIREMENTS

It will take about three hours to play and finish *Tacoma*. A large portion of the attached handout can be completed while the game is being played, so it will probably only take three class periods to finish this lesson.

SAFETY - TRIGGER WARNING

While *Tacoma* covers some mature themes, there is not much in the game that you will have to provide a trigger warning for. It is pretty tame overall.

Assemble With Care

SEE PAGE 74 IN THE STUDENT PACKET

- Content Area/s: English Language Arts
- Developed by UsTwoGames
- Rated: 8+

WHERE TO PLAY

- Available on iOS, Microsoft Windows, macOS

CONTEXT

This lesson should take place during a unit on

- Literary Elements
- Moral

DO BEFORE - PREP

- Choose the texts that you want to teach alongside this game. Some examples are:

  > Polygon: Apple Arcade's fixer-upper game isn't short on irony
  > Any other text that you already use to teach morals as a literary device

OVERVIEW

Assemble With Care is a puzzle game that uses its gameplay to reinforce the morals presented in its story. It is available to play on Apple Arcade, a subscription service that lets people play a large number of mobile games. Luckily, Apple Arcade is always free for the first month. So you can have students sign up in order to play this game for free. You just need to remember to have them cancel the subscription before it automatically renews.

Mobile games offer a unique opportunity for storytellers. While there are plenty of fun games to be found on mobile, touch screens are still not the best way to play games. Most people would prefer to play almost any game with a controller or a keyboard and mouse. Mobile phones, however, are an ideal place to experiment with narrative games that utilize new forms of storytelling. *Assemble With Care* is a perfect example of the type of story that can be enhanced by the gaming experience found on a mobile phone.

The developers of the game describe *Assemble With Care* as, "a story about taking things apart and putting ourselves back together. When Maria, a globe-trotting antique restorer, arrives in the sun-soaked town of Bellariva, she has no idea just how broken it will turn out to be. She wants nothing more than to help the town's inhabitants save their most beloved possessions, but when it's their personal lives that are starting to fracture, she'll need to find a way to hold them together, one spare screw at a time." The simplicity of the game is part of its appeal. Each level starts off like a typical story. You are introduced to the characters and a problem that they are currently facing. They always contain some item that has been broken, leaving you with the task of reassembling the pieces. As you repair a number of miscellaneous items it becomes apparent that you are actually aiding in repairing people's lives and relationships, as well. It is not a profound metaphor, but it is really refreshing to find this kind of narrative embedded in a puzzle game.

For this lesson, you can have students analyze how the gameplay in *Assemble With Care* reinforces the moral of the story. Have them keep track of the various items they reassemble for the characters in the game. Each item holds sentimental significance for a character. When these items are fixed, there is something fixed inside the object's owner, as well. Something that may seem insignificant to me may be of great importance to another person. The relationships of people are often forged by the items they possess. It›s not so often that a simple puzzle game is capable of getting the player to form an emotional connection with its characters and narrative. Each level acts as a chapter, which contains an introduction, a puzzle, and then a conclusion.

DESCRIPTION OF ACTIVITY

- Amount of copies needed is at the discretion of the teacher
  - > The class can play together with the game projected in the front of the room
  - > Students can play in pairs/groups on computers - consoles - smartphone
  - > Or students can play individually on computers - consoles - smartphone
- Go over the definition of "moral" with the class.
  - > **Moral**: The moral of a story is supposed to teach you how to be a better person. If moral is used as an adjective, it means good, or ethical. If you have a strong moral character, you are a good member of society. It is not necessary that the author or the poet has clearly stated it. It can be left for the audiences or the learners to determine.
- Explain the premise of *Assemble With Care*.
  - > *"Assemble With Care* is a story about taking things apart and putting ourselves back together. When Maria, a globe-trotting antique restorer, arrives in the sun-soaked town of Bellariva, she has no idea just how broken it will turn out to be. She wants nothing more than to help the town's inhabitants save their most beloved possessions, but when it's their personal lives that are starting to fracture, she'll need to find a way to hold them together, one spare screw at a time." - Ustwogames
  - > Play your way through 13 different levels, each with their own story and puzzle. It is your job to repair various items for the people of Bellariva. Pay close attention: it's not just their belongings you are repairing.
- Provide an accompanying handout before starting the game, as students will be answering questions as they play through the story.
- Be prepared to help students who may end up stuck on one of the puzzles.

OBJECTIVES

- Students will make connections between the gameplay in *Assemble With Care* and the moral of its narrative.

CORRELATION TO COMMON CORE STANDARDS

English Language Arts Anchor Standards

GRADES K-12

- College and Career Readiness Anchor Standards for Reading

  Key Ideas and Details

  > CCSS.ELA-LITERACY.CCRA.R.2

  Determine central ideas or themes of a text and analyze their development; summarize the key supporting details and ideas.

  > CCSS.ELA-LITERACY.CCRA.R.3

  Analyze how and why individuals, events, or ideas develop and interact over the course of a text.

- College and Career Readiness Anchor Standards for Writing

  Production and Distribution of Writing

  > CCSS.ELA-LITERACY.CCRA.W.4

  Produce clear and coherent writing in which the development, organization, and style are appropriate to task, purpose, and audience.

- College and Career Readiness Anchor Standards for Speaking and Listening

  Comprehension and Collaboration

  > CCSS.ELA-LITERACY.CCRA.SL.1

  Prepare for and participate effectively in a range of conversations and collaborations with diverse partners, building on others› ideas and expressing their own clearly and persuasively.

  > CCSS.ELA-LITERACY.CCRA.SL.2

  Integrate and evaluate information presented in diverse media and formats, including visually, quantitatively, and orally.

English Language Arts

Reading Literature

GRADE 6

Key Ideas and Details

> CCSS.ELA-LITERACY.RL.6.2

Determine a theme or central idea of a text and how it is conveyed through particular details; provide a summary of the text distinct from personal opinions or judgments.

Craft and Structure

> CCSS.ELA-LITERACY.RL.6.4

Determine the meaning of words and phrases as they are used in a text, including figurative and connotative meanings; analyze the impact of a specific word choice on meaning and tone

Teaching with Video Games

GRADE 7

Key Ideas and Details

> CCSS.ELA-LITERACY.RL.7.2

Determine a theme or central idea of a text and analyze its development over the course of the text; provide an objective summary of the text.

Craft and Structure

> CCSS.ELA-LITERACY.RL.7.4

Determine the meaning of words and phrases as they are used in a text, including figurative and connotative meanings; analyze the impact of rhymes and other repetitions of sounds (e.g., alliteration) on a specific verse or stanza of a poem or section of a story or drama.

GRADE 8

Key Ideas and Details

> CCSS.ELA-LITERACY.RL.8.2

Determine a theme or central idea of a text and analyze its development over the course of the text, including its relationship to the characters, setting, and plot; provide an objective summary of the text.

Craft and Structure

> CCSS.ELA-LITERACY.RL.8.4

Determine the meaning of words and phrases as they are used in a text, including figurative and connotative meanings; analyze the impact of specific word choices on meaning and tone, including analogies or allusions to other texts.

GRADES 9-10

Key Ideas and Details

> CCSS.ELA-LITERACY.RL.9-10.2

Determine a theme or central idea of a text and analyze in detail its development over the course of the text, including how it emerges and is shaped and refined by specific details; provide an objective summary of the text.

Craft and Structure

> CCSS.ELA-LITERACY.RL.9-10.4

Determine the meaning of words and phrases as they are used in the text, including figurative and connotative meanings; analyze the cumulative impact of specific word choices on meaning and tone (e.g., how the language evokes a sense of time and place; how it sets a formal or informal tone).

GRADES 11-12

Key Ideas and Details

> CCSS.ELA-LITERACY.RL.11-12.2

Determine two or more themes or central ideas of a text and analyze their development over the course of the text, including how they interact and build on one another to produce a complex account; provide an objective summary of the text.

Craft and Structure

> CCSS.ELA-LITERACY.RL.11-12.4

Determine the meaning of words and phrases as they are used in the text, including figurative and connotative meanings; analyze the impact of specific word choices on meaning and tone, including words with multiple meanings or language that is particularly fresh, engaging, or beautiful. (Include Shakespeare as well as other authors.)

Reading Informational Texts

GRADE 6

Key Ideas and Details

> CCSS.ELA-LITERACY.RI.6.2

Determine a central idea of a text and how it is conveyed through particular details; provide a summary of the text distinct from personal opinions or judgments.

> CCSS.ELA-LITERACY.RI.6.3

Analyze in detail how a key individual, event, or idea is introduced, illustrated, and elaborated in a text (e.g., through examples or anecdotes).

Craft and Structure

> CCSS.ELA-LITERACY.RI.6.4

Determine the meaning of words and phrases as they are used in a text, including figurative, connotative, and technical meanings.

GRADE 7

Key Ideas and Details

> CCSS.ELA-LITERACY.RI.7.2

Determine two or more central ideas in a text and analyze their development over the course of the text; provide an objective summary of the text.

> CCSS.ELA-LITERACY.RI.7.3

Analyze the interactions between individuals, events, and ideas in a text (e.g., how ideas influence individuals or events, or how individuals influence ideas or events).

Craft and Structure

> CCSS.ELA-LITERACY.RI.7.4

Determine the meaning of words and phrases as they are used in a text, including figurative, connotative, and technical meanings; analyze the impact of a specific word choice on meaning and tone.

GRADE 8

Key Ideas and Details

> CCSS.ELA-LITERACY.RI.8.2

Determine a central idea of a text and analyze its development over the course of the text, including its relationship to supporting ideas; provide an objective summary of the text.

> CCSS.ELA-LITERACY.RI.8.3

Teaching with Video Games

Analyze how a text makes connections among and distinctions between individuals, ideas, or events (e.g., through comparisons, analogies, or categories).

Craft and Structure

> CCSS.ELA-LITERACY.RI.8.4

Determine the meaning of words and phrases as they are used in a text, including figurative, connotative, and technical meanings; analyze the impact of specific word choices on meaning and tone, including analogies or allusions to other texts.

GRADES 9-10

Key Ideas and Details

> CCSS.ELA-LITERACY.RI.9-10.2

Determine a central idea of a text and analyze its development over the course of the text, including how it emerges and is shaped and refined by specific details; provide an objective summary of the text.

> CCSS.ELA-LITERACY.RI.9-10.3

Analyze how the author unfolds an analysis or series of ideas or events, including the order in which the points are made, how they are introduced and developed, and the connections that are drawn between them.

Craft and Structure

> CCSS.ELA-LITERACY.RI.9-10.4

Determine the meaning of words and phrases as they are used in a text, including figurative, connotative, and technical meanings; analyze the cumulative impact of specific word choices on meaning and tone (e.g., how the language of a court opinion differs from that of a newspaper).

GRADES 11-12

Key Ideas and Details

> CCSS.ELA-LITERACY.RI.11-12.2

Determine two or more central ideas of a text and analyze their development over the course of the text, including how they interact and build on one another to provide a complex analysis; provide an objective summary of the text.

> CCSS.ELA-LITERACY.RI.11-12.3

Analyze a complex set of ideas or sequence of events and explain how specific individuals, ideas, or events interact and develop over the course of the text.

Craft and Structure

> CCSS.ELA-LITERACY.RI.11-12.4

Determine the meaning of words and phrases as they are used in a text, including figurative, connotative, and technical meanings; analyze how an author uses and refines the meaning of a key term or terms over the course of a text (e.g., how Madison defines faction in Federalist No. 10).

Speaking and Listening

GRADE 6

Comprehension and Collaboration

> **CCSS.ELA-LITERACY.SL.6.1**

Engage effectively in a range of collaborative discussions (one-on-one, in groups, and teacher-led) with diverse partners on grade 6 topics, texts, and issues, building on others› ideas and expressing their own clearly.

> **CCSS.ELA-LITERACY.SL.6.2**

Interpret information presented in diverse media and formats (e.g., visually, quantitatively, orally) and explain how it contributes to a topic, text, or issue under study.

GRADE 7

Comprehension and Collaboration

> **CCSS.ELA-LITERACY.SL.7.1**

Engage effectively in a range of collaborative discussions (one-on-one, in groups, and teacher-led) with diverse partners on grade 7 topics, texts, and issues, building on others› ideas and expressing their own clearly.

> **CCSS.ELA-LITERACY.SL.7.2**

Analyze the main ideas and supporting details presented in diverse media and formats (e.g., visually, quantitatively, orally) and explain how the ideas clarify a topic, text, or issue under study.

GRADE 8

Comprehension and Collaboration

> **CCSS.ELA-LITERACY.SL.8.1**

Engage effectively in a range of collaborative discussions (one-on-one, in groups, and teacher-led) with diverse partners on grade 8 topics, texts, and issues, building on others› ideas and expressing their own clearly.

> **CCSS.ELA-LITERACY.SL.8.2**

Analyze the purpose of information presented in diverse media and formats (e.g., visually, quantitatively, orally) and evaluate the motives (e.g., social, commercial, political) behind its presentation.

GRADES 9-10

Comprehension and Collaboration

> **CCSS.ELA-LITERACY.SL.9-10.1**

Initiate and participate effectively in a range of collaborative discussions (one-on-one, in groups, and teacher-led) with diverse partners on grades 9-10 topics, texts, and issues, building on others› ideas and expressing their own clearly and persuasively.

> **CCSS.ELA-LITERACY.SL.9-10.2**

Integrate multiple sources of information presented in diverse media or formats (e.g., visually, quantitatively, orally) evaluating the credibility and accuracy of each source.

GRADES 11-12

Comprehension and Collaboration

> **CCSS.ELA-LITERACY.SL.11-12.1**

Initiate and participate effectively in a range of collaborative discussions (one-on-one, in groups, and teacher-led) with diverse partners on grades 11-12 topics, texts, and issues, building on others› ideas and expressing their own clearly and persuasively.

> CCSS.ELA-LITERACY.SL.11-12.2
  Integrate multiple sources of information presented in diverse formats and media (e.g., visually, quantitatively, orally) in order to make informed decisions and solve problems, evaluating the credibility and accuracy of each source and noting any discrepancies among the data.

TIME REQUIREMENTS

Assemble With Care will only take about 90 minutes to play through the entire game (assuming students do not get too stuck on one of the puzzles).

SAFETY - TRIGGER WARNING

Nothing to warn students about beforehand. It is a very accessible game.

Kind Words

SEE PAGE 76 IN THE STUDENT PACKET

- Content Area/s: English Language Arts - Social Emotional Learning
- Developed by Popcannibal
- Rated: 10+

WHERE TO PLAY

- Available on Microsoft Windows, Linux, macOS

CONTEXT

This lesson should take place during a unit on

- Anxiety
- Depression
- Writing Letters
- Author's Purpose

DO BEFORE - PREP

- Choose the texts that you want to teach alongside this game. Some examples are:

  > Game Industry: Kind Words: A game of lo-fi beats, letters to strangers, and feeling less alone. Popcannibal›s Ziba Scott on designing and moderating a game exclusively about being kind to other people

OVERVIEW

Sometimes we just need to give our students time to be positive. School comes with a lot of stress and providing time for positivity can be a really refreshing experience. An easy way to do this is through free writing. *Kind Words* is a game that can aid in this process. The game provides the players with several opportunities to write. It is an online game where the player anonymously interacts with other people that are playing. The player can send a letter out to the game's community, respond to messages sent by other players online, and write up a concern of theirs for other players to respond to. All of this is set to a playlist of Lo-Fi music beats. The game is set up to be as relaxing as possible in order to build a sense of comfort for the player. There is no end goal of this game other than writing. This lesson will get students accustomed to thinking positively and provide a space to actually give advice to others in a completely non-threatening and anonymous setting. The game even provides links to mental health resources for any of the players that may need them.

This game can be very personal, so for the sake of this lesson, make it clear that the students should be writing something they are willing to share with their peers. This is with the assumption that students are playing together. If they all have their own copy, then they could write something more private if they want. Students are going to take turns "playing." You can repeat the following steps with each student in the class:

Teaching with Video Games

1. Each player will read out loud, one of the paper planes flying through the room in the game. Each plane has a message written by another player online.

2. Each player will write one nice thing on their own paper plane to send out to the online community.

3. Each player can share a concern they have with the game›s community. Players online will eventually respond to these messages. We will play the game over two days, so during the second day, they will actually get to read the responses to their message.

4. Each player will read a concern from an anonymous online player and then offer advice to them.

Students can also share a concern they have. This is really the focus of *Kind Words*. They write their message down and send it out to everyone else playing *Kind Words*. Then over time, they will receive responses from other players, who take the time to write back to a complete stranger on the internet with the hopes of making me feel better. From here, students can go on to offer their own advice to other players who shared concerns. Offering advice is not always the easiest task. The game provides a space to sit and think intently about how you want to respond to these strangers. Your words after all, may end up having a big impact on someone›s life. The hope is that students will come away from this activity feeling as positive because they can take an active role in helping others without the expectation of receiving something in return. This is a great way to teach empathy in the classroom.

One potential issue that could arise is an online troll who sends out hurtful messages. This does not seem to ever happen, but it is always a possibility on the Internet. These messages can be reported, but my overall experience with the game indicates that this is very unlikely.

While this game is suited to Social Emotional Learning, it also has a place in an ELA classroom. Teaching the author›s purpose is an aspect of many teachers' curriculum. While *Kind Words* is not a story, it can lead to interesting conversations about why students think the developer Popcannibal created the game. Just like any story, there were many choices that went into the creation of the game. Here you can see the thought process of one student who played this game in class. They were concerned about their chemistry class which they found particularly difficult. They shared nice messages like "Life is Beautiful." Another online player responded to them letting them know it is normal to struggle with things like chemistry. And they felt that the author's purpose was to create a platform where people can share opinions and find solutions together.

DESCRIPTION OF ACTIVITY

- Amount of copies needed is at the discretion of the teacher
  > The class can play together with the game projected in the front of the room
  > Students can play in pairs/groups on computers
  > Or students can play individually on computers
- Go over the following vocabulary terms with the students
  > Author's Purpose
    An author's purpose is his reason for or intent in writing. An author's purpose may be to amuse the reader, to persuade the reader, to inform the reader, or to satirize a condition.

> Mental Health

The condition of being sound mentally and emotionally that is characterized by the absence of mental illness and by adequate adjustment, especially as reflected in feeling comfortable about oneself, positive feelings about others, and the ability to meet the demands of daily life.

- Go over the premise of the game *Kind Words*.

    > We will read positive letters from other players online

    We will write our own positive letters to send out online for other players to read.

    > We will write letters about some of the concerns we have this school year. Other players online will respond to these, which we can read in the following lesson.

    We can also respond to other players' concerns.

- Provide an accompanying handout before starting the game, as students will be answering questions as they play through the story.

OBJECTIVES

- Students will determine the author's purpose in the creation of the game *Kind Words*.

CORRELATION TO COMMON CORE STANDARDS

English Language Arts Anchor Standards

GRADES K-12

- College and Career Readiness Anchor Standards for Reading

    Key Ideas and Details

    > CCSS.ELA-LITERACY.CCRA.R.2

    Determine central ideas or themes of a text and analyze their development; summarize the key supporting details and ideas.

    > CCSS.ELA-LITERACY.CCRA.R.3

    Analyze how and why individuals, events, or ideas develop and interact over the course of a text.

- College and Career Readiness Anchor Standards for Writing

    Production and Distribution of Writing

    > CCSS.ELA-LITERACY.CCRA.W.4

    Produce clear and coherent writing in which the development, organization, and style are appropriate to task, purpose, and audience.

- College and Career Readiness Anchor Standards for Speaking and Listening

    Comprehension and Collaboration

    > CCSS.ELA-LITERACY.CCRA.SL.1

    Prepare for and participate effectively in a range of conversations and collaborations with diverse partners, building on others› ideas and expressing their own clearly and persuasively.

    > CCSS.ELA-LITERACY.CCRA.SL.2

Teaching with Video Games

Integrate and evaluate information presented in diverse media and formats, including visually, quantitatively, and orally.

English Language Arts

Writing

Grade 6

Text Types and Purposes

> CCSS.ELA-LITERACY.W.6.1
Write arguments to support claims with clear reasons and relevant evidence.

> CCSS.ELA-LITERACY.W.6.1.A

Introduce claim(s) and organize the reasons and evidence clearly.

GRADE 7

Text Types and Purposes

> CCSS.ELA-LITERACY.W.7.1
Write arguments to support claims with clear reasons and relevant evidence.

> CCSS.ELA-LITERACY.W.7.1.A
Introduce claim(s), acknowledge alternate or opposing claims, and organize the reasons and evidence logically.

GRADE 8

Text Types and Purposes

> CCSS.ELA-LITERACY.W.8.1
Write arguments to support claims with clear reasons and relevant evidence

> CCSS.ELA-LITERACY.W.8.1.A
Introduce claim(s), acknowledge and distinguish the claim(s) from alternate or opposing claims, and organize the reasons and evidence logically.

GRADES 9-10

Text Types and Purposes

> CCSS.ELA-LITERACY.W.9-10.1
Write arguments to support claims in an analysis of substantive topics or texts, using valid reasoning and relevant and sufficient evidence.

> CCSS.ELA-LITERACY.W.9-10.1.A
Introduce precise claim(s), distinguish the claim(s) from alternate or opposing claims, and create an organization that establishes clear relationships among claim(s), counterclaims, reasons, and evidence.

GRADES 11-12

Text Types and Purposes

> CCSS.ELA-LITERACY.W.11-12.1
Write arguments to support claims in an analysis of substantive topics or texts, using valid reasoning and relevant and sufficient evidence.

> CCSS.ELA-LITERACY.W.11-12.1.A

Introduce precise, knowledgeable claim(s), establish the significance of the claim(s), distinguish the claim(s) from alternate or opposing claims, and create an organization that logically sequences claim(s), counterclaims, reasons, and evidence.

TIME REQUIREMENTS

Kind Words takes as long as you want. There is no story that needs to be finished. It is recommended to play the game over the course of two class periods because part of this activity relies on other players online responding to the letters that the students send out. It might take a day for everyone to get a response.

SAFETY - TRIGGER WARNING

A couple of things to note: this is an online game. While the player base has proven to be very responsible, there is always the chance of coming across a troll (I have never experienced this). Keep that in mind in case something negative does pop up. This game is also deeply personal. Students will share their anxieties and the sources of their depression. The whole point of the game is to read these messages and send out advice to others. Students can always skip over certain messages if they do not want to provide feedback on something that makes them uncomfortable. Students also do not need to share their own concerns to the online community. They can share positive messages or celebrations instead.

- Teaching Tolerance
- Beyond the Empathy Games 101: Digging Deep into Empathy, Ethics, and Design with Kelli Dunlap
- An Introduction to Content Warnings and Trigger Warnings

Teaching with Video Games

Florence

SEE PAGE 77 IN THE STUDENT PACKET

- Content Area/s: English Language Arts - Social Emotional Learning
- Developed by Mountains
- Rated: 12+

WHERE TO PLAY

- Available on iOS, Android, Nintendo Switch, Microsoft Windows, macOS

CONTEXT

This lesson should take place during a unit on

- Love
- Relationships

DO BEFORE - PREP

- Choose the texts that you want to teach alongside this game. Some examples are:
  - > Polygon: Apple Arcade's fixer-upper game isn't short on irony
  - > Any other text that you already use to teach the literary device "moral"

OVERVIEW

Florence is a wonderful game that focuses on the ups and downs of relationships. It is a mobile game, so you will need to find a way to project it in the front of the room while one student plays on a phone. You can use an HDMI adapter that connects a smartphone to a screen in the font of the room. If it is possible then you can also assign tablets with the game preloaded, which will allow the class to work in groups. The Aim of the lesson is for them to answer the question, «What can we learn from failed relationships?» To many people this may seem silly, but many students and even adults do not handle breakups well.

«*Florence* is the story of a young woman and the heartracing highs and heartbreaking lows of her very first love.» It tells this story through short, easy puzzles. There are zero spoken words in the game, which makes it very accessible to diverse groups of students. Language is not a barrier. The game also relies heavily on music and colors to convey the mood and feelings of the two characters in the game. It›s also a very realistic portrayal of the ups and downs of a relationship. Spoiler, the relationship does not last. But students will see that what is important is how one moves on after experiencing a breakup with someone with whom they thought they could spend the rest of their life.

The game is told in six acts, each of which contains several chapters. The first three acts are really about introducing the two main characters, Florence and Krish, and building up the relationship between them. A really unique gameplay mechanic is introduced in Act two when Florence and Krish go on their first date. The conversation is told through a series of jigsaw puzzles. Each time you want Florence to say something you must complete a little puzzle first. The puzzles are never difficult, but they get easier as Florence and Krish become more comfortable around each other. For many people, holding a conversation with someone new can be really challenging. Through its visual storytelling, this game conveys that these conversations become easier overtime as you become more comfortable with someone.

From there, Florence and Krish begin a long, healthy relationship and improve each other's lives. They encourage each other to do what they love the most and experience life together. They travel together, Florence makes Krish pursue an education in music, and Krish buys Florence a paint set since she is an aspiring artist who is currently working at a boring office job. We see the two characters move in together and live happily for several months. This will force the player to make space for both characters' belongings. Both of them will have to give up some of their possessions due to lack of space. Students will see how Florence became more productive in her normal life outside of the relationship. She is more productive at work because she is happy. This part allows students to make connections to their own lives and reflect how they often do better in school when their home life is better.

The relationship deteriorates in act five. In the reverse of earlier chapters, the puzzles in this section get more difficult to show how they drift apart. The pieces will even drift away from each other as the relationship breaks apart. The puzzles represent the ups and downs of their relationship. These things happen and it can be really special to hear students speak openly about how they have reacted in similar circumstances. Like in real life, Florence is able to move on after breaking up with Krish. It is not easy, but she manages to put the fragments of her life back together. She doesn't just get back on her feet. She actually ends up better off than before, or even during, her relationship. Krish pushed her to pursue her dream of being an artist and she finally decides to take the plunge after some self reflection. From here the students can answer the Aim: "How can we learn from failed relationships?"

It is for this reason that this game works so well as a Social Emotional Learning lesson. It is not necessarily the job of teachers to guide students in their relationships, but teachers can absolutely help students manage their feelings in a healthy way. Students need to talk about relationships and why they often fail. How many students think they are going to end up marrying their high school sweetheart? *Florence* can show our students that not all relationships will end up in marriage, and that is okay.

DESCRIPTION OF ACTIVITY

- Amount of copies needed is at the discretion of the teacher
  > The class can play together with the game projected in the front of the room
  > Students can play in pairs/groups on computers - consoles - smartphone
  > Or students can play individually on computers - consoles - smartphone
- Give a very basic summary of the game, but try not to spoil it too much. You control Florence, a twenty-five-year-old woman who meets and falls in love with Krish, a musician. Also worth mentioning that it is an interracial relationship. Florence is Japanese while Krish is Indian. While this is not as uncommon as it once was, it is still fairly rare to see interracial relationships in media. This game portrays this type of relationship without pandering to any stereotypes.
- Provide some screenshots on the board to show what kind of puzzles will be in the

Teaching with Video Games

game. While most students will have no problem figuring them out, it is always useful to frontload information to make sure everyone will have a general understanding of how the game will play out.

- Florence is separated into six acts with a total of 20 chapters. Have student volunteers come up to play the game and one student can play one act. You will be handing your phone to the student so remember to turn on Do Not Disturb so that no notifications come through while you are playing.

- If playing together as a class, you will need to connect your phone to whatever projection device you have. I used an HDMI to lightning adapter for my iphone.

- Have the students play through the game, guiding them through the puzzles when necessary.

- The different parts of the game are:

  > Act I: Adult Life, Memories, Music
  > Act II: Crash, First Dates
  > Act III: Dreams, Inspiration, Exploration
  > Act IV: Groceries, Moving In, Happy Together
  > Act V: Routine, Erosion, Fight, Drifting, Moving Out
  > Act VI: Fragments, Let Go, Waking Up, Moving On

- Provide an accompanying handout before starting the game, as students will be answering questions as they play through the story.

- Be prepared to help students who may end up stuck on one of the puzzles.

OBJECTIVES

- Students will discuss what healthy relationships look like.
- Students will extrapolate from the game what can be learned from failed relationships.

CORRELATION TO COMMON CORE STANDARDS

English Language Arts Anchor Standards

GRADES K-12

- College and Career Readiness Anchor Standards for Reading

  Key Ideas and Details

  > CCSS.ELA-LITERACY.CCRA.R.2
  > Determine central ideas or themes of a text and analyze their development; summarize the key supporting details and ideas.

  > CCSS.ELA-LITERACY.CCRA.R.3
  > Analyze how and why individuals, events, or ideas develop and interact over the course of a text.

- College and Career Readiness Anchor Standards for Writing

  Production and Distribution of Writing

  > CCSS.ELA-LITERACY.CCRA.W.4

Produce clear and coherent writing in which the development, organization, and style are appropriate to task, purpose, and audience.

- College and Career Readiness Anchor Standards for Speaking and Listening

Comprehension and Collaboration

> CCSS.ELA-LITERACY.CCRA.SL.1

Prepare for and participate effectively in a range of conversations and collaborations with diverse partners, building on others› ideas and expressing their own clearly and persuasively.

> CCSS.ELA-LITERACY.CCRA.SL.2

Integrate and evaluate information presented in diverse media and formats, including visually, quantitatively, and orally.

English Language Arts

Reading Literature

GRADE 6

Key Ideas and Details

> CCSS.ELA-LITERACY.RL.6.2

Determine a theme or central idea of a text and how it is conveyed through particular details; provide a summary of the text distinct from personal opinions or judgments.

Craft and Structure

> CCSS.ELA-LITERACY.RL.6.4

Determine the meaning of words and phrases as they are used in a text, including figurative and connotative meanings; analyze the impact of a specific word choice on meaning and tone

GRADE 7

Key Ideas and Details

> CCSS.ELA-LITERACY.RL.7.2

Determine a theme or central idea of a text and analyze its development over the course of the text; provide an objective summary of the text.

Craft and Structure

> CCSS.ELA-LITERACY.RL.7.4

Determine the meaning of words and phrases as they are used in a text, including figurative and connotative meanings; analyze the impact of rhymes and other repetitions of sounds (e.g., alliteration) on a specific verse or stanza of a poem or section of a story or drama.

GRADE 8

Key Ideas and Details

> CCSS.ELA-LITERACY.RL.8.2

Determine a theme or central idea of a text and analyze its development over the course of the text, including its relationship to the characters, setting, and plot; provide an objective summary of the text.

Craft and Structure

> CCSS.ELA-LITERACY.RL.8.4

Determine the meaning of words and phrases as they are used in a text, including figurative and connotative meanings; analyze the impact of specific word choices on meaning and tone, including analogies or allusions to other texts.

GRADES 9-10

Key Ideas and Details

> CCSS.ELA-LITERACY.RL.9-10.2

Determine a theme or central idea of a text and analyze in detail its development over the course of the text, including how it emerges and is shaped and refined by specific details; provide an objective summary of the text.

Craft and Structure

> CCSS.ELA-LITERACY.RL.9-10.4

Determine the meaning of words and phrases as they are used in the text, including figurative and connotative meanings; analyze the cumulative impact of specific word choices on meaning and tone (e.g., how the language evokes a sense of time and place; how it sets a formal or informal tone).

GRADES 11-12

Key Ideas and Details

> CCSS.ELA-LITERACY.RL.11-12.2

Determine two or more themes or central ideas of a text and analyze their development over the course of the text, including how they interact and build on one another to produce a complex account; provide an objective summary of the text.

Craft and Structure

> CCSS.ELA-LITERACY.RL.11-12.4

Determine the meaning of words and phrases as they are used in the text, including figurative and connotative meanings; analyze the impact of specific word choices on meaning and tone, including words with multiple meanings or language that is particularly fresh, engaging, or beautiful. (Include Shakespeare as well as other authors.)

Reading Informational Texts

GRADE 6

Key Ideas and Details

> CCSS.ELA-LITERACY.RI.6.2

Determine a central idea of a text and how it is conveyed through particular details; provide a summary of the text distinct from personal opinions or judgments.

> CCSS.ELA-LITERACY.RI.6.3

Analyze in detail how a key individual, event, or idea is introduced, illustrated, and elaborated in a text (e.g., through examples or anecdotes).

Craft and Structure

> CCSS.ELA-LITERACY.RI.6.4

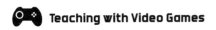

Determine the meaning of words and phrases as they are used in a text, including figurative, connotative, and technical meanings.

GRADE 7

Key Ideas and Details

> CCSS.ELA-LITERACY.RI.7.2

Determine two or more central ideas in a text and analyze their development over the course of the text; provide an objective summary of the text.

> CCSS.ELA-LITERACY.RI.7.3

Analyze the interactions between individuals, events, and ideas in a text (e.g., how ideas influence individuals or events, or how individuals influence ideas or events).

Craft and Structure

> CCSS.ELA-LITERACY.RI.7.4

Determine the meaning of words and phrases as they are used in a text, including figurative, connotative, and technical meanings; analyze the impact of a specific word choice on meaning and tone.

GRADE 8

Key Ideas and Details

> CCSS.ELA-LITERACY.RI.8.2

Determine a central idea of a text and analyze its development over the course of the text, including its relationship to supporting ideas; provide an objective summary of the text.

> CCSS.ELA-LITERACY.RI.8.3

Analyze how a text makes connections among and distinctions between individuals, ideas, or events (e.g., through comparisons, analogies, or categories).

Craft and Structure

> CCSS.ELA-LITERACY.RI.8.4

Determine the meaning of words and phrases as they are used in a text, including figurative, connotative, and technical meanings; analyze the impact of specific word choices on meaning and tone, including analogies or allusions to other texts.

GRADES 9-10

Key Ideas and Details

> CCSS.ELA-LITERACY.RI.9-10.2

Determine a central idea of a text and analyze its development over the course of the text, including how it emerges and is shaped and refined by specific details; provide an objective summary of the text.

> CCSS.ELA-LITERACY.RI.9-10.3

Analyze how the author unfolds an analysis or series of ideas or events, including the order in which the points are made, how they are introduced and developed, and the connections that are drawn between them.

Craft and Structure

> CCSS.ELA-LITERACY.RI.9-10.4

Teaching with Video Games

Determine the meaning of words and phrases as they are used in a text, including figurative, connotative, and technical meanings; analyze the cumulative impact of specific word choices on meaning and tone (e.g., how the language of a court opinion differs from that of a newspaper).

GRADES 11-12

Key Ideas and Details

> CCSS.ELA-LITERACY.RI.11-12.2

Determine two or more central ideas of a text and analyze their development over the course of the text, including how they interact and build on one another to provide a complex analysis; provide an objective summary of the text.

> CCSS.ELA-LITERACY.RI.11-12.3

Analyze a complex set of ideas or sequence of events and explain how specific individuals, ideas, or events interact and develop over the course of the text.

Craft and Structure

CCSS.ELA-LITERACY.RI.11-12.4

Determine the meaning of words and phrases as they are used in a text, including figurative, connotative, and technical meanings; analyze how an author uses and refines the meaning of a key term or terms over the course of a text (e.g., how Madison defines faction in Federalist No. 10).

Speaking and Listening

GRADE 6

Comprehension and Collaboration

> CCSS.ELA-LITERACY.SL.6.1

Engage effectively in a range of collaborative discussions (one-on-one, in groups, and teacher-led) with diverse partners on grade 6 topics, texts, and issues, building on others› ideas and expressing their own clearly.

> CCSS.ELA-LITERACY.SL.6.2

Interpret information presented in diverse media and formats (e.g., visually, quantitatively, orally) and explain how it contributes to a topic, text, or issue under study.

GRADE 7

Comprehension and Collaboration

> CCSS.ELA-LITERACY.SL.7.1

Engage effectively in a range of collaborative discussions (one-on-one, in groups, and teacher-led) with diverse partners on grade 7 topics, texts, and issues, building on others› ideas and expressing their own clearly.

> CCSS.ELA-LITERACY.SL.7.2

Analyze the main ideas and supporting details presented in diverse media and formats (e.g., visually, quantitatively, orally) and explain how the ideas clarify a topic, text, or issue under study.

GRADE 8

Comprehension and Collaboration

> CCSS.ELA-LITERACY.SL.8.1

Engage effectively in a range of collaborative discussions (one-on-one, in groups, and teacher-led) with diverse partners on grade 8 topics, texts, and issues, building on others› ideas and expressing their own clearly.

> CCSS.ELA-LITERACY.SL.8.2

Analyze the purpose of information presented in diverse media and formats (e.g., visually, quantitatively, orally) and evaluate the motives (e.g., social, commercial, political) behind its presentation.

GRADES 9-10

Comprehension and Collaboration

> CCSS.ELA-LITERACY.SL.9-10.1

Initiate and participate effectively in a range of collaborative discussions (one-on-one, in groups, and teacher-led) with diverse partners on grades 9-10 topics, texts, and issues, building on others› ideas and expressing their own clearly and persuasively.

> CCSS.ELA-LITERACY.SL.9-10.2

Integrate multiple sources of information presented in diverse media or formats (e.g., visually, quantitatively, orally) evaluating the credibility and accuracy of each source.

GRADES 11-12

Comprehension and Collaboration

> CCSS.ELA-LITERACY.SL.11-12.1

Initiate and participate effectively in a range of collaborative discussions (one-on-one, in groups, and teacher-led) with diverse partners on grades 11-12 topics, texts, and issues, building on others› ideas and expressing their own clearly and persuasively.

> CCSS.ELA-LITERACY.SL.11-12.2

Integrate multiple sources of information presented in diverse formats and media (e.g., visually, quantitatively, orally) in order to make informed decisions and solve problems, evaluating the credibility and accuracy of each source and noting any discrepancies among the data.

TIME REQUIREMENTS

Florence will take 40-50 minutes, depending on how quickly the students can solve a couple of the puzzles in the game.

SAFETY - TRIGGER WARNING

Nothing to warn about beforehand. It is a very accessible game.

Teaching with Video Games

Night in the Woods

SEE PAGE 80 IN THE STUDENT PACKET

- Content Area/s: English Language Arts - Social Emotional Learning
- Developed by Infinite Fall
- Rated: 13+

WHERE TO PLAY

- Available on Nintendo Switch, PlayStation 4, Xbox One, Macintosh operating systems, Microsoft Windows, Linux

CONTEXT

This lesson should take place during a unit on

- Growing Up
- Mental Health
- Rural/Suburban Life

DO BEFORE - PREP

- Choose the texts that you want to teach alongside this game. Some examples are:

  > The Verge: Night in the Woods isn't about growing up, but becoming an adult

OVERVIEW

Night in the Woods, developed by Infinite Fall, is about college dropout Mae Borowski who returns home to the crumbling former mining town of Possum Springs. How many games feature a college dropout as the protagonist? This game is a unique experience, like a mashup of a graphic novel and a video game. Gameplay, while fun at times, takes a back seat to telling a strong narrative with believable characters. It is a game that does an amazing job of showing us what it means to become an adult. Spoiler: age is not what defines you as an adult. We are presented with a wonderfully diverse cast of characters with unique personalities. Anyone from a small suburban town will instantly connect with the entire cast. There is love and care put into not only the characters› personalities, but into each person›s transition into becoming an adult. We are asked to consider whether it is okay to still smash lightbulbs with a bat when you are in your twenties. Run along power lines? Go shoplifting? Or drop out of college and continue to live with your parents with no future plan? Well, Mae and her friends do all of these things. It is a real look at different forms of inner struggle like depression, contempt, self-image, mental health, and dissatisfaction, that most video games never attempt to shed a light on. Playing this game will offer students the chance to analyze these factors while also reflecting on their own struggles and hopes.

This game can easily be used in an English Language Arts class, but it is an examination of human nature as much as a piece of literature and could work perfectly in a Social Emotional Learning (SEL) lesson. The Aim of the lesson is: «What does it mean to become an adult?» The story focuses on a group of high school best friends set two years after their graduation. All of the characters in the game are presented as animals, although they act and appear human. Each of the cast comes with an enormous amount of emotional and mental baggage that they must reconcile with as the game progresses. The core cast includes:

- Mae Borowski, a pansexual cat and the protagonist, has dropped out of college because of depression, anxiety, and issues with self-image. She has a troubled past and anger issues. She was even instructed to «repress» these issues by her doctor and to journal as a means of coping. She only gets along with a select few people in town, as most find her to be very rude. She has moved back into her parents' home with a somewhat judgmental mother and a father who works a minimum wage job at the grocery store because all of the manufacturing jobs left town.

- Her best friend Bea Santello is a crocodile and was the valedictorian of her graduating class. She was on track to go to college, but her mother died of cancer in her senior year of high school. The costs of her mom›s medical care and funeral forced Bea and her father to sell the family home and move into a small apartment. Her father ends up having a mental breakdown, forcing Bea to sacrifice her dreams of going to college and remain in Possum Springs in order to help him recover and to take over the family business. She is seen smoking constantly throughout the game as a means of dealing with the stress of working a dead-end job.

- Gregg Lee, a fox, is another one of Mae›s friends. He is talkative and always wearing a punk leather jacket. He also commits petty crimes, like breaking into abandoned buildings and smashing stuff in a junkyard. He always seems to be in a good mood, but he will bring up that how he presents himself does not always match how he feels. He has his up days and down days, and tends to lie awake at night while thinking about what he dislikes about himself. He always wants to make others happy and is constantly afraid of ruining his relationship with his boyfriend Angus, whom he lives with.

- Angus Delaney, a bear, is Gregg›s boyfriend. He is much quieter and more reserved than the rest of the crew. He is shy and often disinterested in some of the antics that the other three get into. He mostly tags along because he loves Gregg. He loves to cook and bake food for others, partly because his parents withheld food from him when he was younger. He is not proud, and he mentions that he sometimes feels like a failure. He and Gregg are saving up money to move out of Possum Springs because they are uncomfortable being the only queer couple in town. Not everyone is as open-minded as their friends.

Does this sound like any other game you›ve played before? In all likelihood, it will be a new experience for any player to watch as each of these four animals grapples with the struggles of adulthood. It touches on problems that many students are dealing with themselves. The idea of going to college is a huge source of stress from the moment they enter school, and here we have a protagonist who quit before the end of her second year. The conversations this can lead to about why this happens to so many people is absolutely necessary to have with our students. **Only about 60% of students finish their four-year degrees over the course of six years.** A lot of people head to college and never finish. It is an unfortunate but normal aspect of life that our students need to know exists. Any teacher would love for each and every one of their students to graduate and attend a great post-secondary school, but the reality is that more schooling is not for everyone. And like Bea, not every student that wants to go to college will even be able to.

Teaching with Video Games

All of this subject matter is where the game shines. The narrative thread in *Night in the Woods* is actually about the mysterious disappearances of a number of townspeople. Hence the reason why Mae and her friends will eventually end up spending a night in the woods, trying to solve the mystery.

DESCRIPTION OF ACTIVITY

- Amount of copies needed is at the discretion of the teacher
    - > The class can play together with the game projected in the front of the room
    - > Students can play in pairs/groups on computers - consoles
    - > Or students can play individually on computers - consoles
- Go over the following vocabulary terms with the class:
    - > Mental Health: The condition of being sound mentally and emotionally that is characterized by the absence of mental illness and by adequate adjustment, especially as reflected in feeling comfortable about oneself, positive feelings about others, and the ability to meet the demands of daily life.
    - > Self-image: A mental picture of yourself, both as a physical body and an individual. When you think about yourself, the feelings and images that come up are important. A healthy body image means that you see yourself as you really are and that you feel good in your own skin.
    - > Social Circle: A group of socially interconnected people.
- Go over *Night in the Woods* with your class.
    - > There are 4 Parts in the Game

        Part 1: Home Again

        Part 2: Weird Autumn

        Part 3: The Long Fall

        Part 4: The End of Everything
    - > You play as Mae, a sarcastic twenty-year-old who has just returned to her hometown after dropping out of college.
    - > Between Mae's friends, family, and local townspeople of Possum Springs, there is a wonderful cast of characters with diverse and interesting backgrounds. Talk to everyone! You are sure to learn something new and unique.
- Provide an accompanying handout before starting the game, as students will be answering questions as they play through the story.
- Be prepared to help students who may end up stuck on one of the puzzles.

OBJECTIVES

- Students will discuss what it means to become an adult.
- Students will empathize with the struggles each core character in *Night in the Woods* faces as they enter adulthood.

CORRELATION TO COMMON CORE STANDARDS

English Language Arts Anchor Standards

GRADES K-12

- College and Career Readiness Anchor Standards for Reading

  Key Ideas and Details

  > CCSS.ELA-LITERACY.CCRA.R.2

  Determine central ideas or themes of a text and analyze their development; summarize the key supporting details and ideas.

  > CCSS.ELA-LITERACY.CCRA.R.3

  Analyze how and why individuals, events, or ideas develop and interact over the course of a text.

- College and Career Readiness Anchor Standards for Writing

  Production and Distribution of Writing

  > CCSS.ELA-LITERACY.CCRA.W.4

  Produce clear and coherent writing in which the development, organization, and style are appropriate to task, purpose, and audience.

- College and Career Readiness Anchor Standards for Speaking and Listening

  Comprehension and Collaboration

  > CCSS.ELA-LITERACY.CCRA.SL.1

  Prepare for and participate effectively in a range of conversations and collaborations with diverse partners, building on others› ideas and expressing their own clearly and persuasively.

  > CCSS.ELA-LITERACY.CCRA.SL.2

  Integrate and evaluate information presented in diverse media and formats, including visually, quantitatively, and orally.

English Language Arts

Reading Literature

GRADE 6

Key Ideas and Details

> CCSS.ELA-LITERACY.RL.6.2

Determine a theme or central idea of a text and how it is conveyed through particular details; provide a summary of the text distinct from personal opinions or judgments.

Craft and Structure

> CCSS.ELA-LITERACY.RL.6.4

Determine the meaning of words and phrases as they are used in a text, including figurative and connotative meanings; analyze the impact of a specific word choice on meaning and tone

GRADE 7

Key Ideas and Details

> CCSS.ELA-LITERACY.RL.7.2

Determine a theme or central idea of a text and analyze its development over the course of the text; provide an objective summary of the text.

Craft and Structure

> CCSS.ELA-LITERACY.RL.7.4

Determine the meaning of words and phrases as they are used in a text, including figurative and connotative meanings; analyze the impact of rhymes and other repetitions of sounds (e.g., alliteration) on a specific verse or stanza of a poem or section of a story or drama.

GRADE 8

Key Ideas and Details

> CCSS.ELA-LITERACY.RL.8.2

Determine a theme or central idea of a text and analyze its development over the course of the text, including its relationship to the characters, setting, and plot; provide an objective summary of the text.

Craft and Structure

> CCSS.ELA-LITERACY.RL.8.4

Determine the meaning of words and phrases as they are used in a text, including figurative and connotative meanings; analyze the impact of specific word choices on meaning and tone, including analogies or allusions to other texts.

GRADES 9-10

Key Ideas and Details

> CCSS.ELA-LITERACY.RL.9-10.2

Determine a theme or central idea of a text and analyze in detail its development over the course of the text, including how it emerges and is shaped and refined by specific details; provide an objective summary of the text.

Craft and Structure

> CCSS.ELA-LITERACY.RL.9-10.4

Determine the meaning of words and phrases as they are used in the text, including figurative and connotative meanings; analyze the cumulative impact of specific word choices on meaning and tone (e.g., how the language evokes a sense of time and place; how it sets a formal or informal tone).

GRADES 11-12

Key Ideas and Details

> CCSS.ELA-LITERACY.RL.11-12.2

Determine two or more themes or central ideas of a text and analyze their development over the course of the text, including how they interact and build on one another to produce a complex account; provide an objective summary of the text.

Craft and Structure

> CCSS.ELA-LITERACY.RL.11-12.4

Determine the meaning of words and phrases as they are used in the text, including figurative and connotative meanings; analyze the impact of specific word choices on meaning and tone, including words with multiple meanings or language that is particularly fresh, engaging, or beautiful. (Include Shakespeare as well as other authors.)

Reading Informational Texts

GRADE 6

Key Ideas and Details

> CCSS.ELA-LITERACY.RI.6.2

Determine a central idea of a text and how it is conveyed through particular details; provide a summary of the text distinct from personal opinions or judgments.

> CCSS.ELA-LITERACY.RI.6.3

Analyze in detail how a key individual, event, or idea is introduced, illustrated, and elaborated in a text (e.g., through examples or anecdotes).

Craft and Structure

> CCSS.ELA-LITERACY.RI.6.4

Determine the meaning of words and phrases as they are used in a text, including figurative, connotative, and technical meanings.

GRADE 7

Key Ideas and Details

> CCSS.ELA-LITERACY.RI.7.2

Determine two or more central ideas in a text and analyze their development over the course of the text; provide an objective summary of the text.

> CCSS.ELA-LITERACY.RI.7.3

Analyze the interactions between individuals, events, and ideas in a text (e.g., how ideas influence individuals or events, or how individuals influence ideas or events).

Craft and Structure

> CCSS.ELA-LITERACY.RI.7.4

Determine the meaning of words and phrases as they are used in a text, including figurative, connotative, and technical meanings; analyze the impact of a specific word choice on meaning and tone.

GRADE 8

Key Ideas and Details

> CCSS.ELA-LITERACY.RI.8.2

Determine a central idea of a text and analyze its development over the course of the text, including its relationship to supporting ideas; provide an objective summary of the text.

> CCSS.ELA-LITERACY.RI.8.3

Analyze how a text makes connections among and distinctions between individuals, ideas, or events (e.g., through comparisons, analogies, or categories).

Craft and Structure

> CCSS.ELA-LITERACY.RI.8.4

Determine the meaning of words and phrases as they are used in a text, including figurative, connotative, and technical meanings; analyze the impact of specific word choices on meaning and tone, including analogies or allusions to other texts.

GRADES 9–10

Key Ideas and Details

> CCSS.ELA-LITERACY.RI.9-10.2

Determine a central idea of a text and analyze its development over the course of the text, including how it emerges and is shaped and refined by specific details; provide an objective summary of the text.

> CCSS.ELA-LITERACY.RI.9-10.3

Analyze how the author unfolds an analysis or series of ideas or events, including the order in which the points are made, how they are introduced and developed, and the connections that are drawn between them.

Craft and Structure

> CCSS.ELA-LITERACY.RI.9-10.4

Determine the meaning of words and phrases as they are used in a text, including figurative, connotative, and technical meanings; analyze the cumulative impact of specific word choices on meaning and tone (e.g., how the language of a court opinion differs from that of a newspaper).

GRADES 11–12

Key Ideas and Details

> CCSS.ELA-LITERACY.RI.11-12.2

Determine two or more central ideas of a text and analyze their development over the course of the text, including how they interact and build on one another to provide a complex analysis; provide an objective summary of the text.

> CCSS.ELA-LITERACY.RI.11-12.3

Analyze a complex set of ideas or sequence of events and explain how specific individuals, ideas, or events interact and develop over the course of the text.

Craft and Structure

> CCSS.ELA-LITERACY.RI.11-12.4

Determine the meaning of words and phrases as they are used in a text, including figurative, connotative, and technical meanings; analyze how an author uses and refines the meaning of a key term or terms over the course of a text (e.g., how Madison defines faction in Federalist No. 10).

Speaking and Listening

GRADE 6

Comprehension and Collaboration

> CCSS.ELA-LITERACY.SL.6.1

Engage effectively in a range of collaborative discussions (one-on-one, in groups, and teacher-led) with diverse partners on grade 6 topics, texts, and issues, building on others› ideas and expressing their own clearly.

> CCSS.ELA-LITERACY.SL.6.2

Interpret information presented in diverse media and formats (e.g., visually, quantitatively, orally) and explain how it contributes to a topic, text, or issue under study.

GRADE 7

Comprehension and Collaboration

> CCSS.ELA-LITERACY.SL.7.1

Engage effectively in a range of collaborative discussions (one-on-one, in groups, and teacher-led) with diverse partners on grade 7 topics, texts, and issues, building on others› ideas and expressing their own clearly.

> CCSS.ELA-LITERACY.SL.7.2

Analyze the main ideas and supporting details presented in diverse media and formats (e.g., visually, quantitatively, orally) and explain how the ideas clarify a topic, text, or issue under study.

GRADE 8

Comprehension and Collaboration

> CCSS.ELA-LITERACY.SL.8.1

Engage effectively in a range of collaborative discussions (one-on-one, in groups, and teacher-led) with diverse partners on grade 8 topics, texts, and issues, building on others› ideas and expressing their own clearly.

> CCSS.ELA-LITERACY.SL.8.2

Analyze the purpose of information presented in diverse media and formats (e.g., visually, quantitatively, orally) and evaluate the motives (e.g., social, commercial, political) behind its presentation.

GRADES 9-10

Comprehension and Collaboration

> CCSS.ELA-LITERACY.SL.9-10.1

Initiate and participate effectively in a range of collaborative discussions (one-on-one, in groups, and teacher-led) with diverse partners on grades 9-10 topics, texts, and issues, building on others› ideas and expressing their own clearly and persuasively.

> CCSS.ELA-LITERACY.SL.9-10.2

Integrate multiple sources of information presented in diverse media or formats (e.g., visually, quantitatively, orally) evaluating the credibility and accuracy of each source.

Comprehension and Collaboration

> CCSS.ELA-LITERACY.SL.11-12.1

Initiate and participate effectively in a range of collaborative discussions (one-on-one, in groups, and teacher-led) with diverse partners on grades 11-12 topics, texts, and issues, building on others› ideas and expressing their own clearly and persuasively.

> CCSS.ELA-LITERACY.SL.11-12.2

Integrate multiple sources of information presented in diverse formats and media (e.g., visually, quantitatively, orally) in order to make informed decisions and solve problems, evaluating the credibility and accuracy of each source and noting any discrepancies among the data.

TIME REQUIREMENTS

Night in the Woods takes about eight to nine hours of playtime. It is, however, easy to lose track of time since there is a lot to explore in the game. Make sure to keep students on track and plan to spend a couple of weeks with the game.

SAFETY - TRIGGER WARNING

Night in the Woods is visually tame, but its dialogue and narrative can be very mature at times. The main characters are often having conversations about mental health, death, child abuse, and depression. It is best to prepare your students for these discussions beforehand.

- Teaching Tolerance
- Beyond the Empathy Games 101: Digging Deep into Empathy, Ethics, and Design with Kelli Dunlap
- An Introduction to Content Warnings and Trigger Warnings

Brothers: A Tale of Two Sons

SEE PAGE 87 IN THE STUDENT PACKET

- Content Area/s: English Language Arts - Social Emotional Learning
- Developed by 505 Games: Starbreeze Studios
- Rated: 13+

WHERE TO PLAY

- Available on Playstation 4, Playstation 3, Xbox One, Xbox 360, Microsoft Windows, Android, iOS.

CONTEXT

This lesson should take place during a unit on

- Family
- Death
- Literary Elements

DO BEFORE - PREP

- Choose the texts that you want to teach alongside this game. Some examples are:
  - > About Authoring: Brothers: A Tale of Two Sons as a Semiotic, Narrative, and Rhetorical Text
  - > Brothers: A Tale of Two Sons tells a love story through simple gameplay

OVERVIEW

Two brothers, Naiee and Naia, set off on an adventure to find a cure for their father's illness. Having already lost their mother, the brothers are willing to put their lives on the line in order to make sure that their father stays alive. *Brothers: A Tale of Two Sons* is a game about death. It is about how all of us will experience death at some point and quite often there is nothing we can do to stop its course. As the saying goes, death comes for us all. This game is perfect to get students talking about death and mortality. Everyone goes through a period of their life where we feel invincible, but that facade shatters when someone we know and love dies. All of a sudden, death is a reality in our lives. This game, spoken in an entirely fabricated language, communicates to the players through body language. We physically see how the brothers support each other when dealing with regret, trauma, and PTSD. We feel what they feel. And by the end of the game, the class may be ready to talk about death on a personal level rather than as something that happens to strangers we read about in class.

The gameplay focuses on solving fairly simple puzzles. The challenge is that every task requires the two brothers to work together. The older brother is stronger and is able to lift or move heavy objects. The younger brother is smaller and can squeeze in between places his older brother cannot. While *Brothers* is technically a single player game, the two playable characters are independently controlled by the two joysticks. For this lesson it could be fun to have two students holding the controller together. This will allow each student to control one of the brothers. Each player only has three actions. The joystick will move their respective character. The trigger buttons will cause the brothers to interact with the environment or another person and the bumper buttons rotate the camera. The simple control scheme will allow both players to be able to play with only one hand on the controller at a time. The students will need to communicate in order to progress through the game. If you have the game on Nintendo Switch, then two students do not even need to hold the same controller. Each student can simply hold one of the console's Joycons.

DESCRIPTION OF ACTIVITY

- Only one copy of the game is necessary. Project it in the front of the class and have one student play at a time.

- The story begins with a boy named Naiee paying his respects at the tombstone of his dead mother, who drowned at sea while he remained unable to save her.

  > He will need his brother's help coping with this traumatic experience.

- A man, clinging to life, and his two sons, desperate to cure their ailing father, are left with only one option: they must set out on a journey to find and bring back the «Water of Life» as they come to rely on one another to survive. One must be strong where the other is weak, brave where the other is fearful, they must be... Brothers. - Brothers Wiki

- *Brothers: A Tale of Two Sons* is a single player, co-op game.

  > Only one player plays at a time while controlling two different characters, one with each Joy-stick.

  You can play with two students sharing a single controller

- The game has no dialogue. The language spoken in the game is a fictional language based on Lebanese, the home country of the game's creator, Josef Fares.

  > The characters use their body language in order to get their points across to the player.

- The game focuses on a universal language to teach us about the nature of death and the lengths people will go to make sure their loved ones can escape death.

- There are two ways to play the game. You can have one student playing at a time while controlling both brothers. You can also have two students play together, but they need to share the controller as both brothers are controlled by one controller.

- Provide an accompanying handout before starting the game, as students will be answering questions as they play through the story.

OBJECTIVES

- Students will have meaningful conversations about death.

- Students will make connections between the game *Brothers: A Tale of Two Sons* and their own lives or experiences.

CORRELATION TO COMMON CORE STANDARDS

English Language Arts Anchor Standards

GRADES K-12

- College and Career Readiness Anchor Standards for Reading

  ### Key Ideas and Details

  > CCSS.ELA-LITERACY.CCRA.R.2

  Determine central ideas or themes of a text and analyze their development; summarize the key supporting details and ideas.

  > CCSS.ELA-LITERACY.CCRA.R.3

  Analyze how and why individuals, events, or ideas develop and interact over the course of a text.

- College and Career Readiness Anchor Standards for Writing

  ### Production and Distribution of Writing

  > CCSS.ELA-LITERACY.CCRA.W.4

  Produce clear and coherent writing in which the development, organization, and style are appropriate to task, purpose, and audience.

- College and Career Readiness Anchor Standards for Speaking and Listening

  ### Comprehension and Collaboration

  > CCSS.ELA-LITERACY.CCRA.SL.1

  Prepare for and participate effectively in a range of conversations and collaborations with diverse partners, building on others› ideas and expressing their own clearly and persuasively.

  > CCSS.ELA-LITERACY.CCRA.SL.2

  Integrate and evaluate information presented in diverse media and formats, including visually, quantitatively, and orally.

English Language Arts

Reading Literature

GRADE 6

Key Ideas and Details

> CCSS.ELA-LITERACY.RL.6.2

Determine a theme or central idea of a text and how it is conveyed through particular details; provide a summary of the text distinct from personal opinions or judgments.

Craft and Structure

> CCSS.ELA-LITERACY.RL.6.4

Determine the meaning of words and phrases as they are used in a text, including figurative and connotative meanings; analyze the impact of a specific word choice on meaning and tone

GRADE 7

Key Ideas and Details

> CCSS.ELA-LITERACY.RL.7.2

Determine a theme or central idea of a text and analyze its development over the course of the text; provide an objective summary of the text.

Craft and Structure

> CCSS.ELA-LITERACY.RL.7.4

Determine the meaning of words and phrases as they are used in a text, including figurative and connotative meanings; analyze the impact of rhymes and other repetitions of sounds (e.g., alliteration) on a specific verse or stanza of a poem or section of a story or drama.

GRADE 8

Key Ideas and Details

> CCSS.ELA-LITERACY.RL.8.2

Determine a theme or central idea of a text and analyze its development over the course of the text, including its relationship to the characters, setting, and plot; provide an objective summary of the text.

Craft and Structure

> CCSS.ELA-LITERACY.RL.8.4

Determine the meaning of words and phrases as they are used in a text, including figurative and connotative meanings; analyze the impact of specific word choices on meaning and tone, including analogies or allusions to other texts.

GRADES 9-10

Key Ideas and Details

> CCSS.ELA-LITERACY.RL.9-10.2

Determine a theme or central idea of a text and analyze in detail its development over the course of the text, including how it emerges and is shaped and refined by specific details; provide an objective summary of the text.

Craft and Structure

> CCSS.ELA-LITERACY.RL.9-10.4

Determine the meaning of words and phrases as they are used in the text, including figurative and connotative meanings; analyze the cumulative impact of specific word choices on meaning and tone (e.g., how the language evokes a sense of time and place; how it sets a formal or informal tone).

GRADES 11-12

Key Ideas and Details

> CCSS.ELA-LITERACY.RL.11-12.2

Determine two or more themes or central ideas of a text and analyze their development over the course of the text, including how they interact and build on one another to produce a complex account; provide an objective summary of the text.

Craft and Structure

> CCSS.ELA-LITERACY.RL.11-12.4

Determine the meaning of words and phrases as they are used in the text, including figurative and connotative meanings; analyze the impact of specific word choices on meaning and tone, including words with multiple meanings or language that is particularly fresh, engaging, or beautiful. (Include Shakespeare as well as other authors.)

Reading Informational Texts

GRADE 6

Key Ideas and Details

> CCSS.ELA-LITERACY.RI.6.2

Determine a central idea of a text and how it is conveyed through particular details; provide a summary of the text distinct from personal opinions or judgments.

> CCSS.ELA-LITERACY.RI.6.3

Analyze in detail how a key individual, event, or idea is introduced, illustrated, and elaborated in a text (e.g., through examples or anecdotes).

Craft and Structure

> CCSS.ELA-LITERACY.RI.6.4

Determine the meaning of words and phrases as they are used in a text, including figurative, connotative, and technical meanings.

GRADE 7

Key Ideas and Details

> CCSS.ELA-LITERACY.RI.7.2

Determine two or more central ideas in a text and analyze their development over the course of the text; provide an objective summary of the text.

> CCSS.ELA-LITERACY.RI.7.3

Analyze the interactions between individuals, events, and ideas in a text (e.g., how ideas influence individuals or events, or how individuals influence ideas or events).

Craft and Structure

> CCSS.ELA-LITERACY.RI.7.4

Determine the meaning of words and phrases as they are used in a text, including figurative, connotative, and technical meanings; analyze the impact of a specific word choice on meaning and tone.

GRADE 8

Key Ideas and Details

> CCSS.ELA-LITERACY.RI.8.2

Determine a central idea of a text and analyze its development over the course of the text, including its relationship to supporting ideas; provide an objective summary of the text.

> CCSS.ELA-LITERACY.RI.8.3

Analyze how a text makes connections among and distinctions between individuals, ideas, or events (e.g., through comparisons, analogies, or categories).

Craft and Structure

> CCSS.ELA-LITERACY.RI.8.4

Determine the meaning of words and phrases as they are used in a text, including figurative, connotative, and technical meanings; analyze the impact of specific word choices on meaning and tone, including analogies or allusions to other texts.

GRADES 9-10

Key Ideas and Details

> CCSS.ELA-LITERACY.RI.9-10.2

Determine a central idea of a text and analyze its development over the course of the text, including how it emerges and is shaped and refined by specific details; provide an objective summary of the text.

> CCSS.ELA-LITERACY.RI.9-10.3

Analyze how the author unfolds an analysis or series of ideas or events, including the order in which the points are made, how they are introduced and developed, and the connections that are drawn between them.

Craft and Structure

> CCSS.ELA-LITERACY.RI.9-10.4

Determine the meaning of words and phrases as they are used in a text, including figurative, connotative, and technical meanings; analyze the cumulative impact of specific word choices on meaning and tone (e.g., how the language of a court opinion differs from that of a newspaper).

GRADES 11-12

Key Ideas and Details

> CCSS.ELA-LITERACY.RI.11-12.2

Determine two or more central ideas of a text and analyze their development over the course of the text, including how they interact and build on one another to provide a complex analysis; provide an objective summary of the text.

> CCSS.ELA-LITERACY.RI.11-12.3

Analyze a complex set of ideas or sequence of events and explain how specific individuals, ideas, or events interact and develop over the course of the text.

Craft and Structure

> CCSS.ELA-LITERACY.RI.11-12.4

Determine the meaning of words and phrases as they are used in a text, including figurative, connotative, and technical meanings; analyze how an author uses and refines the meaning of a key term or terms over the course of a text (e.g., how Madison defines faction in Federalist No. 10).

Speaking and Listening

GRADE 6

Comprehension and Collaboration

> CCSS.ELA-LITERACY.SL.6.1

Engage effectively in a range of collaborative discussions (one-on-one, in groups, and teacher-led) with diverse partners on grade 6 topics, texts, and issues, building on others› ideas and expressing their own clearly.

> CCSS.ELA-LITERACY.SL.6.2

Interpret information presented in diverse media and formats (e.g., visually, quantitatively, orally) and explain how it contributes to a topic, text, or issue under study.

GRADE 7

Comprehension and Collaboration

> CCSS.ELA-LITERACY.SL.7.1

Engage effectively in a range of collaborative discussions (one-on-one, in groups, and teacher-led) with diverse partners on grade 7 topics, texts, and issues, building on others› ideas and expressing their own clearly.

> CCSS.ELA-LITERACY.SL.7.2

Analyze the main ideas and supporting details presented in diverse media and formats (e.g., visually, quantitatively, orally) and explain how the ideas clarify a topic, text, or issue under study.

GRADE 8

Comprehension and Collaboration

> CCSS.ELA-LITERACY.SL.8.1

Engage effectively in a range of collaborative discussions (one-on-one, in groups, and teacher-led) with diverse partners on grade 8 topics, texts, and issues, building on others› ideas and expressing their own clearly.

> CCSS.ELA-LITERACY.SL.8.2

Analyze the purpose of information presented in diverse media and formats (e.g., visually, quantitatively, orally) and evaluate the motives (e.g., social, commercial, political) behind its presentation.

GRADES 9-10

Comprehension and Collaboration

> CCSS.ELA-LITERACY.SL.9-10.1

Initiate and participate effectively in a range of collaborative discussions (one-on-one, in groups, and teacher-led) with diverse partners on grades 9-10 topics, texts, and issues, building on others› ideas and expressing their own clearly and persuasively.

> CCSS.ELA-LITERACY.SL.9-10.2

Integrate multiple sources of information presented in diverse media or formats (e.g., visually, quantitatively, orally) evaluating the credibility and accuracy of each source.

Teaching with Video Games

Comprehension and Collaboration

> CCSS.ELA-LITERACY.SL.11-12.1

Initiate and participate effectively in a range of collaborative discussions (one-on-one, in groups, and teacher-led) with diverse partners on grades 11-12 topics, texts, and issues, building on others› ideas and expressing their own clearly and persuasively.

> CCSS.ELA-LITERACY.SL.11-12.2

Integrate multiple sources of information presented in diverse formats and media (e.g., visually, quantitatively, orally) in order to make informed decisions and solve problems, evaluating the credibility and accuracy of each source and noting any discrepancies among the data.

TIME REQUIREMENTS

A playthrough of *Brothers: A Tale of Two Sons* takes about three hours. Taking into account time for discussion, it would be best to set aside four to five hours for this activity.

SAFETY - TRIGGER WARNING

This game is rated 13+, but it does deal with death. It can be very emotionally heavy.

- Beyond the Empathy Games 101: Digging Deep into Empathy, Ethics, and Design with Kelli Dunlap
- An Introduction to Content Warnings and Trigger Warnings

Before I Forget

SEE PAGE 90 IN THE STUDENT PACKET

- Content Area/s: English Language Arts - Social Emotional Learning
- Developed by 3-Fold Games
- Rated: 13+

WHERE TO PLAY

- Available on Microsoft Windows, Linux, macOS

CONTEXT

This lesson should take place during a unit on

- Dementia
- Alzheimer›s Disease

DO BEFORE - PREP

- Choose the texts that you want to teach alongside this game. Some examples are:
  > What is Alzheimer's Disease?
  > Losing My Mother Again and Again: My Story With Alzheimer's Disease
  > ALZHEIMER'S STORIES: HELLO, GOODBYE

OVERVIEW

Before I Forget is not what will come to mind for most people when they think of video games. You play and progress through the story using a controller, despite the lack of interactivity. But you are in the passenger seat of a heartbreaking story of Sutina, who is a woman struggling with Alzheimer›s Disease. The player moves throughout different rooms in her home, each of which help piece together her fragmented memory. Yes, you hold the controller and move the narrative along, but there is ultimately nothing you can do to alter the course of the game.

Before I Forget is not meant to be a fun game; instead, it is a game about what happens when someone is unable to remember the things they have done or the people they have loved. It's a love story that puts you in the shoes of someone who is no longer able to remember the entire story; the protagonist›s memories are constantly jumbled and fading away.

Before I Forget is a genuinely sad game from start to finish. It intentionally tries to visualize what it might be like to live with dementia. From forgetting certain memories, to getting lost in your home, it is a portrait of mental illness that has afflicted the loved ones of so many people. Some of our students most likely have family members that are currently affected by dementia. Playing this game can provide an outlet for students to discuss this mental affliction, and mental health in general, in a class setting. Providing a safe discussion space in a classroom can help students unpack all of the emotions that come with that. The game is also a perfect example of how video games have evolved beyond just "play."

The game starts with the player in a completely colorless room. Sutina can›t seem to remember where everyone is or even if she is supposed to be there. The player can examine post-it notes, postcards, and photographs that help Sutina piece together her life-story and understand her current surroundings. The layout of the player›s home is disorienting as the protagonist can›t seem to remember which room is where. There is a tear-jerking moment when you are in search of the bathroom, but you end up in the closet every time you try to open the bathroom door. This ultimately leads to your character having an accident, as she couldn›t make it to the bathroom in time. There is nothing the player can do to stop this, even though they know where the bathroom is.

You find different items that begin to jog Sutina›s memory as you work your way through the home. The layout of the home was clearly put together in a way that would allow Sutina to figure out where she is every day. There are photos placed at her bedside, magazines with Sutina on the cover to help her remember her career as a cosmologist, and post-it notes reminding her where she can find food to eat. A number of these items will even trigger flashback sequences to earlier times in Sutina›s life. Part of what makes this game unique is that both the player and Sutina are learning about her own past together. Every twist and turn for the player is equally, if not more so, shocking to Sutina.

Color will slowly fill out Sutina›s home as she sorts through her confusion and regains her memories. It›s a simple but effective way to convey how someone with Alzheimer›s can start their day confused, but gradually become more aware of their surroundings as the day progresses. Even after completely filling a room with color, however, there is still a chance of walking into the next room and ending up lost. And as you get closer to the end of the game, Sutina gradually becomes more distressed as she begins to piece together her own life story.

This entire game is a lesson in empathy. *Before I Forget* is a clear example of how video games have evolved into something more than their entertainment origins. It›s first and foremost a story and it is one that deserves to be taught within an educational setting.

DESCRIPTION OF ACTIVITY

- Only one copy of the game is necessary. Project in the front of the class and have one student play at a time.
- Go over the following vocabulary terms with the class (definitions from the Alzheimer's Association):
  > Mental Health: Refers to cognitive, behavioral, and emotional well-being. It is all about how people think, feel, and behave.
  > Dementia: a general term for memory loss and other cognitive abilities serious enough to interfere with daily life. Alzheimer›s disease accounts for 60-80% of dementia cases.
  > Alzheimer's: Alzheimer›s is a type of dementia that affects memory, thinking, and behavior. It is a progressive disease, where dementia symptoms gradually worsen over a number of years. In its early stages, memory loss is mild, but with late-stage Alzheimer›s, individuals lose the ability to carry on a conversation and respond to their environment.
- Go over *Before I Forget* with your class.
  > *Before I Forget* tells the story of a woman alone in a house. It is both a mystery and

a love story where you must explore the present in order to uncover the past. It's a short story of love, loss, and a life well-lived.

> It is a narrative exploration that examines a world where memories are constantly fading and jumbled. It is also a game about dementia and what happens when you can't hold onto the things you've done or the people you've loved.

> *Before I Forget* is a Walking Simulator. There is no action or fighting. You simply play as a woman walking through and exploring her own home.

> Doing so will be challenging as the protagonist struggles remembering exactly where everything is supposed to be.

- Provide an accompanying handout before starting the game, as students will be answering questions as they play through the story.

OBJECTIVES

- Students will discuss representations of dementia and Alzheimer's Disease.

- Students will discuss the ways in which gameplay in *Before I Forget* is explicitly tied to the symptoms experienced by those with Alzheimer's Disease.

- Students will acknowledge the challenges faced by those with Alzheimer's Disease.

CORRELATION TO COMMON CORE STANDARDS

English Language Arts Anchor Standards

GRADES K-12

- College and Career Readiness Anchor Standards for Reading

  Key Ideas and Details

  > CCSS.ELA-LITERACY.CCRA.R.2

  Determine central ideas or themes of a text and analyze their development; summarize the key supporting details and ideas.

  > CCSS.ELA-LITERACY.CCRA.R.3

  Analyze how and why individuals, events, or ideas develop and interact over the course of a text.

- College and Career Readiness Anchor Standards for Writing

  Production and Distribution of Writing

  > CCSS.ELA-LITERACY.CCRA.W.4

  Produce clear and coherent writing in which the development, organization, and style are appropriate to task, purpose, and audience.

- College and Career Readiness Anchor Standards for Speaking and Listening

  Comprehension and Collaboration

  > CCSS.ELA-LITERACY.CCRA.SL.1

  Prepare for and participate effectively in a range of conversations and collaborations with diverse partners, building on others› ideas and expressing their own clearly and persuasively.

Teaching with Video Games

> CCSS.ELA-LITERACY.CCRA.SL.2

Integrate and evaluate information presented in diverse media and formats, including visually, quantitatively, and orally.

English Language Arts

Reading Literature

GRADE 6

Key Ideas and Details

> CCSS.ELA-LITERACY.RL.6.2

Determine a theme or central idea of a text and how it is conveyed through particular details; provide a summary of the text distinct from personal opinions or judgments.

Craft and Structure

> CCSS.ELA-LITERACY.RL.6.4

Determine the meaning of words and phrases as they are used in a text, including figurative and connotative meanings; analyze the impact of a specific word choice on meaning and tone

GRADE 7

Key Ideas and Details

> CCSS.ELA-LITERACY.RL.7.2

Determine a theme or central idea of a text and analyze its development over the course of the text; provide an objective summary of the text.

Craft and Structure

> CCSS.ELA-LITERACY.RL.7.4

Determine the meaning of words and phrases as they are used in a text, including figurative and connotative meanings; analyze the impact of rhymes and other repetitions of sounds (e.g., alliteration) on a specific verse or stanza of a poem or section of a story or drama.

GRADE 8

Key Ideas and Details

> CCSS.ELA-LITERACY.RL.8.2

Determine a theme or central idea of a text and analyze its development over the course of the text, including its relationship to the characters, setting, and plot; provide an objective summary of the text.

Craft and Structure

> CCSS.ELA-LITERACY.RL.8.4

Determine the meaning of words and phrases as they are used in a text, including figurative and connotative meanings; analyze the impact of specific word choices on meaning and tone, including analogies or allusions to other texts.

GRADES 9-10

Key Ideas and Details

> CCSS.ELA-LITERACY.RL.9-10.2

Determine a theme or central idea of a text and analyze in detail its development over the course of the text, including how it emerges and is shaped and refined by specific details; provide an objective summary of the text.

Craft and Structure

> CCSS.ELA-LITERACY.RL.9-10.4

Determine the meaning of words and phrases as they are used in the text, including figurative and connotative meanings; analyze the cumulative impact of specific word choices on meaning and tone (e.g., how the language evokes a sense of time and place; how it sets a formal or informal tone).

GRADES 11-12

Key Ideas and Details

> CCSS.ELA-LITERACY.RL.11-12.2

Determine two or more themes or central ideas of a text and analyze their development over the course of the text, including how they interact and build on one another to produce a complex account; provide an objective summary of the text.

Craft and Structure

> CCSS.ELA-LITERACY.RL.11-12.4

Determine the meaning of words and phrases as they are used in the text, including figurative and connotative meanings; analyze the impact of specific word choices on meaning and tone, including words with multiple meanings or language that is particularly fresh, engaging, or beautiful. (Include Shakespeare as well as other authors.)

Reading Informational Texts

GRADE 6

Key Ideas and Details

> CCSS.ELA-LITERACY.RI.6.2

Determine a central idea of a text and how it is conveyed through particular details; provide a summary of the text distinct from personal opinions or judgments.

> CCSS.ELA-LITERACY.RI.6.3

Analyze in detail how a key individual, event, or idea is introduced, illustrated, and elaborated in a text (e.g., through examples or anecdotes).

Craft and Structure

> CCSS.ELA-LITERACY.RI.6.4

Determine the meaning of words and phrases as they are used in a text, including figurative, connotative, and technical meanings.

Teaching with Video Games

GRADE 7

Key Ideas and Details

> CCSS.ELA-LITERACY.RI.7.2

Determine two or more central ideas in a text and analyze their development over the course of the text; provide an objective summary of the text.

> CCSS.ELA-LITERACY.RI.7.3

Analyze the interactions between individuals, events, and ideas in a text (e.g., how ideas influence individuals or events, or how individuals influence ideas or events).

Craft and Structure

> CCSS.ELA-LITERACY.RI.7.4

Determine the meaning of words and phrases as they are used in a text, including figurative, connotative, and technical meanings; analyze the impact of a specific word choice on meaning and tone.

GRADE 8

Key Ideas and Details

> CCSS.ELA-LITERACY.RI.8.2

Determine a central idea of a text and analyze its development over the course of the text, including its relationship to supporting ideas; provide an objective summary of the text.

> CCSS.ELA-LITERACY.RI.8.3

Analyze how a text makes connections among and distinctions between individuals, ideas, or events (e.g., through comparisons, analogies, or categories).

Craft and Structure

> CCSS.ELA-LITERACY.RI.8.4

Determine the meaning of words and phrases as they are used in a text, including figurative, connotative, and technical meanings; analyze the impact of specific word choices on meaning and tone, including analogies or allusions to other texts.

GRADES 9-10

Key Ideas and Details

> CCSS.ELA-LITERACY.RI.9-10.2

Determine a central idea of a text and analyze its development over the course of the text, including how it emerges and is shaped and refined by specific details; provide an objective summary of the text.

> CCSS.ELA-LITERACY.RI.9-10.3

Analyze how the author unfolds an analysis or series of ideas or events, including the order in which the points are made, how they are introduced and developed, and the connections that are drawn between them.

Craft and Structure

> CCSS.ELA-LITERACY.RI.9-10.4

Determine the meaning of words and phrases as they are used in a text, including figurative, connotative, and technical meanings; analyze the cumulative impact of specific word choices on meaning and tone (e.g., how the language of a court opinion differs from that of a newspaper).

GRADES 11-12

Key Ideas and Details

> CCSS.ELA-LITERACY.RI.11-12.2

Determine two or more central ideas of a text and analyze their development over the course of the text, including how they interact and build on one another to provide a complex analysis; provide an objective summary of the text.

> CCSS.ELA-LITERACY.RI.11-12.3

Analyze a complex set of ideas or sequence of events and explain how specific individuals, ideas, or events interact and develop over the course of the text.

Craft and Structure

CCSS.ELA-LITERACY.RI.11-12.4

Determine the meaning of words and phrases as they are used in a text, including figurative, connotative, and technical meanings; analyze how an author uses and refines the meaning of a key term or terms over the course of a text (e.g., how Madison defines faction in Federalist No. 10).

Speaking and Listening

GRADE 6

Comprehension and Collaboration

> CCSS.ELA-LITERACY.SL.6.1

Engage effectively in a range of collaborative discussions (one-on-one, in groups, and teacher-led) with diverse partners on grade 6 topics, texts, and issues, building on others› ideas and expressing their own clearly.

> CCSS.ELA-LITERACY.SL.6.2

Interpret information presented in diverse media and formats (e.g., visually, quantitatively, orally) and explain how it contributes to a topic, text, or issue under study.

GRADE 7

Comprehension and Collaboration

> CCSS.ELA-LITERACY.SL.7.1

Engage effectively in a range of collaborative discussions (one-on-one, in groups, and teacher-led) with diverse partners on grade 7 topics, texts, and issues, building on others› ideas and expressing their own clearly.

> CCSS.ELA-LITERACY.SL.7.2

Analyze the main ideas and supporting details presented in diverse media and formats (e.g., visually, quantitatively, orally) and explain how the ideas clarify a topic, text, or issue under study.

Teaching with Video Games

GRADE 8

Comprehension and Collaboration

> CCSS.ELA-LITERACY.SL.8.1

Engage effectively in a range of collaborative discussions (one-on-one, in groups, and teacher-led) with diverse partners on grade 8 topics, texts, and issues, building on others› ideas and expressing their own clearly.

> CCSS.ELA-LITERACY.SL.8.2

Analyze the purpose of information presented in diverse media and formats (e.g., visually, quantitatively, orally) and evaluate the motives (e.g., social, commercial, political) behind its presentation.

GRADES 9-10

Comprehension and Collaboration

> CCSS.ELA-LITERACY.SL.9-10.1

Initiate and participate effectively in a range of collaborative discussions (one-on-one, in groups, and teacher-led) with diverse partners on grades 9-10 topics, texts, and issues, building on others› ideas and expressing their own clearly and persuasively.

> CCSS.ELA-LITERACY.SL.9-10.2

Integrate multiple sources of information presented in diverse media or formats (e.g., visually, quantitatively, orally) evaluating the credibility and accuracy of each source.

GRADES 11-12

Comprehension and Collaboration

> CCSS.ELA-LITERACY.SL.11-12.1

Initiate and participate effectively in a range of collaborative discussions (one-on-one, in groups, and teacher-led) with diverse partners on grades 11-12 topics, texts, and issues, building on others› ideas and expressing their own clearly and persuasively.

> CCSS.ELA-LITERACY.SL.11-12.2

Integrate multiple sources of information presented in diverse formats and media (e.g., visually, quantitatively, orally) in order to make informed decisions and solve problems, evaluating the credibility and accuracy of each source and noting any discrepancies among the data.

TIME REQUIREMENTS

Before I Forget is on the shorter side, lasting for only about 50 minutes, though a playthrough can easily last over an hour if discussions are conducted while playing the game. This activity will take at most two full class periods.

SAFETY - TRIGGER WARNING

This game is rated 13+, but it does deal with death. It can be very emotionally heavy.

- [Beyond the Empathy Games 101: Digging Deep into Empathy, Ethics, and Design with Kelli Dunlap](#)
- [An Introduction to Content Warnings and Trigger Warnings](#)

Gris

SEE PAGE 92 IN THE STUDENT PACKET

- Content Area/s: Social Emotional Learning
- Developed by Nomada Studio
- Rated: 6+

WHERE TO PLAY

- Available on iOS, Nintendo Switch, PlayStation 4, PlayStation 5, Microsoft Windows, macOS

CONTEXT

This lesson should take place during a unit on

- Grief

DO BEFORE - PREP

- Choose the texts that you want to teach alongside this game. Some examples are:
    - > Healthline: <u>What You Should Know About the Stages of Grief</u>

OVERVIEW

The phrase "video games are art" gets thrown around a lot in the video game industry. That phrase really applies to the game *Gris*. *Gris* is not just a game. It is literally art: a beautiful watercolor painting that we have the privilege of interacting with. Take a screenshot of any scene and it would look like a painting. It is beautifully animated by artist Conrad Roset to make the whole game seem like a watercolor painting come to life.

Beyond the aesthetics, the game is a story of grief, something everyone will experience at one point or another. The experience of losing a loved one and all the emotions and baggage that comes with it. The story follows a girl going through the stages of bringing color back to her life. The game starts with a girl who safely sings in the hands of a giant statue, which then begins to crumble. The girl, grief stricken, loses her voice and tumbles below. She has clearly lost someone important to her and begins the first stage of grief: denial. The world has lost all color and the girl cannot sing and can barely walk.

Over the course of the game, you will guide this girl through each step of the grieving process and bring color back to her bleak world. Denial, anger, bargaining, and depression, and acceptance. These are the five stages of grief. The player must help the protagonist overcome her internal struggles in order to arrive at a place of acceptance. One must help her find her voice and ultimately accept that what is lost can never come back. It teaches us that we will all recover after losing a loved one, and it does so without an ounce of dialogue. It relies on its visuals and music. *Gris* is an experience and an artistic spectacle.

DESCRIPTION OF ACTIVITY

- Only one copy of the game is necessary
  - > The class can play together with the game projected in the front of the room
- Losing someone you love can occur for different reasons:
  - > Death
  - > Break-up
  - > Moving Away
- *Gris* is a video game that revolves around grief. Gris, the titular character, is grieving, presumably from the death of a loved one.
- Art is often used as a medium of expressing emotions. The developers partnered with artist Conrad Roset to illustrate Gris in its distinctive watercolor style.
- As you progress through the game, Gris will experience the five stages of grief.
  - > Denial: In this stage, the world becomes meaningless and overwhelming. Life makes no sense. We are in a state of shock and denial (grief.com).
  - > Anger: Anger is a necessary stage of the healing process. Be willing to feel your anger, even though it may seem endless. The more you truly feel it, the more it will begin to dissipate and the more you will heal (grief.com).
  - > Bargaining: After a loss, bargaining may take the form of a temporary truce. "What if I devote the rest of my life to helping others. Then can I wake up and realize this has all been a bad dream?" We become lost in a maze of "If only..." or "What if..." statements. We want life returned to what is was; we want our loved one restored. We want to go back in time (grief.com).
  - > Depression: After bargaining, our attention moves squarely into the present. Empty feelings present themselves, and grief enters our lives on a deeper level, deeper than we ever imagined. This depressive stage feels as though it will last forever (grief.com).
  - > Acceptance: This stage is about accepting the reality that our loved one is physically gone and recognizing that this new reality is the permanent reality. We will never like this reality or make it OK, but eventually we accept it. We learn to live with it (grief.com).
- Have a small discussion about how not everyone will necessarily experience these emotions in this order, or even feel all of them when they grieve. Every person is different and grieves differently, but these are established norms that aid conversation about the subject.
- Now introduce the type of gameplay that will be found in *Gris*.
  - > It is a platformer with some mild puzzles scattered throughout.
  - > You can move, jump, and sing, although in the beginning of the game, you cannot sing because you have lost your voice.
- More important is the art style, colors, and music.
  - > Gris is presented as a luscious watercolor painting.
  - > After the initial loss, the game is bleak and colorless.
    As we progress through and "grieve" in a healthy way, more color is added to the game.

- Provide an accompanying handout before starting the game, as students will be answering questions as they play through the story.
- Be prepared to help students who may end up stuck on one of the puzzles.

OBJECTIVES

- Students will discuss the five stages of grief.
- Students will identify how color is used as a representation of the five stages of grief.

CORRELATION TO COMMON CORE STANDARDS

English Language Arts Anchor Standards

GRADES K-12

- College and Career Readiness Anchor Standards for Reading

  Key Ideas and Details

  > CCSS.ELA-LITERACY.CCRA.R.2

  Determine central ideas or themes of a text and analyze their development; summarize the key supporting details and ideas.

  > CCSS.ELA-LITERACY.CCRA.R.3

  Analyze how and why individuals, events, or ideas develop and interact over the course of a text.

- College and Career Readiness Anchor Standards for Writing

  Production and Distribution of Writing

  > CCSS.ELA-LITERACY.CCRA.W.4

  Produce clear and coherent writing in which the development, organization, and style are appropriate to task, purpose, and audience.

- College and Career Readiness Anchor Standards for Speaking and Listening

  Comprehension and Collaboration

  > CCSS.ELA-LITERACY.CCRA.SL.1

  Prepare for and participate effectively in a range of conversations and collaborations with diverse partners, building on others› ideas and expressing their own clearly and persuasively.

  > CCSS.ELA-LITERACY.CCRA.SL.2

  Integrate and evaluate information presented in diverse media and formats, including visually, quantitatively, and orally.

English Language Arts

Reading Literature

GRADE 6

  Key Ideas and Details

  > CCSS.ELA-LITERACY.RL.6.2

Determine a theme or central idea of a text and how it is conveyed through particular details; provide a summary of the text distinct from personal opinions or judgments.

GRADE 7

Key Ideas and Details

> CCSS.ELA-LITERACY.RL.7.2

Determine a theme or central idea of a text and analyze its development over the course of the text; provide an objective summary of the text.

GRADE 8

Key Ideas and Details

> CCSS.ELA-LITERACY.RL.8.2

Determine a theme or central idea of a text and analyze its development over the course of the text, including its relationship to the characters, setting, and plot; provide an objective summary of the text.

GRADES 9-10

Key Ideas and Details

> CCSS.ELA-LITERACY.RL.9-10.2

Determine a theme or central idea of a text and analyze in detail its development over the course of the text, including how it emerges and is shaped and refined by specific details; provide an objective summary of the text.

GRADES 11-12

Key Ideas and Details

> CCSS.ELA-LITERACY.RL.11-12.2

Determine two or more themes or central ideas of a text and analyze their development over the course of the text, including how they interact and build on one another to produce a complex account; provide an objective summary of the text.

Speaking and Listening

GRADE 6

Comprehension and Collaboration

> CCSS.ELA-LITERACY.SL.6.1

Engage effectively in a range of collaborative discussions (one-on-one, in groups, and teacher-led) with diverse partners on grade 6 topics, texts, and issues, building on others› ideas and expressing their own clearly.

> CCSS.ELA-LITERACY.SL.6.2

Interpret information presented in diverse media and formats (e.g., visually, quantitatively, orally) and explain how it contributes to a topic, text, or issue under study.

GRADE 7

Comprehension and Collaboration

> CCSS.ELA-LITERACY.SL.7.1

Engage effectively in a range of collaborative discussions (one-on-one, in groups, and teacher-led) with diverse partners on grade 7 topics, texts, and issues, building on others› ideas and expressing their own clearly.

> CCSS.ELA-LITERACY.SL.7.2

Analyze the main ideas and supporting details presented in diverse media and formats (e.g., visually, quantitatively, orally) and explain how the ideas clarify a topic, text, or issue under study.

GRADE 8

Comprehension and Collaboration

> CCSS.ELA-LITERACY.SL.8.1

Engage effectively in a range of collaborative discussions (one-on-one, in groups, and teacher-led) with diverse partners on grade 8 topics, texts, and issues, building on others› ideas and expressing their own clearly.

> CCSS.ELA-LITERACY.SL.8.2

Analyze the purpose of information presented in diverse media and formats (e.g., visually, quantitatively, orally) and evaluate the motives (e.g., social, commercial, political) behind its presentation.

GRADES 9-10

Comprehension and Collaboration

> CCSS.ELA-LITERACY.SL.9-10.1

Initiate and participate effectively in a range of collaborative discussions (one-on-one, in groups, and teacher-led) with diverse partners on grades 9-10 topics, texts, and issues, building on others› ideas and expressing their own clearly and persuasively.

> CCSS.ELA-LITERACY.SL.9-10.2

Integrate multiple sources of information presented in diverse media or formats (e.g., visually, quantitatively, orally) evaluating the credibility and accuracy of each source.

GRADES 11-12

Comprehension and Collaboration

> CCSS.ELA-LITERACY.SL.11-12.1

Initiate and participate effectively in a range of collaborative discussions (one-on-one, in groups, and teacher-led) with diverse partners on grades 11-12 topics, texts, and issues, building on others› ideas and expressing their own clearly and persuasively.

> CCSS.ELA-LITERACY.SL.11-12.2

Integrate multiple sources of information presented in diverse formats and media (e.g., visually, quantitatively, orally) in order to make informed decisions and solve problems, evaluating the credibility and accuracy of each source and noting any discrepancies among the data.

TIME REQUIREMENTS

Plan to spend between three and four hours of playtime to finish Gris.

SAFETY - TRIGGER WARNING

Nothing on screen in Gris will be triggering, though the conversations and visualizations of grief and loss may be difficult for some students.

- Beyond the Empathy Games 101: Digging Deep into Empathy, Ethics, and Design with Kelli Dunlap
- An Introduction to Content Warnings and Trigger Warnings

Teaching with Video Games

Celeste

SEE PAGE 96 IN THE STUDENT PACKET

- Content Area/s: Social Emotional Learning
- Developed by Matt Makes Games
- Rated: 10+

WHERE TO PLAY

- Available on Microsoft Windows, Nintendo Switch, Playstation 4, PlayStation 5, Xbox One, Xbox Series X/S, macOS, Linux, Google Stadia

CONTEXT

This lesson should take place during a unit on

- Growth Mindset
- Depression
- Anxiety

DO BEFORE - PREP

- Choose the texts that you want to teach alongside this game. Some examples are:
  - > Brain Pickings: Fixed vs. Growth Mindset
  - > Kotaku: Celeste Taught Fans And Its Own Creator To Take Better Care Of Themselves

OVERVIEW

Celeste is one of the most important games to come out this decade. It is an indie screen-by-screen platform game. Basically, with each screen, you need to figure out how to jump across from one side to another. It is simple, but developers used this mechanic to tell a sweet story with an incredibly important message. The plot of the game is about a girl named Madeline trying to climb a mountain named Celeste. You play as Madeline and work your way up the mountain. As you progress, however, it becomes clear that the mountain is a metaphor for anxiety, depression, and other mental health issues that Madeline faces in her life.

Madeline is attempting to climb Celeste Mountain as proof that she can accomplish something. Along the way she will meet and help people who are also dealing with their own issues. Theo, who helps Madeline on her journey, is obsessed with social media and self-image. He wants to make sure people always see the pleasant parts of his life. Mr. Oshiro is a lost soul who manages a resort that he has completely neglected. There is trash and laundry everywhere that Madeline will need to help clean up. Finally, Badeline is a mirror image of Madeline. She is a physical manifestation of all of Madeline's insecurities.

Madeline is an instantly relatable protagonist. She suffers from depression and anxiety and will endure several panic attacks during the events of the game. She constantly doubts whether or not she can actually scale Celeste Mountain. Despite her challenges, she is strong-willed, and with the support of her friends, she overcomes her various adversities. These are real issues that people deal with on a daily basis in the real world.

This game is extraordinarily challenging, but intentionally so. Overcoming and healing from anxiety and depression is no easy task. That difficulty is represented in the platforming mechanics. You will die hundreds or thousands of times playing this game. The game will even keep a death count for each level. The game wants you to die and wants you to experience failure, but it is teaching you how to have a growth mindset in the process. And it is designed in a way that lets the player know each and every task is doable. It will just take some practice. They can do it on their own, or they can enable any number of accessibility options to differentiate various aspects of the gameplay for different types of players. It is one of the few games out there where the message of the story is formally intertwined with the gameplay.

The accessibility features in this game ensure that the game could be played by anyone.

This game can be utilized to show your students that failure is okay so long as we keep moving forward and learn from those experiences. Not everyone naturally has a growth mindset, and a game like *Celeste* can help get students to think in that way. And the students do not need to play the entire game. They can, but playing through just one level will take up an entire class period, and that is more than enough to get them thinking and conversing about overcoming adversity. Just like most other games, *Celeste* can also be played together as a class. Even if it is just one student holding the controller, other students can help the player figure out what to do next. Each screen is a platforming puzzle that will take many attempts to solve. Students can collaborate to finish the level and then have a conversation about the message of the game. You can see in the following student sample that a student died 71 times while making their way through the first level of the game. They noted that in the game, just like in real life, it is okay if you fail at something your first time. You can keep trying because there are always new opportunities for success.

DESCRIPTION OF ACTIVITY

- Only one copy of the game is necessary. Project in the front of the class and have one student play at a time.

- In this game, you play as a girl named Madeline. She has decided that she wants to climb to the top of Celeste Mountain. There will be many obstacles, both physical and mental in her way. It is your job to learn from your past mistakes to get Madeline to the top.

- It is okay to spoil some of the game as you likely won't play through the entire game with your students. In this lesson, we will only be playing through the tutorial and the first level.

- Explain how we do not really know exactly why Madeline is attempting to climb Celeste Mountain, but that she is there to prove to herself that she is capable of doing so.

- It is okay to explain that Madeline suffers from depression and that climbing this mountain is a metaphor for her overcoming her own depression and anxiety.

- Have a volunteer from the class come play the tutorial and first level.
    - > Preferably someone with a background playing games because this is a hard game.
    - > Later on, give all the other students a chance to play, but for the context of this lesson, there will not be enough time to let everyone play.

Teaching with Video Games

- Provide an accompanying handout before starting the game, as students will be answering questions as they play through the story.
- Be prepared to help students who may end up stuck on one of the puzzles.

OBJECTIVES

- Students will discuss the various obstacles in the way of their own goals.
- Students will offer advice to other students in the room about how to overcome these challenges.

CORRELATION TO COMMON CORE STANDARDS

English Language Arts Anchor Standards

GRADES K-12

- College and Career Readiness Anchor Standards for Reading

  Key Ideas and Details

  > CCSS.ELA-LITERACY.CCRA.R.2

  Determine central ideas or themes of a text and analyze their development; summarize the key supporting details and ideas.

  > CCSS.ELA-LITERACY.CCRA.R.3

  Analyze how and why individuals, events, or ideas develop and interact over the course of a text.

- College and Career Readiness Anchor Standards for Writing

  Production and Distribution of Writing

  > CCSS.ELA-LITERACY.CCRA.W.4

  Produce clear and coherent writing in which the development, organization, and style are appropriate to task, purpose, and audience.

- College and Career Readiness Anchor Standards for Speaking and Listening

  Comprehension and Collaboration

  > CCSS.ELA-LITERACY.CCRA.SL.1

  Prepare for and participate effectively in a range of conversations and collaborations with diverse partners, building on others› ideas and expressing their own clearly and persuasively.

  > CCSS.ELA-LITERACY.CCRA.SL.2

  Integrate and evaluate information presented in diverse media and formats, including visually, quantitatively, and orally.

English Language Arts

Reading Literature

GRADE 6

    Key Ideas and Details

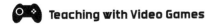

> CCSS.ELA-LITERACY.RL.6.2

Determine a theme or central idea of a text and how it is conveyed through particular details; provide a summary of the text distinct from personal opinions or judgments.

GRADE 7

Key Ideas and Details

> CCSS.ELA-LITERACY.RL.7.2

Determine a theme or central idea of a text and analyze its development over the course of the text; provide an objective summary of the text.

GRADE 8

Key Ideas and Details

> CCSS.ELA-LITERACY.RL.8.2

Determine a theme or central idea of a text and analyze its development over the course of the text, including its relationship to the characters, setting, and plot; provide an objective summary of the text.

GRADES 9-10

Key Ideas and Details

> CCSS.ELA-LITERACY.RL.9-10.2

Determine a theme or central idea of a text and analyze in detail its development over the course of the text, including how it emerges and is shaped and refined by specific details; provide an objective summary of the text.

GRADES 11-12

Key Ideas and Details

> CCSS.ELA-LITERACY.RL.11-12.2

Determine two or more themes or central ideas of a text and analyze their development over the course of the text, including how they interact and build on one another to produce a complex account; provide an objective summary of the text.

Speaking and Listening

GRADE 6

Comprehension and Collaboration

> CCSS.ELA-LITERACY.SL.6.1

Engage effectively in a range of collaborative discussions (one-on-one, in groups, and teacher-led) with diverse partners on grade 6 topics, texts, and issues, building on others› ideas and expressing their own clearly.

> CCSS.ELA-LITERACY.SL.6.2

Interpret information presented in diverse media and formats (e.g., visually, quantitatively, orally) and explain how it contributes to a topic, text, or issue under study.

GRADE 7

Comprehension and Collaboration

> CCSS.ELA-LITERACY.SL.7.1

Engage effectively in a range of collaborative discussions (one-on-one, in groups, and teacher-led) with diverse partners on grade 7 topics, texts, and issues, building on others› ideas and expressing their own clearly.

> CCSS.ELA-LITERACY.SL.7.2

Analyze the main ideas and supporting details presented in diverse media and formats (e.g., visually, quantitatively, orally) and explain how the ideas clarify a topic, text, or issue under study.

GRADE 8

Comprehension and Collaboration

> CCSS.ELA-LITERACY.SL.8.1

Engage effectively in a range of collaborative discussions (one-on-one, in groups, and teacher-led) with diverse partners on grade 8 topics, texts, and issues, building on others› ideas and expressing their own clearly.

> CCSS.ELA-LITERACY.SL.8.2

Analyze the purpose of information presented in diverse media and formats (e.g., visually, quantitatively, orally) and evaluate the motives (e.g., social, commercial, political) behind its presentation.

GRADES 9-10

Comprehension and Collaboration

> CCSS.ELA-LITERACY.SL.9-10.1

Initiate and participate effectively in a range of collaborative discussions (one-on-one, in groups, and teacher-led) with diverse partners on grades 9-10 topics, texts, and issues, building on others› ideas and expressing their own clearly and persuasively.

> CCSS.ELA-LITERACY.SL.9-10.2

Integrate multiple sources of information presented in diverse media or formats (e.g., visually, quantitatively, orally) evaluating the credibility and accuracy of each source.

GRADES 11-12

Comprehension and Collaboration

> CCSS.ELA-LITERACY.SL.11-12.1

Initiate and participate effectively in a range of collaborative discussions (one-on-one, in groups, and teacher-led) with diverse partners on grades 11-12 topics, texts, and issues, building on others› ideas and expressing their own clearly and persuasively.

> CCSS.ELA-LITERACY.SL.11-12.2

Integrate multiple sources of information presented in diverse formats and media (e.g., visually, quantitatively, orally) in order to make informed decisions and solve problems, evaluating the credibility and accuracy of each source and noting any discrepancies among the data.

TIME REQUIREMENTS

This lesson only requires the class to play through the first level of the game, though teachers are more than welcome to play more.

SAFETY - TRIGGER WARNING

While there is not much to warn students about the game itself, the conversations around depression and anxiety might be difficult for some students.

- Teaching Tolerance
- Beyond the Empathy Games 101: Digging Deep into Empathy, Ethics, and Design with Kelli Dunlap
- An Introduction to Content Warnings and Trigger Warnings

References

Playdius Entertainment. (2017). *Bury me, my Love – A Story of Love, Hope and Migration*. Bury me my Love. http://burymemylove.arte.tv/.

Barlow, S. (2015). *Her Story*. HER STORY. http://www.herstorygame.com/about/.

Campbell, J. (2004). *The hero with a thousand faces*. Princeton University Press.

Clement, J. (2020, January 8). *WhatsApp Status daily active users 2019*. Statista. https://www.statista.com/statistics/730306/whatsapp-status-dau/.

Dark Realm Studios. (2008). *Pandemic 2 - Kill Everyone in the World!* Play Pandemic 2 Game Full Screen | TRY TO KILL EVERYONE IN THE WORLD. http://pandemic2.org/.

E-Line Media. (2014). *Never Alone*. http://neveralonegame.com/game/.

Flower. thatgamecompany. (2009). https://thatgamecompany.com/flower/.

Fullbright. (2017). *Tacoma*. https://tacoma.game/.

Gusmanson.nl, D. (2018, February 20). *From fake news to chaos! How bad are you? Get as many followers as you can*. Bad News. https://www.getbadnews.com/.

Hartzman, Z. (2019, April 13). *I Taught Papers, Please*. Hey Listen Games. https://www.heylisten-games.org/post/i-taught-papers-please.

Hartzman, Z. (2019, April 25). *I Taught The Republia Times*. Hey Listen Games. https://www.heylistengames.org/post/i-taught-the-republia-times.

Hartzman, Z. (2019, August 11). *Why You Should Play Pokémon Go on Your Next Field Trip*. Hey Listen Games. https://www.heylistengames.org/post/why-you-should-play-pok%C3%A9mon-go-on-your-next-field-trip.

Hartzman, Z. (2019, December 27). *I Taught With Emily is Away*. Hey Listen Games. https://www.heylistengames.org/post/i-taught-with-emily-is-away.

Hartzman, Z. (2019, July 17). *New Lesson on Pandemic II Now Available*. Hey Listen Games. https://www.heylistengames.org/post/new-lesson-on-pandemic-ii-now-available.

Hartzman, Z. (2019, July 31). *Why You Should Teach With the Bad News Game*. Hey Listen Games. https://www.heylistengames.org/post/why-you-should-teach-with-the-bad-news-game.

Hartzman, Z. (2019, June 15). *New Lesson on Journey Now Available*. Hey Listen Games. https://www.heylistengames.org/post/new-lesson-on-journey-now-available.

Hartzman, Z. (2019, June 22). *New Lesson on Never Alone Now Available*. Hey Listen Games. https://www.heylistengames.org/post/new-lesson-on-never-alone-now-available.

Hartzman, Z. (2019, June 6). *New Lesson on Flower Now Available*. Hey Listen Games. https://www.heylistengames.org/post/new-lesson-on-flower-now-available.

Hartzman, Z. (2019, March 19). *I Taught Celeste*. Hey Listen Games. https://www.heylisten-games.org/post/i-taught-celeste.

Hartzman, Z. (2019, May 27). *New Lesson on Her Story Now Available*. Hey Listen Games. https://www.heylistengames.org/post/new-lesson-on-her-story-now-available.

Hartzman, Z. (2019, November 11). *Why You Should Teach With Emily is Away*. Hey Listen Games. https://www.heylistengames.org/post/why-you-should-teach-with-emily-is-away.

Hartzman, Z. (2019, November 17). *I Taught With Kind Words*. Hey Listen Games. https://www.heylistengames.org/post/i-taught-with-kind-words.

Hartzman, Z. (2020, April 15). *I Taught With Assemble With Care*. Hey Listen Games. https://www.heylistengames.org/post/i-taught-with-assemble-with-care.

Hartzman, Z. (2019, October 20). *Why You Should Teach With Kind Words*. Hey Listen Games. https://www.heylistengames.org/post/why-you-should-teach-with-kind-words.

Hartzman, Z. (2020, April 30). *Why You Should Teach with Batman: The Telltale Series*. Hey Listen Games. https://www.heylistengames.org/post/why-you-should-teach-with-batman-the-telltale-series.

Hartzman, Z. (2020, February 15). *Why You Should Teach With Tacoma*. Hey Listen Games. https://www.heylistengames.org/post/why-you-should-teach-with-tacoma.

Hartzman, Z. (2020, February 27). *Why You Should Teach With Life is Strange 2*. Hey Listen Games. https://www.heylistengames.org/post/why-you-should-teach-with-life-is-strange-2.

Hartzman, Z. (2020, January 13). *Why You Should Teach With 1979 Revolution: Black Friday*. Hey Listen Games. https://www.heylistengames.org/post/why-you-should-teach-with-1979-revolution-black-friday.

Hartzman, Z. (2020, January 5). *I Taught With Florence*. Hey Listen Games. https://www.heylistengames.org/post/i-taught-with-florence.

Hartzman, Z. (2020, July 13). *I Taught With Super Mario Odyssey*. Hey Listen Games. https://www.heylistengames.org/post/i-taught-with-super-mario-odyssey.

Hartzman, Z. (2020, June 12). *I Taught With Batman: The Telltale Series*. Hey Listen Games. https://www.heylistengames.org/post/i-taught-with-batman-the-telltale-series.

Hartzman, Z. (2020, March 27). *I Taught With Pandemic II*. Hey Listen Games. https://www.heylistengames.org/post/i-taught-with-pandemic-ii.

Hartzman, Z. (2020, May 18). *I Taught With Valiant Hearts: The Great War*. Hey Listen Games. https://www.heylistengames.org/post/i-taught-with-valiant-hearts-the-great-war.

INK Stories. (2016). *1979 Revolution Black Friday*. 1979 Revolution. https://1979revolutiongame.com/.

Journey. thatgamecompany. (2012). https://thatgamecompany.com/journey/.

Life is Strange 2. SQUARE ENIX. (2018). https://lifeisstrange.square-enix-games.com/en-us.

Matt Makes Games. (2018). Celeste. http://www.celestegame.com/.

Maurin, F. (2016, November 18). *What reality-inspired games are*. Gamasutra. https://www.gamasutra.com/blogs/FlorentMaurin/20161118/285793/What_realityinspired_games_are.php.

Metev, D. (2020, July 4). *How Much Time Do People Spend on Social Media in 2020?* Review42. https://review42.com/how-much-time-do-people-spend-on-social-media/.

Montpellier, U. (2014). *Valiant Hearts*. Ubisoft.com. https://www.ubisoft.com/en-us/game/valiant-hearts/.

Mountains. (2019). *Florence*. ANNAPURNA INTERACTIVE. https://annapurnainteractive.com/games/florence/.

National Governors Association Center for Best Practices, & Council of Chief State School Officers. (2010). Common Core State Standards. Common Core State Standards Initiative. http://www.corestandards.org/.

Niantic. (2016). *Pokémon GO!* Pokémon Go. https://www.pokemongo.com/en-us/.

Nintendo. (2017). *Super Mario Odyssey* . Super Mario Odyssey for Nintendo Switch - Nintendo Game Details. https://www.nintendo.com/games/detail/super-mario-odyssey-switch/.

Popcannibal. (2019). *Kind Words (lo fi chill beats to write to)*. Kind Words. https://popcannibal.com/kindwords/.

Pope, L. (2012). Games by Lucas Pope. http://pope.jeffsys.net/.

Reviews for what your kids want to watch (before they watch it): Common Sense Media. Common Sense Media: Ratings, reviews, and advice. (2020). https://www.commonsensemedia.org/.

Soullier, L., & Zerrouky, M. (2015, December 18). *Le voyage d›une migrante syrienne à travers son fil WhatsApp*. Le Monde.fr. https://www.lemonde.fr/international/visuel/2015/12/18/dans-le-telephone-d-une-migrante-syrienne_4834834_3210.html.

Telltale Games. (2016). *Batman: The Telltale Series*. Telltale Games. https://www.telltale.com/batman-a-telltale-story/.

U.S. Department of Health & Human Services. (2018, May 16). *Vaccines: Vac-Gen/Why Are Childhood Vaccines So Important?* Centers for Disease Control and Prevention. https://www.cdc.gov/vaccines/vac-gen/howvpd.htm.

U.S. Department of State. (2020). *The Immigration Act of 1924 (The Johnson-Reed Act)*. Office of the Historian. https://history.state.gov/milestones/1921-1936/immigration-act.

But Our Princess is in Another Castle

Remember when you were a child playing the original *Super Mario Bros.* game and you finally beat the first castle, only to be greeted by a Toad saying, "Thank you Mario! But our princess is another castle"? It became increasingly frustrating as another Toad would greet you at the end of each castle saying the same thing until you finally found Princess Peach at the end of the game. That first castle and the first few levels were basically a tutorial. They introduced the player to all of the concepts and skills they would need to develop in order to finish the rest of the game.

This book is your first castle. It is your game-based learning tutorial. You have made it to the end, but this does not mean your journey is over. There is much more out there for you to learn, both from other educators and from yourself. You probably have a good idea of how to start teaching with video games, but you will learn so much more from your own trials and experiences with them. Every educator teaches in a unique setting with students who have different needs and learn in different ways. Each lesson described here will need to be modified to fit your specific classroom. Not everything will work perfectly, but you will grow as a game based educator with each new video game lesson.

Know that just by reading this book you have made it farther than most. There is still a long way to go to prove that video games should be utilized in schools in the same capacity as other mediums. There are social stigmas attached to gaming that many people need to unlearn. You can be a part of that process. Show your students, their parents, and your colleagues how valuable you know they are. Now continue on to your next castle.

In the meantime, here are actionable next steps you can take:

- Choose a game from this book, or over at heylistengames.org, that could be a good fit in your classroom and start making some lesson plans/curriculum (or use the provided curriculum on Hey Listen Games).

- Acquire the necessary materials and technology needed to play video games. Ask your students for input if you need some help. Some of them will know exactly what technology you need to get started. They are also bound to provide game recommendations as well.

- Discuss with and bounce ideas off other teachers in your school.

- Get on social media. Twitter and Reddit can help put you in contact with other teachers who are implementing this technology in their classrooms, too. There are thousands of people out there interested in helping one another.

- Always feel free to reach out if you need some more help or have specific questions you need answered.
    - > Fill out the contact form on Hey Listen Games.
    - > Email heylistengamesinfo@gmail.com
    - > Twitter: @HeylistenGames_
- Have Fun!!

Acknowledgements

This book is the culmination of several years of work, and I did not get to this point by myself. None of this would have been possible without my students over the past several years. My students are some of the best people I know. Their open-mindedness and trust have allowed me to experiment a lot as an educator. They saw my love for video games and were excited to have me share that passion with them. They are the reason I love my job and why I look forward to my continued time in the classroom.

I have also been lucky enough to work with amazing colleagues and under a wonderful school administration. My school's leadership has never once questioned my ability to appropriately teach my students. Over the years they have trusted me to teach with different mediums like movies, comics, and video games because they knew that whatever the lesson was, I would be putting in one hundred percent of myself. Even though they are not familiar with video games themselves, they understood that I knew enough about them to make these ventures worthwhile.

Even though I wrote this book, it may come as a surprise (or not) that I am not the greatest writer. I was always a better math student than I was an English one. My parents, who wholly enabled my gaming hobbies as a kid, still find it surprising that I have spent so much of my free time writing about my experiences teaching with video games. Luckily, I have an amazing wife who is a much better writer than I am. Over the years she has proofread and edited every single one of my blog posts over at Hey Listen Games. It is because of her that any of my thoughts come out sounding coherent. Annie, I love you and I cannot wait to annoy you with my writing for many more years.

This book would also not exist without the initial push from Dr. Anthony Bean, Geek Therapeutics, and Leyline Publishing. I was perfectly content just sharing and interacting with people online, but Anthony reached out and told me to write a book; so here we are. Your guidance has been much appreciated and I look forward to future collaborations.

About the Author

Zachary Hartzman is a licensed secondary school teacher in New York. He received his Masters in the teaching of social studies from Teachers College at Columbia University. He teaches high school social studies in New York City, and has also taught global history, United States history, economics, and government. He created a new English language arts elective course dedicated to the study of video games as literature. For the past six years, he has served a student population consisting of newly arrived immigrants and English language learners. He specializes in finding ways to incorporate pop culture like movies, TV, and especially comics and video games into the classroom.

He is also the founder of Hey Listen Games, a space where educators can find curriculum and lesson plans for teaching with video games and engage in discourse about their experiences with game-based learning. Zachary has been featured in a number of educational podcasts ,where he advocates for game-based learning in schools as a way to increase engagement among students and social emotional learning. He frequently travels to video game and comic conventions in order to both learn and share how to utilize geek culture as a method of making learning more fun and improving school culture. He reflects on these lessons and games as he incorporates them in his own classroom on his personal blog, which can be found on Hey Listen Games. The Game Awards recognized Zachary for his work on Hey Listen Games in 2020 by making him an inaugural member of The Future Class, a diverse group of thinkers, builders, and dreamers whose voices elevate and diversify the gaming art form. He is active on twitter at @ HeyListenGames_.

CPSIA information can be obtained
at www.ICGtesting.com
Printed in the USA
LVHW020902180723
752608LV00005B/402